The Cooking of the Caribbean Islands

The Cooking of the Caribbean Islands

by

Linda Wolfe

and the Editors of

TIME-LIFE BOOKS

photographed by Richard Meek

THE AUTHOR: Linda Wolfe is the author of *The Literary Gourmet*, published in 1963, a cookery book that investigates the fascination food has always held for fiction writers. Her own fiction has appeared in various literary publications and she has written articles on food for *Gourmet* magazine. Mrs. Wolfe now works for Time Inc. Her daughter Jessica, who appears in this photograph, has often accompanied her on her extensive Caribbean travels.

THE PHOTOGRAPHER: Richard Meek, a member of the original SPORTS ILLUSTRATED photographic staff, is now a free-lance photographer who has covered subjects as varied as the America's Cup races, Shaker furniture and the wild-life of the Canadian Rockies. His first major assignment in food photography was *The Cooking of Scandinavia* in the FOODS OF THE WORLD library.

THE CONSULTING EDITOR: The late Michael Field supervised the adapting and writing of recipes for this book. One of America's foremost food experts and culinary teachers, he wrote many articles for leading magazines. His books include *Michael Field's Cooking School* and *All Manner of Food*.

THE CONSULTANT: Elisabeth Lambert Ortiz lived in Jamaica as a girl and has travelled frequently in the Caribbean. An expert on the cooking of Mexico and South America as well as on that of the islands, she served as principal consultant for *Latin American Cooking* of the FOODS OF THE WORLD library. She contributes articles to *Gourmet* magazine, *House and Garden* and other publications and wrote *The Complete Book of Mexican Cooking*.

THE SPECIAL CONSULTANT FOR THIS EDITION: Margaret Costa (*left*), born in Southern Rhodesia and educated in England, has been "obsessed" with cooking since the age of six. She abandoned theatre work and a job as staff writer for London's *Sunday Pictorial* to write about food—a career that has kept her busy for 20 years. For some 15 of those years, she has helped to compile Raymond Postgate's *Good Food Guide* to eating out in the British Isles. Today, as the wife of one of London's best chefs, an Englishman trained in the Escoffier tradition, she writes about food, wine and restaurants for half a dozen newspapers and magazines, including *The Sunday Times Magazine* and *The Illustrated London News*.

THE ASSISTANT TO THE SPECIAL CONSULTANT: J. Audrey Ellison is a microbiologist, food analyst and home economist. She taught home economics at London University after taking her science degree there. Now, she is consultant to the Norway Food Centre in London and to a number of food manufacturers and importers. She has compiled several cookery books, including *The Great Scandinavian Cook Book*, which she translated from the Swedish and edited for English and American readers.

© Original edition Time-life Books Inc, 1970
© This edition Macmillan Publishers Ltd, 1985

This edition published 1985

Published by *Macmillan Publishers Ltd* London and Basingstoke
Associated companies and representaives in Accra, Auckland, Delhi, Dublin, Gaborone, Hamburg, Harare, Hong Kong, Kuala Lumpur, Lagos, Manzini, Melbourne, Mexico City, Nairobi, New York, Singapore, Tokyo

British Library Cataloguing in Publication Data
Wolfe, Linda
   The cooking of the Caribbean islands.
   1. Cookery, West Indian
   I. Title II. Meek, Richard
   641.3'009729   TX716.W4

ISBN 0-333-40005-4

Printed in Hong Kong

Contents

The Recipe Booklet that accompanies this volume has been designed for use in the kitchen. It contains all of the 85 recipes in this book plus 58 more. It also has a wipe-clean cover and a spiral binding so that it can either stand up or lie flat when open.

The Island Cuisines Are Finally Coming into Their Own

On a July morning in 1929 I saw for the first time the majestic mountains of Martinique. I was travelling to Tahiti via Panama aboard an intermediate class French steamer; we had been 17 days at sea, and I was anxious to feel firm soil beneath my feet. But I was even more anxious to sample a change of food. The menus on board had been good enough, but you get tired of any cuisine after a week, and this particular ship did not pretend to be first rate. The birthplace of the Empress Josephine should surely be able to supply an antidote.

Soon after the ship docked in Fort-de-France I found a café on the main square; the sky was blue, the sun was shining, and the north-east trade wind tempered the midsummer heat. I ordered a rum punch. A waitress set before me a bottle of rum, an earthenware water jug, a small bottle containing some kind of sauce, and a couple of limes. I was invited to help myself. I had, naturally, no idea of how to employ this do-it-yourself kit, and explained this to the waitress. She emitted a high-pitched cackle and gave me my first lesson in concocting the Caribbean's chief potation. First she sliced a lime and squeezed a few drops of its juice into my glass. She then added a minute contribution from the small bottle. It contained cane syrup, I discovered. The rum came next, a two-finger measure. Finally the water.

That is the classic formula for rum punch: one of sour, two of sweet, three of strong and four of weak. The method of making punch varies in the different islands because the flavour of the rum is different everywhere; fruit and other flavours can be added. But I prefer the Martinican method. It is the simplest and the purest and you get the full flavour of the spirit. On French liners I always order it. And as I sip it, I recall that morning when I first tasted it in Fort-de-France, looking across the *savane* to the white statue of Josephine with its circlet of sentinel palms. Peace descended on my spirit then, and I repeated the punch ritual to make sure I had learned my lesson. I clearly had. My euphoria deepened. "And now," I thought, "for lunch."

Lunch, however, was a very different matter. There was fried fish that was rescued from tastelessness only by the lime juice that I squirted over it; then came two slices of dry overcooked beef that were accompanied by a dish of starchy, flavourless yams and bread-fruit. The meal was rounded off by two bananas. It was no better and very little different from the meals that had been served to me on board ship; nor was the wine any better than the *vin compris* Côte de Bourg that had been supplied there. I enjoyed myself because of the setting, because it was a gay and crowded scene, and my spirit was at peace after those two punches. But there was no denying that it had been a very ordinary meal.

That first lunch was to prove typical of many of the meals that I ate in the Caribbean during the next three decades. In the following year I made a five-month tour of the whole area. In 1938 I visited most of the islands that I had missed on that first trip. After World War II, between 1948 and 1958, I went again most years, and I stayed in every kind of hotel and guest house; I visited friends. I always asked for "the special local dish". I always looked forward to my meals; and it is true that I usually enjoyed them. How could I not have in such a setting, either on a shaded porch or high on a veranda, overhung with bougainvillea, looking out "over the bright blue meadow of a bay," my spirits soothed with rum.

And indeed there were many admirable foods to enjoy—particularly the fruits and vegetables. The mango is in a class by itself. Out of the soursop can be made a delicious cool drink—it is almost a soup—with which to begin a lunch. Guava jelly takes the place of marmalade. À cook I had in Martinique greatly enhanced her coffee with a thick white cream she squeezed out of the pulp of the coconut. In St. Lucia I had some excellent wild woodcock. Barbados had its flying fish. Trinidad its pepper-pot, a pungent stew that has been handed down from one generation to another. Dominica has a bullfrog—called "mountain chicken" in case delicate susceptibilities might be affronted by exact definition—that has a most delicate flavour.

Nevertheless, almost everywhere I went in those days I was reminded of that first, disappointing meal in Fort-de-France. There was an uninspired sameness in most of the food served me, and a lack of distinction in the cooking. I always felt that it should somehow have been better, in view of the rich soil and the congenial climate.

The author of this book, Linda Wolfe, formed the same opinion when she first went to the islands in 1958, and in the opening pages she gives the historical reasons for the mediocrity of the cuisine. The greater part of the book, however, is devoted to the changes for the better that have taken place during the 1960s. Partly in response to the tourist boom that has struck the area like a hurricane, and partly out of rising national pride, the West Indians—citizens, restaurateurs and government officials alike—have set themselves the task of fostering a cuisine based on the materials available in and peculiar to the islands. They are, Mrs. Wolfe says, achieving remarkable success.

I was fascinated by her account. It is some years since I have been in the islands, and she told me a great deal I did not know. Her book will be invaluable to the tourist. It will tell him what to look for, explain to him what he is being served. It will also encourage local chefs to further experiment.

I have often wondered during recent years whether I should ever go to the West Indies again. So many of my old friends have vanished, so many familiar beaches have been appropriated by hotels. But now thanks to Mrs. Wolfe I have a powerful inducement to return. With her book in hand, I propose to make a thorough tour of the islands, sampling and savouring the dishes that so long eluded me. It should be one of the most rewarding trips that I have ever made in the Caribbean and I do not propose to hurry it. I am very grateful to Mrs. Wolfe.

—*Alec Waugh*

Mr. Waugh, author of "Island in the Sun", "A Family of Islands" and other books and magazine articles about the West Indies, wrote the volume on "Wines and Spirits" for the Foods of the World Library.

I

A Lively Cuisine in the Making

Opposite: Framed by palm fronds, a laden Grenadian woman walks along a sun-blanched beach. Her large baskets are filled with smaller baskets in turn full of local spices—allspice, nutmeg, cinnamon and other seasonings closely identified with the Caribbean cuisine. She sells the smaller spice baskets to tourists as souvenirs.

The first time I travelled in the Caribbean was in 1958. My husband and I spent ten days in Puerto Rico and the Virgin Islands, staying at hotels whose dining-rooms flaunted plastic greenery embellished with fake tropical fruits and whose bedrooms were furnished with teak chairs from Sweden and inexpensive prints of French Impressionist paintings. In the evening we listened to American girls in strapless gowns singing pop tunes. And we were never once served, anywhere, a breadfruit, a mango or a pawpaw.

One evening we decided to escape from hotel life. We drove to the outskirts of San Juan and stopped at an outdoor restaurant where whole families, babies and all, were eating at long tables beneath coloured lanterns. In the enclosed courtyard we examined the fare, which turned out to be exclusively land crabs. Caged in large wire-netted pens, the dark clawing creatures looked grotesque but, we reasoned, no more so than the costly sea crabs in our New York fish market. We questioned the restaurant owner and learned that land crabs, which are scavengers, must be purged before they can be eaten. This was done by putting the crabs on a strict three-day diet. The first day of their captivity they were fed coconut, the second day corn and water, and the third corn alone. This coarse, bland food both fattened the crabs and cleaned their stomachs. Everyone at the restaurant looked happy and hale, so we decided to have our dinner there. The land crabs that were served to us were boiled, removed from their shells, cut into small pieces, and mixed with a sauce that contained garlic, olive oil, coriander leaves and tomatoes. It was an exhilarating new taste to me, the meat softer and more chewy than that of the sea crab and the sauce glitteringly spicy.

8

A woman from a near-by table stopped to chat with us and regaled us with a story about Sir Francis Drake, one of the early explorers of the Caribbean. Once Drake and his men lay in ambush on Hispaniola, hoping to attack the Spanish, when they were frightened from their hiding place by the terrifying sound of a cavalry onslaught. They rushed back to their boats in alarm only to realize that the sound they had heard was the noisy scuttling of an army of land crabs through the undergrowth.

We enjoyed that dinner far more than the glazed baked ham, the beef Stroganov and the sirloin steaks turned out by the kitchen of our hotel, although I admit it wasn't the crabs, or *jueyes*, alone that delighted us. We were also beguiled by the chance to use our bookish Spanish and listen to the silvery sounds of laughing children and guitar-playing fathers.

For me that evening was the beginning of an enduring interest in both the people and the cooking of the Caribbean. At that time it was very difficult to obtain authentic Caribbean food either in the United States or in the Caribbean itself. I knew of one restaurant in New York City operated by an *émigré* from Trinidad. It was tiny, dark, and redolent of herbs—the living room of the owner's apartment, a room crowded with students who, like me, enjoyed the cheap, filling rice dishes and the peppery sauces that were perfect for our budgets.

In the islands themselves there were only a few restaurants that specialized in local food. Hotel dining-rooms tended to serve a cuisine billed as Continental, an often unsatisfying version of French cooking based on frozen ingredients from the United States. Although there are hundreds of Caribbean dishes that could have been prepared from fresh ingredients, most hoteliers ignored these and often denigrated native Caribbean food. Indeed, on the night my husband and I returned from our land crab dinner, we mentioned it to the hotel manager, an American, who frowned and said, "You shouldn't have gone there. There's no telling how clean those crabs are."

"Then where," we asked, "is a good place to sample Puerto Rican food?"

"No place," he said. "Because there is none. No decent Puerto Rican food anyway. Except, perhaps, the slice of lime we put in the rum punch."

All this is different today. At sophisticated new resorts the furniture is made by local craftsmen out of native woods such as *gommier* and *bois-ti-baume*, and on the walls hang island-made patchwork tapestries or intricate hand-woven straw mats. Calypso singers, steel bands and limbo dancers perform nightly at all the bastions of tourism. Throughout the islands those who cater for the needs of the tourist have come to recognize that he *wants* to experience Caribbean culture, that there *is* a culture in the Caribbean worth experiencing, and that one of the most exciting aspects of that culture is its cuisine.

It is a cuisine based on the treasures of the rich tropical soil of the region—guava, mango, pawpaw, pineapple, coconut, okra, cassava, bread-fruit, plantain and a host of other exotic fruits and vegetables. It is a cuisine that is at its most successful when dealing with the fruits of the tropical sea, the local spiny lobster, conch, prawns and endless varieties of fish. Two foods that Europeans did not know about before Columbus explored the Caribbean—tomatoes and hot peppers—give the island cooking its most important flavours. And spiciness and heartiness are the cuisine's most dominant characteristics.

A term often used in relation to Caribbean cooking is Creole, though it is a word with many meanings. Originally, both in the United States and in the islands, Creole meant a person of pure French or Spanish descent born in the New World. Today in much of the United States and throughout the Caribbean the meaning has changed to describe a person of mixed negro and white descent. Sometimes in the Caribbean it is defined as "all mixed up and born in the islands." That description applies as aptly to much of the cuisine. Except for delicacies straight off a tree or just out of the sea that are served with absolute simplicity, the best Caribbean dishes are spicy mixtures of island flavours, blended often with tomatoes, usually with hot peppers and always with imagination.

It would be foolish to claim that the Caribbean cuisine is on a par with the great cuisines of Europe or that it is as well developed as some of the long-established cuisines of the Orient. At the time of their discovery by Columbus in 1492 the islands of the Caribbean were peopled by primitive Indians. Sizeable colonies did not exist until some hundred years after that. For the next two centuries wars and piracy and poverty ravaged the islands, inhibiting the development of such graces as an intricate cuisine. Furthermore, what indigenous cooking did exist was buried by the colonialist contempt for anything "native" —a derogatory view of the local food that to some extent was shared by the natives themselves. Today, with many of the islands newly independent and with more stable economies developing, a Caribbean cuisine is beginning to flower. It is a cuisine in the making—enticing, exotic and above all experimental.

Because of their great distance from Europe, the Caribbean islands are still a mystery to most Europeans, even to those who have visited them. There are more than 7,000 islands in all in the area, some little more than rocks in the sea, some of considerable size. Cuba, the largest, is almost as big as Bulgaria. Hispaniola, the name for the island that comprises both Haiti and the Dominican Republic, is the next largest, followed by Jamaica and Puerto Rico. These four islands and some 25 other relatively large ones make up most of the land area of the Caribbean; they are known collectively as the West Indies, or, sometimes, the Antilles, a name used by 14th-century Europeans to describe a group of imaginary islands in the Atlantic.

The West Indies form a grand arc that curves east and south from Cuba, just below Florida, to Trinidad, just off the coast of Venezuela, and that encloses the Caribbean Sea in its mountainous embrace. Though the sea itself covers an area of 750,000 square miles, all the islands would fit easily into an area the size of Yugoslavia. Geologists say that during the last Ice Age the islands were part of an unbroken isthmus, a land bridge that spanned the distance between Florida and Venezuela. This land bridge was submerged in later times by a cataclysmic series of earthquakes, hurricanes and volcanic eruptions— three furies that still bedevil the region—and only the tops of the mountains remained above sea level to form the islands we know today.

The first impression they give, of course, is one of unsurpassing beauty. Columbus, the Caribbean's first foreign intruder, was astonished by the natural splendours of the area and his admiration has been

Continued on page 14

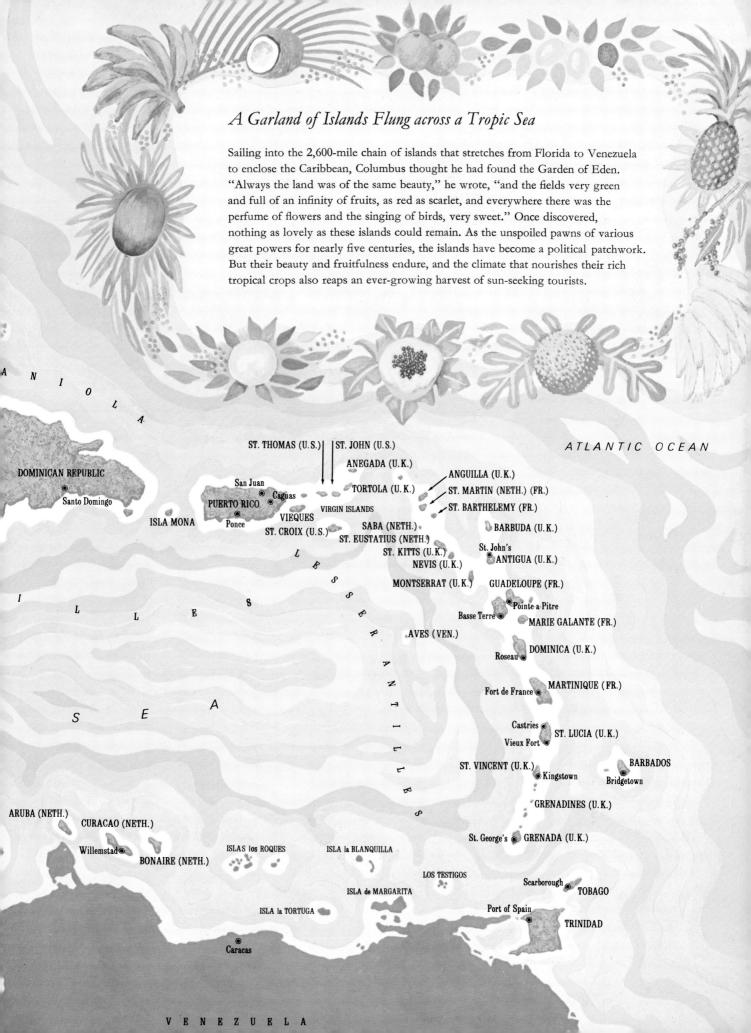

A Garland of Islands Flung across a Tropic Sea

Sailing into the 2,600-mile chain of islands that stretches from Florida to Venezuela to enclose the Caribbean, Columbus thought he had found the Garden of Eden. "Always the land was of the same beauty," he wrote, "and the fields very green and full of an infinity of fruits, as red as scarlet, and everywhere there was the perfume of flowers and the singing of birds, very sweet." Once discovered, nothing as lovely as these islands could remain. As the unspoiled pawns of various great powers for nearly five centuries, the islands have become a political patchwork. But their beauty and fruitfulness endure, and the climate that nourishes their rich tropical crops also reaps an ever-growing harvest of sun-seeking tourists.

ATLANTIC OCEAN

ST. THOMAS (U.S.) ST. JOHN (U.S.)
ANEGADA (U.K.)
ANGUILLA (U.K.)
San Juan
TORTOLA (U.K.)
ST. MARTIN (NETH.) (FR.)
PUERTO RICO
Caguas
ST. BARTHELEMY (FR.)
VIRGIN ISLANDS
DOMINICAN REPUBLIC
Santo Domingo
VIEQUES
Ponce
BARBUDA (U.K.)
ISLA MONA
ST. CROIX (U.S.)
SABA (NETH.)
ST. EUSTATIUS (NETH.)
St. John's
ST. KITTS (U.K.)
ANTIGUA (U.K.)
NEVIS (U.K.)
MONTSERRAT (U.K.)
GUADELOUPE (FR.)
Pointe-a-Pitre
Basse Terre
MARIE GALANTE (FR.)
AVES (VEN.)
Roseau
DOMINICA (U.K.)

LESSER ANTILLES

CARIBBEAN SEA

Fort de France
MARTINIQUE (FR.)
Castries
ST. LUCIA (U.K.)
Vieux Fort
ST. VINCENT (U.K.)
BARBADOS
Kingstown
Bridgetown

ARUBA (NETH.)
CURACAO (NETH.)
GRENADINES (U.K.)
Willemstad
St. George's GRENADA (U.K.)
BONAIRE (NETH.)
ISLAS los ROQUES
ISLA la BLANQUILLA
LOS TESTIGOS
Scarborough
TOBAGO
ISLA de MARGARITA
ISLA la TORTUGA
Port of Spain
TRINIDAD
Caracas

VENEZUELA

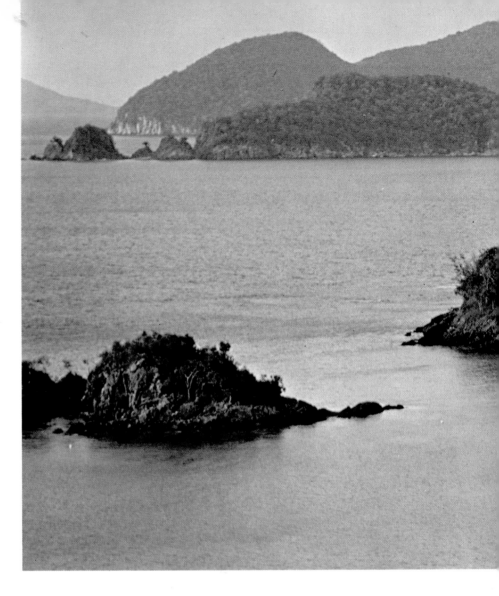

Crystalline water, smooth beaches, wooded hills plunging into the sea, and the sight of other islands—these are some of the enchantments of the Caribbean. This hawk's-eye view shows Trunk Bay on St. John in the Virgin Islands. The houses are part of the Caneel Bay Plantation, a resort developed by the Rockefeller family.

echoed by every traveller since. I myself am overwhelmed every time I go there. First of all, the water of the Caribbean is soft and caressing, buoyant and never cold. It is so radiant with sunlight that its colour is constantly changing from crystal to aquamarine to sapphire to emerald—a perpetual rainbow of white, blue and green. Along the water's edge are the beaches that have made the region a mecca for tourists. Some are rocky, with great cliffs that thrust down fiercely into the water and make even the experienced swimmer uneasy. Others are long, gentle miles of uninterrupted sand either gleaming white or intense lava black. Nor is the beauty of the islands skin deep. Their interiors are lovely too. Some are arid and pricked with cactus; others are gently fertile, with orderly banana groves and fields of waving sugar cane. Still others are crazily overgrown with tumbling vegetation, ferns and palms, flowers and fruits and creepers all entangled. Even more dramatic are the mountains, which look too high and heavy for the floating earth that bears them. They rise skywards like cathedrals, and on their slopes are dark chapels of rain forests, mysterious with the chants of birds and insects.

But perhaps the most breath-taking sight on a Caribbean island is the view of another island. The first time I looked across from one island to another was in Trinidad, where we had been driving in the rain

14

along a scary narrow road. The sea was cloudy and churning all round us. I felt as if I were on a ship rather than on land. Then suddenly the clouds parted and there, quite close, was a great looming mass of land— the island of Tobago. It startled me, and I have never quite grown used to such sudden ghostly appearances. When I left Martinique by boat, I was sad at leaving its beaches and mountains and one of the few really romantic towns in the Caribbean, Fort-de-France, with its secretive old houses and wrought-iron balconies. But no sooner had Martinique disappeared behind us than there on the horizon was fortress-like Dominica, and my spirits leaped at once at the thought of exploring its forests, its waterfalls and its hundreds of streams. From Dominica I could see Guadeloupe, from Guadeloupe the Îles des Saintes. One is really never out of sight of land in the Caribbean and never able to quell one's *wanderlust*. This is the most compelling of all its qualities, as Columbus himself discovered. Like a tourist confronted with too many travel brochures, he wrote, "I saw so many islands that I could not decide to which I would go first." Each island he visited impressed him more than the last with its fertility, its soft breezes, its looming mountains; and time after time he concluded of one island after another, "It is the loveliest thing that I have seen", or, "It is the fairest island that eyes have beheld."

What makes the islands so fair, besides their beauty, is their glorious climate. They bask in the tropical sun, caressed by the boisterous Atlantic Ocean on one side and the gentler Caribbean on the other. They are alternately buffeted and soothed by the trade winds that blow from the ocean, and their tropical heat is often subdued by torrential rains. Though the weather can change dramatically from one minute to the next, climatic conditions in the course of a year are remarkably constant and, with some exceptions, are much the same from island to island. It is a climate in which a man can grow lazy but in which plants grow with abandon. This means that a great variety of trees and plants— including those basic to the local cuisine, such as coconut, mango and bread-fruit trees, peppers, plantains, sugar-cane—grow naturally and profusely from one end of the Caribbean to the other.

The political history of the area has been much less equable than its climate. Today a good many of the islands are self-governing countries. But independence has come to them only in the last few decades. For most of the last four and a half centuries the islands have been under the continuous domination of various European powers. Sometimes a single island has belonged successively to several owners. Jamaica was Spanish for 146 years, then English for 307 years; Guadeloupe was Spanish, then English, then French; St. Lucia changed hands six times in 20 years. Not only Spain, England and France, the chief colonial powers, but also Holland, Denmark and the United States have owned Caribbean islands.

Because of this historical pattern it has long been usual to view the islands not as a cultural entity but more as appendages of their European owners. Before I began seeing them for myself I shared this view, particularly where food was concerned. I expected that if an island was owned by France or Holland, Spain or England, not only the hotel but also the local fare would be French or Dutch, Spanish or English.

Then I began travelling among the islands and paying close attention to what I was eating. Sometimes my husband went with me, sometimes I took our daughter Jessica, sometimes I went with friends. I went whenever possible to those islands most famous for their cuisine or for their cultural contribution to the area as a whole—to Jamaica, Trinidad, Barbados, Dominica, Guadeloupe, Martinique, Puerto Rico, the Dominican Republic and Curaçao—though I have not been to two other places that have had an important influence on the cooking of the region: I was unable to make arrangements to visit Cuba and unwilling to visit inhospitable Haiti. To understand the cooking on these two islands I have had to content myself with reading about it, and with eating with and talking to Cubans and Haitians living in other parts of the Caribbean and in the United States.

I survived dozens of airports, and—coping haltingly with the various languages of the Caribbean—enjoyed hundreds of meals with friends and new acquaintances and ate in restaurants great and small; and I came to a very surprising conclusion. There *is* a cuisine common to all the islands, whatever their colonial past. It is not accurate, I decided, to discuss the cuisine of the West Indies strictly in terms of "Spanish islands", "French islands", "English islands" and so on. Most of us were taught history as the history of nations rather than of peoples, but the fact is that a Martinican does not have a closer cultural resemblance to a Frenchman than he does to a Jamaican, nor a Curaçaoan a closer resemblance to a Dutchman than to a Puerto Rican. Caribbean culture and Caribbean cuisine are based not on the various European nations that have ruled there for periods of time but on four waves of influence shared by all the islands: what might be called intercontinental rather than international waves.

To start with, there were the native inhabitants of the region—Carib and Arawak Indians originally from South America, who had started out from what is now Venezuela and the Guianas and spread north-wards through the islands. They were displaced and dispersed by the settlers who followed upon the voyages of Columbus—Spanish soldiers, English pirates, Dutch merchants, Irishmen, Scotsmen, Frenchmen, fortune-seekers from everywhere in Europe. After the Europeans came Africans from the Congo, Guinea and the Gold Coast, enslaved and brought in to work the sugar-cane fields the Europeans had planted. The negroes were followed by Orientals, indentured servants from China and India. Not all but most islands in the Caribbean have experienced these four waves of settlement, their mixed populations testify.

You quickly become aware in the Caribbean of how much the races have mixed and, more than that, of how beneficial the social results have been. This is a matter of pride for many islanders, whatever their colour. I was first struck by this fact one morning some years ago during a visit to Jamaica. I was travelling with a friend, a blue-eyed golden-haired girl. I myself am dark-haired and dark-eyed. The policeman in front of our hotel, trim in his red-striped uniform, greeted us with characteristic Jamaican courtesy. "Good morning," he said as I came out, trailed at some distance by my friend. "It's a lovely morning, isn't it? And you're looking lovely this morning to match it." Then seeing my companion, he added, "and your sister is too." Priscilla and I laughed. "Sisters?" I asked. "How can we be sisters with her so fair and me so dark?" He laughed and said, "Why not? Jamaica does that all the time to families."

He was exaggerating, but the islanders are indeed ethnically mixed. And so too is their cuisine. The same amalgam of races that created the population also created Caribbean cooking.

The first influence was a primitive one. Some of the Indians were farmers of sorts, raising starchy roots like cassava—from which they made bread—sweet potatoes and arrowroot; others were hunters and gatherers of game and fish, of guava and cashew fruit and pineapple. The Europeans had never seen many of these, and they learned the dangers and the delights of native Caribbean foods from the Indians.

But the Indians' foods were not sufficient to sustain the large numbers of European colonists who followed the discoverers. Columbus, charged by the Spanish monarchs with colonial responsibility, learned this quickly, and he soon began demanding that Spain send flour and meat, oil, vinegar and wine. The Spanish priest Las Casas, who came to settle in Hispaniola only eight years after it had been discovered, wrote that only the finding of gold—a rare occurrence—brought as much happiness to the colonists there as the arrival of food from Spain. But it was risky to rely on such shipments and so the settlers were forced to experiment with new crops that might take hold in the hospitable climate. Thus they initiated the second culinary wave in the area. Many of the foods we now consider virtually synonymous with the word Caribbean, including bread-fruit, oranges, limes, mangoes, rice, coffee and

Overleaf: A typical scene in the Caribbean can be bustling as well as languid. Clustered in the early morning sunlight, farmers and their customers fill the noisy Market Square in the town of St. George's, in Grenada. Everybody's Store, whose front is on the square, has not even opened for business yet; but the fruit and vegetable sellers—who rose long before dawn to pack up and travel to town in lorries and the local buses with names like *Show Time* and *St. Andrew's Pride*—are already briskly selling such staple foods as bananas, plantains, bread-fruit, tomatoes, yams and peppers.

17

even sugar-cane, were introduced to the West Indies by European colonists.

The next great influence in Caribbean cooking was the result of the influx of African slaves. Fifteen million slaves were imported into the Americas between 1518 and 1865. Exactly how many of these were taken to which islands is not certain, but it is known that during one century at the height of the slave trade two million Africans went to the British West Indies alone. Besides bringing some of their own foods with them—plants like okra and callaloo, taro and akee—the Africans developed a style of cooking that is the basis of food in the Caribbean today. Because they were so often fed with foods their masters rejected or that were cheap to raise and had little taste, they learned how to flavour their food cleverly. Pungent seasoning and spicing were essential to make poor foods palatable.

Today, no stew in the English-speaking islands starts without the cook's first buying "a bunch of sive", and the "sive", which is spring onion that is tied up in a bouquet with parsley or coriander leaves and thyme. On the Spanish-speaking islands dozens of dishes are made from the same herb and vegetable base; dish after dish begins with *sofrito*, a sauce made from annatto seeds, coriander leaves, tiny green peppers, onions, garlic and tomatoes. In all the islands meat and fish will usually have been marinated and seasoned with herbs before anything else is done to them. Ginger, nutmeg, cloves and allspice are

Fine French cooking is rare in most of the Caribbean but easy to find in Martinique, where there are several restaurants that could hold their own in Paris. Le Foyal, on the harbour front of Fort-de-France, is one of the best. The waitress is dressed in the old Martinican fashion, with a traditional *madwas* on her head.

lavishly used. So is cinnamon; in fact, if you ask simply for "spice" in the islands, cinnamon is what you will get. But the most important element in Caribbean seasoning is the hot pepper—which in the United States is more often called the chilli pepper. To a palate unfamiliar with them, one hot pepper is indistinguishable from another except in the degree to which it burns the mouth. But to an islander each variety of hot pepper has a quality and flavour of its own; Jamaicans, for instance, will argue endlessly over the comparative virtues of the Scotch bonnet and the country pepper. Good island cooks recognize, however, that even their favourite peppers must be handled with discretion if they are to enhance, not annihilate, other flavours. There is a French Creole story that makes this point, mocking a foolish woman who found that she had no ingredients but hot peppers in her kitchen and who thought that because they were so tasty she could make a palatable soup of them for the family's dinner. Her children took one sip of the soup, ran to the river to cool their mouths, and drank and drank until they drowned.

The fourth intercontinental wave reached the Caribbean only in the last century. In the early 1800s agitation against the slave system began to be heard in Europe, particularly in England, and pressure was gradually applied to the colonialists to free their slaves. By 1850 the French and English colonies had grudgingly granted emancipation to their slaves. But although they were then offered wages, working conditions were still brutal and degrading, and many ex-slaves chose to leave the fields entirely. Where this occurred, and also on islands such as Trinidad, where large-scale sugar production did not begin until the emancipation, plantation owners desperately needed a new labour force. Their solution was to import large numbers of indentured servants from the Orient, some from China, most from India. Thus emerged the fourth influence on Caribbean food. While curry may have been eaten in the Caribbean before the 1830s, perhaps prepared in the kitchen of an Englishman who knew about Indian cooking, its prevalence throughout the region today is due to the presence of East Indians. In some islands, particularly Hispaniola and Puerto Rico, where there were fewer slaves in the first place, there was no Oriental influx. Elsewhere, however, curry has become as Caribbean a dish as it is Indian. The Dutch islanders call it *kerry* and the French islanders call it *colombo*. All agree that they need curry because it causes them to perspire and thus cools off the body.

Other Oriental influences can be seen in the concern with the correct way of cooking rice, in the presence of Chinese vegetables in many of the islands' markets, and in the increasing popularity of the Trinidad *roti*, a flat Indian bread, and of Indian dishes like Jamaica's *katarri*, which one Jamaican defined as "an Indian delicacy of Irish potato, rice, and other else things."

It is the interplay of aboriginal, European, African and Oriental influences that has given the Caribbean cuisine its own distinct formula—an amalgam that can be found in all the islands. Thus a traveller will find many of the same dishes in a Caribbean meal no matter where he eats. To begin at the beginning, there are a number of interesting foods that we would think of as hors d'oeuvre, readily available in most of the islands whether they were once French or Spanish, English or Dutch. My favourite dish is a crisp vegetable fritter most often made of mashed black-eyed peas or beans, perked up with hot peppers and so

This is the oldest kitchen in the Americas, re-created in Santo Domingo, capital of the Dominican Republic. In 1509 Columbus' son Diego arrived in the island of Hispaniola as Viceroy for the Spanish kingdom of Castile and Léon. His palace, known as the Alcazar, or fortress, was restored in 1957. The kitchen, despite its single fire-place, furnished food even for state dinners.

finely ground and thoroughly beaten before it is deep-fried that it seems to double in bulk like a yeast cake. These ubiquitous fritters are called *cala* in the Dutch islands; French and English islanders call them akkra, a name that comes from the African Yoruba language.

In Puerto Rico drinks are frequently served with little fritters of mashed spicy salt fish, called *bacalaitos* or *hojuelas de bacalao*. These are known as *acrat de morue* or *marinades* in the French islands and by a number of wonderful names in the English islands: sometimes poor man's fritters, sometimes macadam—because some cooks make them as flat and hard as paving stones—sometimes John Staggerback, for the same reason. In Jamaica the most popular name for the cakes is stamp and go (*Recipe Index*), an oddity that reflects the Jamaican's penchant for nautical language. The phrase "stamp and go" was a command given to 17th-century English sailors when they were to perform certain duties —to step out round the capstan, for instance, or to haul on a line. The words struck the people's fancy in Jamaica, came ashore, and were put to a new use.

Crisp, finger-thin fried corn sticks called *surullitos* (*Recipe Index*) in Puerto Rico are also found under a variety of names in different islands. So are *morcillas*, or blood sausages. Called pudding in the English-speaking islands, blood sausage is inevitably accompanied by souse, which is the lime-marinated meat of pig's head, tongue and trotters. Pudding and souse can be found on the table at Sunday brunch or at an afternoon gathering almost anywhere in Trinidad or Barbados.

I like best the blood pudding of the French islands, perhaps because there they always mix the blood with bread, while in other islands it is sometimes mixed with sweet potatoes, rice or cassava flour instead. Other islanders sometimes seem ashamed of their fondness for this humble dish, but not the French islanders. It is "dear to the Creole heart," says a French island cookery-book writer, Marie-Eugenie Bourgeois, and she adds, "It is the snack of one's dreams."

Stuffed land-crab backs are another inter-island first-course speciality. The meat of the land crab, which is superior in flavour to that of the local sea crab, is boiled, minced and sautéed with hot peppers and herbs, spices and breadcrumbs, then stuffed appetisingly back into the shells. There are any number of ways of varying the ingredients.

Wherever one goes in the Caribbean one will find these dishes and many more, and the experienced island hopper can tell you which speciality he prefers in which island. Curiously, however, when you talk to an islander, he is very likely to tell you that the akkra fritters or the pudding or the crab back is a particular speciality of his island; he is not aware that it is a speciality everywhere. This is so partly because the international rivalry that for so long dominated Caribbean history produced an intense isolationism; islands were not encouraged to communicate with one another but only with their European owners. I had this dramatically brought home to me one night at dinner in Bar-

The food for a meal at the Alcazar was carried upstairs from the kitchen to this serving room before being taken into the dining-room next door. Most of the great Spanish *conquistadores* visited the Alcazar, perhaps to eat from china such as the emblazoned plate below. "A Castilla y a Leon Nuevo Mundo Dio Colon," it reads, "To Castile and Léon, Columbus gave a New World".

23

bados, during which we ate akkra and blood pudding and sautéed sea eggs. My host, a radical who claimed ties with Africa, declared that he did not feel at all English although he was English educated. Since I was going on to Guadeloupe, I asked him whether he felt any ties with the people in the French islands. I spoke rhetorically, expecting that he would of course say yes, we are all African and have all been exploited in similar ways by Europeans. But surprisingly he said, "No. They are French". I argued that they were African by his own definition. "No," he said, and then, "not like us. Perhaps they are from Algeria. In any case they are not like us." I was not surprised, when I was invited to dinner on Guadeloupe a few days later, to be served akkra and blood sausage and sea eggs. The region and the heritage decreed it. And naturally my host explained to me that these delicacies were Guadeloupe's own specialities.

Certainly there are differences in the cuisine of the Caribbean. There are islands that have special dishes not to be found elsewhere, sometimes because a certain ingredient cannot be grown or obtained anywhere else. There are differences, too, in methods of cooking. One Haitian I know swears that he cannot abide eating with Jamaicans because, although they cook virtually the same dishes he makes at home, they use coconut oil for sautéeing while the Haitians prefer butter and olive oil, in the French style. More important, there are different attitudes towards food. In Barbados an islander of English descent warned me not to bother tasting callaloo—a thick spicy soup that is a local favourite, made of okra, salt pork, crab meat and a leafy spinach-like vegetable that is also called callaloo. But on Guadeloupe a French-descended islander kissed her finger-tips at the mention of callaloo. "The Creole cuisine is superb," she glowed, "and callaloo with crab is the king."

There is even a fifth intercontinental wave now in the process of changing the Caribbean culinary scene. It is, of course, the growing wave of tourism. On many islands the tourist boom has brought a general upgrading of the food and an interest in new dishes that draw upon local ingredients in an imaginative way. An hotelier will wrap bacon round banana to produce a new hors-d'oeuvre. Or he will offer pawpaw and prosciutto, a variation on the standard melon and prosciutto. Islanders like hot soups, but tourists prefer something cool to start their meals, so to suit them a rainbow of new cold soups has been devised from local ingredients. Chilled orange soup and chilled avocado soup are among the most successful.

The Caribbean is undergoing dynamic changes. Islands that were colonies are now independent; islands that survived for centuries on a one-crip economy are growing a greater variety of foodstuffs; islands that were once remote and isolated are now visited daily by travellers from all over the world. There is an exciting, simmering feeling in the Caribbean these days and it can certainly be sensed in food as well as in politics and economics. The situation reminds me of a classic Caribbean dish, pepper-pot, a stew the aboriginal Indians made. Kept going on the fire, with new ingredients added each day over the course of weeks or months—or even, legend says, for generations— pepper-pot is enhanced by age. To me Caribbean cooking is itself a pepper-pot with new elements constantly being added and the old ones constantly being blended in, refined and absorbed. The pepper-pot is maturing and the longer it simmers the better it gets.

Opposite: Pudding and souse are a familiar pair throughout the Caribbean, and a good excuse for an afternoon party in this Trinidadian house. The pudding is blood, or black, sausage; the souse is lime-marinated pork. Conveniently for the hostess, the combination may be served at room temperature. Here they are accompanied by a loaf of banana bread and iced drinks.

24

Green Plantain Crisps (Jamaica)

To serve 4

Vegetable oil or fat for deep-
    frying
1 large green plantain (about 1 lb.)
Salt

Fill a deep-frying pan or large, heavy saucepan with vegetable oil or cooking fat to a depth of 2 or 3 inches and heat to a temperature of 375° F. on a deep-frying thermometer.

Trim off the ends of the plantain with a small, sharp knife, and cut it in half crosswise. Following the diagram (*Banana Pésé: Recipe Index*), cut four evenly spaced slits lengthways in each half. Pull the skin away from the white banana-like fruit inside with your fingers and pull or cut off the fibrous strings. Slice the plantain crosswise into paper-thin rounds.

Deep-fry the plantain slices, a dozen or so at a time, for 3 to 4 minutes turning them over with a perforated spoon until they are golden brown on both sides. Transfer them to kitchen paper to drain as they brown.

Sprinkle with salt and serve the crisps warm or at room temperature.

Pudding and Souse (Trinidad)

BLACK PUDDING WITH COLD LIME-MARINATED PORK HOCKS

To serve 6 to 8 as a first course

4 lb. fresh pork hocks (*see note*)
1 large onion, peeled and quartered
3 teaspoons salt
½ pint strained fresh lime juice
1 large cucumber
1 teaspoon finely chopped fresh hot
    chillies (*caution: see "How to Handle
    Chillies"*)
Watercress or whole fresh hot
    chillies for garnish
1 to 1½ lb. commercially made
    black pudding (blood sausage)

Note. It is not always possible to find butchers who will sell pork hocks as such but they may be willing to cut them from the more familiar joint, a hand of pork, a large joint which includes what is known as the "hock end".
Alternatively, forehock of bacon could be substituted using the meat from the leaner end and giving it a preliminary salting. No salt would probably be needed in the lime juice marinade.

Wash the pork hocks thoroughly under cold running water, then place them in a large pan or flame-proof casserole and pour in enough cold water to cover them by about 1 inch. Bring to the boil over a high heat, meanwhile skimming off the scum and foam that rise to the surface. Add the onion and 2 teaspoons of the salt, and reduce the heat to low. Simmer with the pan partly covered for about 2 hours. (Keep the pork covered with water and add more boiling water to the pan if necessary.) When they are done, they should show no resistance when pierced with the point of a sharp knife. Transfer the pork to a plate, strain the cooking liquid through a fine sieve set over a bowl, and put it aside.

While the pork is still warm, remove and discard the skin and bones. Cut the meat into ½-inch cubes, drop them into a bowl, and add ⅜ pint of the lime juice and the remaining teaspoon of salt. Turn the meat over with a spoon to coat it evenly and marinate it in the refrigerator for at least 12 hours, turning over the meat occasionally to keep it well moistened.

Before serving, prepare the sauce in the following way: Trim and peel the cucumber with a small sharp knife or swivel-bladed vegetable parer. Grate enough of the cucumber to fill 1 tablespoon and slice the rest of the cucumber crosswise into ¼-inch-thick rounds. Set the slices aside.

Put the grated cucumber, 6 tablespoons of the reserved cooking liquid, the rest of the lime juice and the chillies into a serving bowl and stir together until well mixed. Taste the sauce and add salt and freshly ground pepper if desired.

To serve, drain the diced meat thoroughly and discard the marinade. Add the meat and the cucumber slices to the sauce and turn them over and over with a spoon until the pieces are evenly coated. Garnish the bowl with watercress or whole fresh chillies.

The black pudding or blood sausage, which is traditionally served with souse, may be poached or fried and presented whole or sliced into ½-inch-thick pieces arranged attractively on a dish.

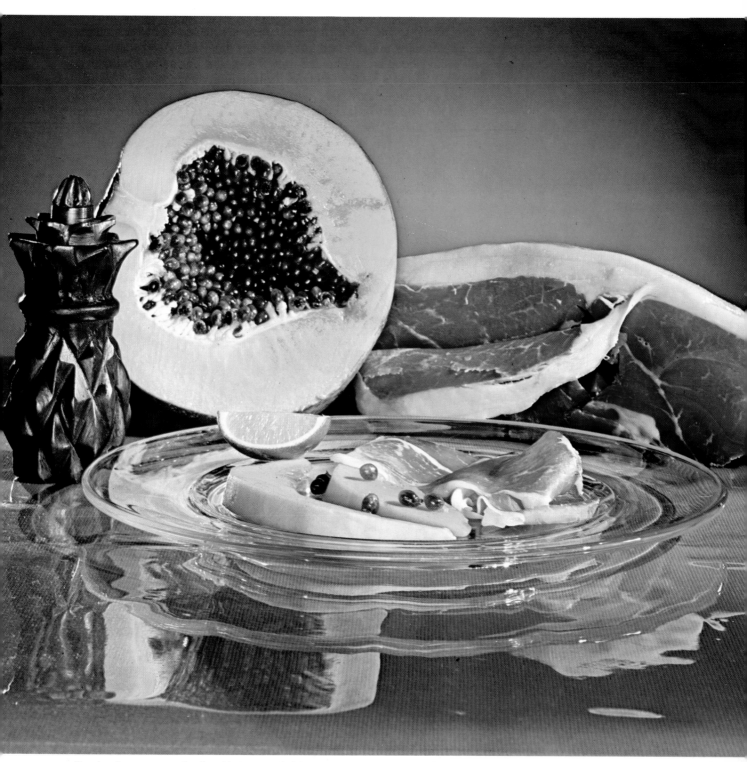

Serving home-grown foods with imported delicacies is a
popular practice among islanders and often produces
unexpected delights such as this first course of fresh colourful
pawpaw with prosciutto. The fruit is peeled, seeded and cut
into wedges, the prosciutto is sliced paper thin, and the two
are served with a wedge of lime and a sprinkling of capers,
with a pepper mill handy. (*See box on page 116.*)

Jellied Orange Consommé *(Grenada)*

To serve 6

1½ pints cold chicken stock
½ oz. powdered gelatine
2 egg whites, beaten
1¼ pints strained fresh orange juice
Salt
1 unpeeled orange, cut crosswise into
 paper-thin slices

Skim the surface of the chicken stock of all fat, using a large spoon. Pour the stock into a deep bowl, sprinkle the gelatine on top, and let it soften for 5 minutes. Then pour the stock into a large, heavy saucepan and add the beaten egg whites. Bring the stock to the boil over a high heat, stirring constantly with a whisk.

When the stock begins to froth and rise, remove the pan from the heat. Let the mixture rest for 5 minutes, then pour it into a large sieve set over a deep bowl and lined with a double thickness of cheesecloth or a damp tea towel.

Allow the liquid to drain through into the bowl without disturbing it at any point. Then stir in the strained orange juice, taste the soup, and season it with salt if desired.

Refrigerate the consommé for at least 4 to 6 hours, until it is thoroughly chilled and firm enough to hold its shape lightly in a spoon.

Serve the jellied consommé in chilled soup plates and garnish each portion with slices of orange.

Stamp and Go *(Jamaica)*
CODFISH CAKES

To make about 2 dozen 1½ inch
 cakes

½ lb. salt cod
1½ tablespoons vegetable oil mixed
 with ½ teaspoon liquid annatto
4 oz. finely chopped onions
4 oz. flour
1 teaspoon baking powder
½ teaspoon salt
1 egg, lightly beaten
9 tablespoons milk
2½ teaspoons melted butter
1½ teaspoons finely chopped fresh hot
 chillies (*caution: see "How to Handle
 Chillies"*)
Vegetable oil

Starting a day in advance, place the cod in a glass, enamel or stainless-steel pan or bowl, cover it with cold water, and soak for at least 12 hours, changing the water 3 or 4 times.

Drain the cod, rinse under cold running water, place in a saucepan, and add enough fresh water to cover the fish by 1 inch. Bring to the boil over a high heat. (Taste the water. If it seems excessively salty, drain, cover with fresh water, and bring to the boil again.) Reduce the heat to low and simmer with the saucepan uncovered for about 20 minutes, until the fish flakes apart easily when prodded gently with a fork. Drain thoroughly. Remove and discard any skin and bones using a small knife, and separate the fish into coarse flakes. Set aside.

Heat the annatto-flavoured oil over a moderate heat in a heavy, medium-sized frying-pan until a light haze forms above it. Add the onions and cook for about 5 to 8 minutes, stirring frequently, until they are soft and transparent but not brown. Remove the pan from the heat.

Sift the flour, baking powder and salt into a deep bowl. Make a well in the centre of the flour and pour the egg, milk and butter into it. Mix together using a wooden spoon for just long enough to blend, then add the onions and their oil, the flaked cod and the chillies, and stir until the ingredients are well mixed and form a fairly smooth batter.

Pour vegetable oil to a depth of about ½ inch into a large, heavy frying-pan and heat until it is very hot but not smoking.

Drop the batter, a tablespoon or so at a time, into the hot oil. Do not crowd the cakes; the batter will spread quickly into rounds about 1½ inches in diameter. Fry the cakes for about 3 to 4 minutes, turning them over using a perforated spoon or a fish slice until they are golden brown on both sides. Transfer the cakes to kitchen paper to drain.

Stamp and go should be served hot or at room temperature either with drinks or as a first course accompanied by "floats" (*Recipe Index*).

The vivid orange slices are for effect, but it is the freshly squeezed juice that gives jellied orange consommé its tangy flavour.

Surullitos *(Puerto Rico)*
CHEESE CORN STICKS

Put the water and salt into a heavy, medium-sized saucepan and bring to the boil over a high heat. Pour in the cornmeal in a slow, thin stream so that the water does not stop boiling, stirring constantly; continue to stir for 10 to 15 minutes, until the porridge is smooth and thick. Remove the pan from the heat and beat in the grated cheese, using a spoon.

Cool to room temperature, then, moistening your hands from time to time in cold water, shape the mixture, 1½ tablespoons at a time, into cylinders about 3 inches long and 1 inch in diameter. The *surullitos* may be kept at room temperature for 2 to 3 hours or in the refrigerator for a day or two, covered with a sheet of plastic or greaseproof paper.

When you are ready to fry the *surullitos*, preheat the oven to the lowest possible temperature and line a large, shallow baking dish with kitchen paper. Heat the oil over a high heat in a large, heavy frying-pan until a light haze forms above it. Fry 4 or 5 *surullitos* at a time, turning them over with a perforated spoon or a fish slice for about 5 minutes, until they are crisp and golden brown. Transfer the corn sticks to the lined baking dish as they brown, and keep them warm in the oven.

Serve the *surullitos* hot or at room temperature either as an accompaniment to drinks or as a hot bread.

To make about 2 dozen sticks

1¼ pints water
1½ teaspoons salt
6¾ oz. yellow cornmeal
2½ oz. freshly grated Edam or Gouda or a mild Cheddar cheese
⅝ pint vegetable oil

29

Crisply fried *bombas de camarones y papas* make substantial savouries to serve with drinks or as a first course. Shown before, during and after cooking, the *bombas* are cylindrical cakes made from chopped prawns (*camarones*) and mashed potatoes (*papas*), flavoured with grated cheese and onions, and lightly coated with egg and breadcrumbs. The frying oil is being kept hot over the embers of a clay West Indian coal pot.

To make about 14 two-inch-long cylinders

2 medium-sized baking potatoes (about ½ lb.), peeled and quartered

2 oz. butter, cut into ½-inch pieces, plus 1 oz. butter

4 oz. freshly grated Münster cheese

1 egg yolk

3 tablespoons finely chopped fresh parsley

1¼ teaspoons salt

¼ teaspoon white pepper

1 lb. raw prawns in their shells

4 oz. finely chopped onions

2 oz. flour

1 egg, lightly beaten

1 oz. soft fresh crumbs made from white bread, prepared in a blender or finely shredded with a fork

Vegetable oil for deep frying

Bombas de Camarones y Papas (Dominican Republic)
PRAWN AND POTATO CAKES

Drop the potatoes into enough lightly salted boiling water to cover them completely, and cook briskly, uncovered, until they are tender and show no resistance when pierced with the point of a sharp knife. Drain the potatoes in a sieve or colander, return them to the pan and slide the pan backwards and forwards over a moderate heat for 10 to 15 seconds, until they are completely dry.

Force the potatoes through a ricer set over a deep bowl, or mash them with a fork or a potato masher. Add the butter pieces, the cheese, egg yolk, parsley, salt and pepper, and beat vigorously, using a large wooden spoon, until the mixture is smooth. Cover the bowl tightly with foil or a sheet of plastic and set it aside.

Shell the prawns. De-vein each by making a shallow incision down the back with a small, sharp knife and lifting out the black or white intestinal vein with the point of the knife. Chop the prawns coarsely.

Melt the remaining ounce of butter over a moderate heat in a heavy, medium-sized frying-pan. When the foam begins to subside, drop in the onions and cook for about 5 minutes, stirring constantly, until they are soft and transparent but not brown. Add the prawns and stir for 2 to 3 minutes, until they begin to turn pink. Do not overcook. Add the contents of the pan to the potato mixture and stir together gently. Taste for seasoning.

To form each prawn cake, flour your hands lightly, scoop up about 2½ tablespoons of the prawn mixture, and shape it into a cylinder about 2 inches long and ¾ inch in diameter. Roll the cylinder in flour and gently brush or shake off the excess. Paint the entire surface of the cylinder with beaten egg, using a pastry brush, then dip it into the breadcrumbs. Place the *bombas* side by side on greaseproof paper as they are shaped and coated. Refrigerate them for at least 30 minutes to set the coating.

Fill a deep-frying pan or large, heavy saucepan with oil to a depth of 3 to 4 inches, and heat it to a temperature of 375° F. on a deep-frying thermometer.

Fry the *bombas* in the hot oil 4 or 5 at a time, turning them over and over with a perforated spoon for a minute or two until they are golden brown on all sides. Transfer them to kitchen paper to drain.

Serve the *bombas* at once, either as an accompaniment to drinks or as a first course.

Pawpaw and Mango Jam (*Antigua*)

Put the pawpaw, mango, sugar and lime juice into a large, heavy enamel or stainless-steel saucepan. Bring to the boil over a moderate heat, stirring constantly. Reduce the heat to the lowest possible point and simmer uncovered for about 30 to 40 minutes, until most of the liquid has cooked away and the mixture is thick enough to hold its shape in a spoon. Stir it frequently as it begins to thicken, to prevent the jam from sticking to the bottom and sides of the pan.

Remove the pan from the heat. Ladle the jam immediately into hot sterilized preserving or jam jars, using a large spoon. Fill each preserving jar to within ⅛ inch of the top and seal it quickly and tightly with its ring and lid. Fill each jam jar to within ½ inch of the top, and at once pour a thin layer of hot paraffin over the surface of the jam, making sure it covers the jam completely and touches the inside surface all the way around. Let the jars rest until the paraffin cools and hardens, then cover them with metal lids.

Escovitch (*Jamaica*)
PICKLED FISH

Put the onions, carrots, green peppers, bay leaves, red pepper, salt and a few grindings of black pepper into a large enamel or stainless-steel saucepan. Pour in the vinegar, 1½ tablespoons of the oil and the water, and bring to the boil over a high heat. Reduce the heat to low, cover tightly, and simmer for about 30 minutes, until the vegetables are tender but not falling apart.

Meanwhile, pour the remaining 3½ tablespoons of oil into a large, heavy frying-pan and heat over a moderate heat until a light haze forms above it. Add a few fillets of the fish at a time, and cook them for 2 to 3 minutes on each side, until delicately brown. Transfer the fillets as they brown to a large, shallow heatproof serving dish.

Pour the hot vinegar mixture over the fish, arranging the vegetables evenly and attractively on top. Serve escovitch immediately or cool to room temperature, cover tightly, and refrigerate until chilled.

To make about 1½ pints

1 small (1 lb.) firm ripe fresh pawpaw (*see* "*A Note about Mangoes and Pawpaws*"), peeled, seeded and cut into ½-inch cubes

1 large (1½ lb.) firm ripe fresh mango, peeled, cut away from the stone, and then cut into ½-inch cubes

1½ lb. sugar

2½ tablespoons strained fresh lime juice

To serve 4 to 6 as a main course or 8 as a first course

4 medium-sized onions, peeled and cut crosswise into paper-thin slices

2 large carrots, scraped and cut into paper-thin rounds

2 medium-sized green peppers, the seeds and white pith removed, and cut into strips 2 inches long and ¼ inch wide

2 medium-sized bay leaves, crumbled

½ teaspoon crushed hot red pepper

2½ teaspoons salt

Freshly ground black pepper

6 tablespoons white wine vinegar

5 tablespoons olive oil

¾ pint cold water

2 lb. skinned and filleted red snapper

II

The Legacy of the Earliest Islanders

Caribbean islanders, like people in tropical climates everywhere, have a taste for fiery food. The Carib Indians were making hot pepper sauce even before Columbus arrived, and today every island cook has her own version. As these examples show, the sauces may be red tomato mixtures or golden turmeric blends; some are chunky and others are puréed. But all have peppers, and all are hot.

The first Europeans in America had to rely heavily upon the Caribbean Indians in learning about the foods of their strange new world. Bizarre plants and animals bewildered the newcomers, who found almost every growing thing to be different from anything they knew. The Indians could afford to be generous, both with information about how to survive and with actual offers of food itself, and Columbus himself praised them for this. "Of anything that they possess," he wrote, "they invite you to share it and show as much love as if their hearts went with it." Before long the lot of the Caribbean Indians changed drastically for the worse, but most of the foods they introduced to the Spaniards, as well as some of their primitive ways of cooking, still form part of the islands' cuisine. And those Indians who are left today are still generous, as I discovered when I received an explorer's welcome from some of them in the island of Dominica.

When Columbus sailed into the Caribbean Sea, its islands were inhabited by several hundred thousand Indians, divided into two main groups, the placid Arawaks and the belligerent Caribs; both were soon to learn the dangers of being hospitable to the invaders. The Arawaks were cruelly exploited and almost exterminated within a few generations. The Caribs, seasoned by their skirmishes with other tribes, took on the Spanish and later the French and English and fought longer than any other Indian tribe in the New World, including the North American Apaches.

But inexorably they were driven from island to island until finally, harmless in their reduced numbers and tempered disposition, they were allowed to settle in a few scattered groups. One survives in Trinidad, near the town of Arima; the biggest group exists in the mountainous obscurity of the north side of Dominica, the most rugged island of any size in the Caribbean. Fifteen hundred Caribs live there, though probably fewer than one hundred of them are of pure Indian blood, since they have intermarried so much with the negroes in the island. Even so, the Caribs behave like a race apart. They have their own elected chief and they deal separately with the government of the island.

When my husband and I visited their reserve on Dominica, we were accompanied by a young Carib boy called Faustulus Frederick. He was an artist, as were his two brothers Masclem and John, and we had seen their spare, expressive drawings of the life of their people in a local newspaper. We sought them out, and when Faustulus learned I was interested in Carib cooking he offered to introduce me to his mother, "the best cook I know".

We were on our way to meet her, wandering among the wooden cabins in the Carib reserve, when we passed the house of our guide's uncle. The family was having its one meal of the day. Faustulus' aunt and uncle and two young cousins were squatting on the ground outside their cabin, heels under their haunches, balancing their bowls in their laps. They were eating boiled green bananas covered with a yellow egg sauce. Beside the head of the family was piled the dessert, a heap of green coconuts.

Faustulus introduced me to the family, and immediately they gestured at the coconuts. "They want you to have one," Faustulus explained. "Oh, no," I said. "They have so few." But they repeated the offer, and Faustulus said, "They say you look hot and thirsty. They want you to have one."

We accepted, of course, and this meant that their pile of coconuts disappeared, for they gave one to me, one to my husband, one to our driver and one to Faustulus. We squatted beside them and drank the sweet, cooling coconut water, and smiled and tried to communicate our gratitude without words. When we stood up to leave, Faustulus' uncle got up too and went off into the bush with his machete to gather more coconuts for his family. I was touched, and wondered whether I would have given up the last of the milk in my own house to passing strangers if it meant going to the store during the meal to feed my own family.

The generosity of the Indians centuries ago in sharing their knowledge of the local fruits and plants and wild life smoothed the way for the European explorers, who thus learned painlessly which foods were poisonous, which were life sustaining, which were delicacies. In some cases the Indians were directly responsible for the survival of the adventurers.

There are many accounts of this. The most touching—a true story immortalized by Richard Steele in the *Spectator Papers*—is about a Carib Indian girl named Yarico who saved the life of a young English colonist, Thomas Inkle. They met in 1647 when the ship in which Inkle had set out to make his fortune in the New World ran into difficulties somewhere along the Spanish Main—the old name for those parts of the Central and South American mainland that border on the Caribbean Sea. Inkle and other members of the ship's company were forced to land, but as they came ashore they were attacked by hostile Indians who killed all except Inkle. Wounded, the young man managed to escape to a remote part of the forest and was lying there, exhausted, when Yarico came upon him. "If the European was highly charmed with the limbs, features and wild graces of the naked American," wrote Steele, "the American was no less taken with the dress, complexion and shape of a European, covered from head to foot." Yarico fell in love with this covered-up man at first sight and determined to save his life, even from her own people. "She therefore," the story continues, "conveyed him to a cave where she gave him a delicious repast of fruits."

Inkle regained his strength under her careful nursing and eventually the lovers came to understand each other's language. Inkle communicated to his mistress how happy he would be to have her in his country, saying that there she would be clothed in such silks as his waistcoat was made of, and be carried in houses drawn by horses. Yarico agreed to go with him wherever he went and one night succeeded in signalling to a European vessel anchored off the coast. She and Inkle were taken aboard and they set sail for Barbados. But then greed asserted itself in the young fortune seeker. When the ship reached Barbados, Inkle reflected on the money that his loss of time his dalliance with Yarico had cost him, "upon which consideration the prudent and frugal young man sold Yarico to a Barbadian merchant".

This kind of betrayal went on in one form or another for two centuries until there was no vestige of trust left between Indian and European. By then the Europeans had learned to sustain themselves handsomely and they needed no Yarico to help them; they had long since come to value and take advantage of the New World foods the Indians had bestowed on them.

These are the same foods that the present-day Caribbean cuisine still honours as its legacy from the Indians. There are many fruits, for instance, that had never been seen by a European before the voyage of Columbus: the avocado, the cashew fruit, the sour-sop, the mamey, the pawpaw, the guava and the pineapple. The last named is perhaps the Indians' greatest gift of fruit to the world. Gonzalo Fernández de Oviedo, one of the earliest settlers to write about the plants of the New World, recognized its quality immediately and went to great lengths to explain that although the pineapple grew on plants like thistles, it was "in taste one of the best fruits in the world . . . for those who are surfeited and do not wish to eat, it is an excellent appetizer."

The pineapple originated in South America and moved with the Caribs when they migrated to the islands. They esteemed it highly, and like many of their favourite foods it took on a more than material significance. During puberty rites, Carib boys were made to run between rows of spiky pineapple spears to prove their bravery. The fruit itself, when placed on the doors of their huts, served as a symbol of hospitality to strangers. Europeans soon carried the idea back with them to the architects of Spain and England, who made the pineapple a favourite colonial-era motif for decorating gate-posts and door lintels. The fruit itself was welcomed all over the world and was one of the first plants to be carried from America westwards across the Pacific. Many people, of course, associate Hawaii and the pineapple, which, ironically, did not even get to the Polynesian islands until the late 19th century.

Another delicacy the Indians shared with their invaders has remained a local treasure. This is the mangrove-tree oyster, which grows on the roots of mangrove trees along muddy river banks and beaches. Sir Walter Ralegh came upon this phenomenon in Trinidad on a fortune-seeking voyage in 1595 and reported it to Queen Elizabeth on his

Raised off the ground on wooden piles and shored up by poles, this Carib Indian house in Dominica reflects the hazards of Caribbean house building. The poles keep it from blowing over in heavy storms; the piles discourage mongooses as well as the island's voracious termites. John Frederick, 20 years old, drew this sketch of his family's two-room house; the kitchen is in a separate shack a few yards away.

return to England. He was almost laughed out of Court—whoever heard of oysters growing on trees! But there is no doubt about either the existence of the oysters or their excellence. The method of harvesting them is to cut an underwater root or branch and scrape off the dozens of clustered molluscs growing on it. The oysters are elongated and smaller than most well-known oysters—not more than two inches long. They are extremely tender and refreshing, and it takes a great many to satisfy the appetite of an aficionado. In Puerto Rico years ago lovers of the *ostione*, as it is locally known, used to ride from San Juan all the way across the island to Bocheron to buy them from harvesters; they would then eat them by the hundred at a picnic. Now, refrigeration has made it possible for some of San Juan's better seafood restaurants to serve *ostiones*, and they are a speciality well worth the trouble of finding.

The Indian cuisine was too primitive to have contributed many prepared foods to posterity, but one that has survived intact throughout the islands is cassava bread. Cassava, which is called by many names, among them yuca and manioc, is a starchy tuber that was the staple food of most of the Caribbean Indians. It was either boiled and eaten as we eat potatoes, or ground, made into meal, and baked into bread.

Because it was their staff of life, cassava was revered by the Indians. In a Spanish history of the Indies written in 1554, an Indian agricultural ceremony is described in which cassava bread is blessed by Indian priests and pieces of the blessed bread are divided among all the Indians

36

present. Just as some Jews preserve a bit of the Passover matzoh from one year's holiday to the next to ensure their presence at the next year's festivities, so the Indians who received cassava bread at this ceremony preserved it in the belief that a family who did not do so was vulnerable to many dangers throughout the ensuing year.

Their veneration for cassava is understandable. It could not only sustain life but could also take it away. For cassava—there are two kinds, sweet and bitter—contains in its juice varying quantities of prussic acid. This can be removed by cooking or pressing, but the bitter cassava root contains enough acid to be fatally poisonous if eaten raw. A common method used by the Arawak Indians to escape the torments of their Spanish overlords was to commit suicide by eating raw cassava.

Sweet cassava when boiled has a pleasant, bland flavour something like a moist white potato. In the islands today it is a frequent accompaniment to meat and is at its best when sprinkled with salt, freshly ground black pepper and a few drops of lime juice. It can also be prepared in all the same ways as potatoes—mashed, creamed, fried, or made into croquettes. But the most important product of cassava is bread. It is sold everywhere in the islands and can be obtained in the United States in cities where there is a sizeable Puerto Rican, Jamaican or Mexican population. Baked in a flat, round shape, it has an earthy flavour and is eaten plain or, in a favourite Jamaican variation, is fried in butter as a breakfast dish. Slightly different from the bread are the wafers made of cassava and served as accompaniments to soups. These chips (*Recipe Index*) are also round and flat, but they, unlike the bread, have a crisp, airy lightness.

Although the Indians in the Carib reserve in Dominica have very few possessions, every woman owns the necessary equipment for making cassava bread. I watched it being used by Faustulus Frederick's mother during my visit to her village. A stately woman in her middle forties, Mrs. Frederick lived in a two-room cabin that was spotlessly clean and tidy, and very sparsely furnished: just a table and chairs, a chest of drawers and a wood-slatted bed without a mattress. She did have a radio, as did all her neighbours, and it was to the strains of "The Blue Danube" that we inspected her kitchen.

Like the old Carib kitchens, it was outside the house itself—part of it simply outdoors, among the banana and coconut trees, and part of it in a separate cooking shack so that if the open cooking fire spread, it would not destroy the main part of the house. In the shack were a few pots and pans, a three-foot-tall wooden mortar for grinding coffee beans, and the utensils for making cassava bread. First Mrs. Frederick showed me the grater, a wooden-backed steel device with jagged teeth. I feared for her hand when she demonstrated it but she laughed at me; I should have seen her mother's grater, she said; that one was just rusty nails hammered into a piece of wood.

Mrs. Frederick then explained the bread-making process. After the cassava is grated it is heaped in a cassava canoe, a wooden receptacle shaped like the dug-out canoes for which the Caribs are famous. Later the gratings are thoroughly squeezed through a cloth to press out the poisonous juices, and are left to dry in the sun. Next they are passed through a sifter made of woven roots to get the meal to a consistent fineness. The cassava is then ready for baking. Actually it is not baked but cooked on a girdle like a pancake. Like her neighbours, Mrs. Frederick uses a rough-edged circular piece of miscellaneous metal as

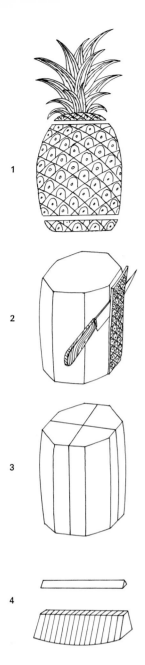

a girdle. Finally the bread is thoroughly dried in the sun until it has a hard, crusty texture throughout. Although non-Carib islanders use more modern methods—they may grate the tubers in a blender and cook them on greased girdles over a gas flame—local cookery books still recommend drying the bread under the tropical sun.

In the outdoor part of Mrs. Frederick's kitchen is her working surface, a board nailed between two trees at a convenient height, and her larder, which consists simply of a tomato plant and a hot pepper plant, one growing at each end of the work-table. She needs only to reach out her arm, she showed me, to obtain the best fresh ingredients for her soups and stews.

Both these plants figure strongly in Caribbean cooking, but the pepper is perhaps the single most important ingredient in the cuisine. The Indians were using capsicum peppers in their cooking when the Spaniards arrived. The plant grows profusely in the islands, and the fruit comes in every imaginable shape, size, colour and degree of pungency and is turned into innumerable varieties of pepper sauces by the islanders. The Caribs were accomplished makers of pepper sauce. Not knowing how to extract salt from the sea, they flavoured their food with *coui*, a sauce of hot peppers and cassava juice. The addiction has persisted: All West Indians like hot peppers in their food, and when a dish is not spicy enough they reach for the ever-present bottle of hot sauce. This is made in most homes by steeping diced hot peppers in vinegar. They may also be soaked in rum or sherry, but every island, indeed every Caribbean kitchen, has its own variation on the theme.

There are few records of other seasonings used by the Indians in their cooking, though it is known that sweet basil, purslane and watercress grew on the islands. The Europeans found another spice, one they had never seen before, growing wild on many of the islands. They decided it tasted like a combination of cinnamon, nutmeg and clove and so it got its name—allspice. Also known as Jamaica pepper, allspice still grows in profusion there and the island supplies a good share of the world's supply.

There is another now popular spice that the Indians put to curious use. The seed of the annatto, a graceful, red-flowering tree, makes an excellent dye; the Indians mixed it with oil and used it to paint their bodies. Its purpose was partly decorative—some historians think it was the American Indians' use of this dye that earned them the name redskins—but also functional: The Indians wore no clothes and were constantly exposed to the sun and to insect bites. Annatto oil protected them from both.

In time annatto achieved culinary importance. Like saffron, it lends a delicate flavour and a strong colour to food, and in the Spanish-speaking islands, where it is called *achiote*, the seed came to be used in making sauces. Today it is an essential ingredient in many Puerto Rican dishes. The dried seeds are stirred into a small amount of lard or oil until a vivid red-orange colour is obtained. The seeds are then removed and into the reddened oil go the chopped leaf of the coriander plant, which in Spanish is called *cilantro*, tiny sweet peppers, onions, garlic, tomatoes and sometimes salt pork. These are simmered in the oil to make a sauce called *sofrito*. There is also a Spanish sauce of the same name that does not include annatto. Now Puerto Rican cooking begins. *Asopao, arroz con pollo*, Puerto Rican *ropa vieja*, and many other vegetable dishes start with the making of *sofrito*. Annatto is used in other

HOW TO PREPARE PINEAPPLE WEDGES
A quick way to peel, core and cut a fresh pineapple into wedges is shown in these drawings. First lay the fruit on its side and, grasping it firmly with one hand, slice off the leafy crown and the base with a large, sharp knife (1). Then stand the pineapple on end and slice off the prickly rind in seven or eight downward strokes, cutting deep enough each time to remove the eyes (2). Now divide the fruit into quarters (3), and cut the triangular section of core away from each quarter. Lay each quarter on its side and slice it crosswise into wedges of the desired thickness (4).

Caribbean islands as well—it is called *rou cou* on Trinidad, Martinique and Guadeloupe, but on Puerto Rico it is as essential as salt is to us.

The Indians' culinary legacy to the modern Caribbean cuisine includes two methods of cooking. To cook a fish or bird, the Indians coated it with mud and baked it in an ash fire made in a pit dug into the sand. When the creature was sufficiently done its mud jacket was scraped away; this pulled off the scales or feathers as well, leaving the flesh clean and unaffected by contact with the fire. In Guadeloupe, among people who live in seaside houses, the method is still popular for cooking fish for twilight picnics. A large fish, generally a red snapper, is preferred. Thyme and hot peppers are placed between its skin and flesh, then mud is tightly packed round the fish; it is placed on hot ashes in a pit, covered with sand and baked while the guests laze in the cool of the evening.

The Indians' other cooking legacy is one to which every enthusiastic outdoor cook in Europe owes an appreciative salute. For it is from the Caribbean Indians that the word barbecue comes. An Arawak *barbacoa* was a grating of thin green sticks upon which meat was grilled above an open fire. The Arawaks also used the word for a stick-frame bed they made in the same fashion. The Indians sliced their meat into thin strips, laid it upon the *barbacoa* and cooked it slowly, exposing it to the smoke of the wood fire below, which was constantly enhanced with the fat of the animal. Cooked and cured in this way, meat took on a more interesting flavour than that obtained by the South American Indians, who cured their meat by drying it in the sun. Some writers have suggested that our word barbecue comes from the French *barbe à queue*, or beard to tail, reasoning that barbecuing sometimes involves spitting whole animals over a cooking fire. I prefer the view of most authorities, that we took the word from the Arawak.

To cook meat on a *barbacoa* was, in the language of the early settlers, to *boucan*. By another curious etymological twist, it is from this word that the pirates who plagued Spanish shipping of the 17th century took their name—buccaneers. Except for the few who struck it rich, these adventurers lived among the Indians in almost as wild a fashion. They sustained themselves by boucaning the islands' birds, small game and fish just as the Indians did.

One of the first men to report on the Indian methods of cooking was Père Labat, an extraordinary French priest who lived in the Caribbean in the late 1600s. Garrulous, argumentative, humorous, inquisitive about everything from priestly intrigue to gardening, Labat wrote a memoir of his life in the islands that is one of the most fascinating of all travel books. An inordinate number of Labat's stories deal with food, and I was puzzled by this preoccupation until I saw a portrait of him. Round-faced and fat as any Chaucerian priest, Labat was plainly a man for whom food was Experience.

My favourite Labat story is one he tells about the day he gave a boucan picnic for some fellow priests. It was held in a forest in Martinique, and all the guests had to pretend to be buccaneers. Their fare was a pig, barbecued in Indian and pirate fashion. No metal implements were allowed, no plates, dishes, spoons or forks. "Even tablecloths are forbidden," the priest's rules read, "as they are too much at variance with buccaneer simplicity."

The guests arrived at 9 a.m. and were immediately put to work constructing the *barbacoa* and building a fire under it. After the fire burned down to charcoal the pig was laid on its back upon the *barbacoa*, its

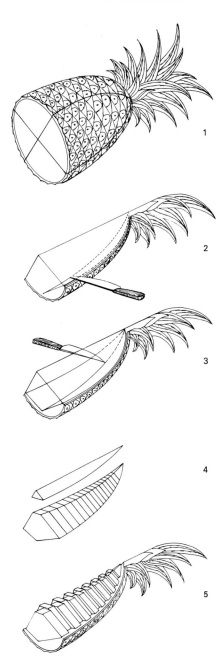

HOW TO PREPARE PINEAPPLE BOATS
A pretty way to serve fresh pineapple is to cut it up and then reassemble the fruit in four boat-like pieces of rind. First lay the pineapple on its side and cut off the base with a large sharp knife. Then, slicing right through the leafy crown, divide the pineapple lengthways into quarters (1). Make diagonal cuts into the quarters from each side to separate the fruit from the rind (2 and 3). Lift out each strip of fruit, cut away the core along the top, and slice the fruit crosswise into wedges (4). Return the fruit to the rinds, staggering the wedges decoratively (5).

belly up and open and sprinkled with lime juice, salt and crushed allspice. When the pig was ready, the priests said a blessing and "sat down at a table so solid that nothing but an earthquake could have shaken it, for our table was the earth itself". There were a few unauthentic touches at the picnic for which Labat apologized: "I had provided napkins and bread though this is really contrary to the rules, for real buccaneers know not the meaning of napkins and use only baked plantains for bread."

But in one respect there was complete authenticity. The priests played their roles of buccaneers to the hilt by drinking their wine neat—not, as in their usual fashion, mixing it with water. It must have been a hilarious afternoon, and Labat is at his wittiest in describing it. "I do not think it necessary to inform the reader that one of the essential things in a boucan is to drink frequently. The law compels it, the sauce invites one to do so, and few err in this respect. But since man is frail and would often fall if he had no one to remind him of his duty and correct him, the master of the boucan has to watch his party. Should he find anyone idle or negligent he must at once call everybody's attention to the fact. The delinquent must then do penance by drinking from the large calabash, no mean punishment since this calabash is always kept full of wine."

Like Labat, the Indians considered pork the most desirable meat for boucaning—though it has been said that the savage Caribs preferred the barbecued limbs of an enemy. Visitors among the Caribs testified to this, and one writer even discussed their favourite victims with the Indians. He reported that they found the French to have the most delicate flavours; the Spanish were stringy and likely to produce indigestion.

The few Indians remaining today rarely barbecue or boucan anything because it is increasingly difficult to obtain game in the islands and they are too poor to buy meat. However, they have developed over the years one dish that is a highlight of the Caribbean cuisine and has been adopted and adapted by all other comers to the island: pepper-pot (*Recipe Index*). If you are travelling in the islands and have not been invited to someone's house to discover its delights, the best place to sample pepper-pot is in the Trinidad restaurant called The Tropical, which serves some of the finest West Indian food in the islands. The Tropical serves curried chicken, stuffed crab back, crisp akkras, thick vegetable soups. But its best dish is pepper-pot, the gift of the Indians.

The traditional pepper-pot is a stew, not to be confused with a soup of the same name widely popular in Jamaica and other islands today. The latter has vegetables in it, which Indian pepper-pot has not. What it does have is meat, though one never knows what kind it will be—sometimes a wild creature, sometimes beef or pork, sometimes chicken or oxtail and calf's head. Or all of these.

Pepper-pot does have one ingredient besides the meat, however, that makes it different from any other stew. This is cassareep, a juice obtained from cassava root. Cassareep gives pepper-pot a flavour that is almost impossible to describe; a flavour often called "subtle" or "haunting" or simply "indescribable". I decided to try to be more specific one day, and prepared some cassareep and tasted it carefully. It was bitter, certainly, but there was more to it—a mysterious something I could not define. Just then my daughter Jessica came in and asked if she could taste it, too. I warned her that she wouldn't like it—and, indeed, she didn't, but she said, "It isn't bitter, Mummy, it's sweet, too sweet." And then she said, with a five-year-old's certainty, "It's both. It's sweet and bitter. How strange." And I realized that that was it, the haunting, subtle flavour of pepper-pot—a finely balanced tug of war between bitter and sweet.

I find it ironic that the basis of pepper-pot is the juice of cassava roots: the substance that brought death for suicide-bent Arawaks prolongs life for the last remaining Caribs. I was moved by this thought when I went to the small town of Arima on Trinidad, and visited the ancient lady who is the titular "Queen" of Trinidad's Caribs. She is Edith Martinez, a wizened woman in her late seventies whose mother was queen before her. The hereditary title passes through the maternal line, so Queen Edith expects her eldest daughter to become queen too. Not too soon, though, she warns you. Her own mother lived to 113 and she herself feels as sprightly as a girl.

The day I met her she had dressed for the occasion. She was wearing three-inch stiletto-heeled shoes and a pink lace dress, undoubtedly bought years ago when she was not so bent, that came down almost to her ankles. I was glad, for my daughter was with me, and when she first saw the Queen's one-room wooden house she refused to believe we were going to meet a queen; but she suspended all her disbelief when the old woman appeared. The length of the dress convinced Jessica that here indeed was a Queen.

I myself needed only to speak to her to be convinced. She spoke about her people with royal concern, and we talked of the help she longed to

Fresh from a garden in Trinidad, this bouquet displays some of the spices, herbs and roots available to Caribbean cooks. Most of them are used for flavouring; the basilisk, worm-grass and jumbie balsam however, are steeped to make tea.

1 Parsley	8 Annatto
2 Thyme	9 Anise
3 Broad-leaved	flowers
thyme	10 Chives
4 Thyme	11 Spanish
5 Basilisk	thyme
6 Worm-grass	12 Geranium
7 Jumbie	13 Anise
balsam	14 Bay leaf

give her people—food, education, a resting place in the town of Arima that would offer them shelter when they came down from the hills. Then we talked about cooking, one of Queen Edith's favourite occupations. She showed me her dirt-floored kitchen. Despite its scanty equipment, its open fire-place and crude cassava-grating tools, it was clearly a well-loved domain.

"What do you like cooking?" I asked. "Cassava bread," she said proudly. "That's our own bread. The Caribs' bread. Although lots of other people eat it now too." I nodded to show that I knew about it. "What do you have with it?" I asked. "A stew we make with cassava juice," she said. "Some people call it pepper-pot. We make it whenever we can afford to buy meat. Or if we catch some." She went on to explain: "We keep it going on the fire for a long time so when there's a pot of it if someone's hungry he can eat it any time of day." Then, looking troubled, she added: "And if we don't have pepper-pot, we have whatever we can find."

The Indians are finding less and less. They are the poorest outcasts of the islands; quite possibly, despite belated governmental efforts to honour and protect them, the Caribs will be as extinct as the Arawaks within a few generations. Yet both peoples live on—in the sense that their foods live on as part of the present. For barbecuing, for cassava bread and hot pepper sauce, for pepper-pot and a host of herbs and fruits, all the islanders today, of whatever background, owe the Indians a debt of gratitude.

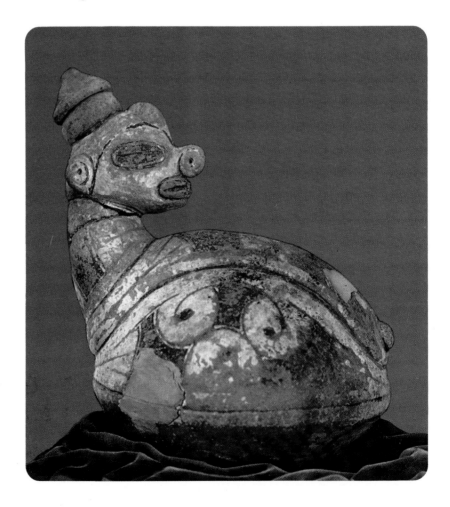

The Arawak Indians, who were part of the aboriginal population of the Caribbean islands, produced pottery and sculptures marked by a lively expressiveness. This water jug, showing a distorted human form, was found in an ancient burial mound in southern Trinidad. It had been placed there, together with food and other domestic amenities, to help ease the passage of an Arawak soul to the world of the dead.

CHAPTER **II** RECIPES

Sopa de Frijol Negro *(Cuba)*
BLACK BEAN SOUP

Wash the beans in a large sieve or colander under cold running water until the draining water runs clear. Transfer them to a large, heavy casserole, add 2½ teaspoons of salt, and pour in enough water to cover the beans by at least 2 inches. Bring to the boil over a high heat, reduce the heat to low, partly cover the pan and simmer for about 2 to 3 hours, until the beans are tender enough to be mashed against the sides of the pan with a spoon.

Drain the beans through a large sieve or colander set over a bowl and put them aside to cool to room temperature. Add enough chicken stock to the bean-cooking liquid to make it up to 2½ pints.

When the beans have cooled, put ⅜ pint of beans and ⅜ pint of the liquid at a time into the jar of an electric blender. Blend at high speed until the beans are well pulped, but do not purée them too finely. As you proceed, scrape the mixture into a large bowl or pan with a rubber spatula. (If you do not have a blender, rub the beans through a food mill into a deep bowl or press them through a fine sieve with a spoon. Stir the liquid into the purée.)

Heat the annatto-flavoured oil over a moderate heat in a large heavy pan until a light haze forms above it. Add the onions and garlic and cook for 5 minutes, stirring frequently, until they are soft and transparent but not brown. Stir in the ham, tomatoes, vinegar, cumin and a few grindings of pepper. Bring to the boil and cook briskly until the mixture thickens enough to coat the spoon heavily, stirring frequently. Add the bean purée and simmer over a low heat for about 15 minutes, until the soup is heated through.

Taste for seasoning. Ladle the soup into a large tureen or individual soup plates and serve it at once.

Sopa de Gandules *(Puerto Rico)*
GREEN PIGEON PEA SOUP

Fry the salt pork over a moderate heat in a large, heavy pan, turning over the pork dice with a spoon until they are crisp and brown and have rendered all their fat. Remove the dice and discard them.

Add the onions and garlic to the fat remaining in the casserole and cook over a moderate heat for 5 minutes, stirring frequently until they are soft and transparent but not brown. Drop in the tomato, green pepper and ham; cover and simmer for 5 minutes longer. Stir the pumpkin, stock and green pigeon peas into the casserole. Bring to the boil over a high heat, reduce the heat to low, cover tightly, and simmer for 20 minutes, until the soup thickens and the pumpkin is soft and begins to fall apart. The soup should still be a bit lumpy. Taste and season with salt and pepper. Ladle into a heated tureen or individual soup plates, and serve at once.

NOTE: To prepare fresh tomatoes, drop the tomato into a pan of boiling water and remove it after 15 seconds. Run it under cold water, and peel it with a small, sharp knife. Cut out the stalk, then slice the tomato in half crosswise. Squeeze the halves gently to remove the seeds and juice, and chop the tomato coarsely.

To serve 6 to 8

1 lb. dried black beans
Salt
1½ pints chicken stock
1½ tablespoons vegetable oil mixed with ½ teaspoon liquid annatto
4 oz. finely chopped onions
1½ teaspoons finely chopped garlic
8-oz. finely chopped lean cooked ham
1 large firm ripe tomato, peeled, seeded and finely chopped (*see sopa de gandules, Recipe Index*), or an 8-oz. can chopped drained tomatoes
1½ tablespoons malt vinegar
½ teaspoon ground cumin
Freshly ground black pepper

To serve 6

4 oz. lean salt pork, cut into ¼-inch dice
4 oz. finely chopped onions
1 teaspoon finely chopped garlic
1 large firm ripe tomato, peeled, seeded and coarsely chopped, or substitute an 8-oz. can chopped drained tomatoes
1 medium-sized green pepper, the seeds and white pith removed, and finely chopped
4 oz. lean boneless cooked ham, cut into ¼-inch dice
1 lb. fresh West Indian pumpkin (calabaza, *see Glossary*), or substitute firm-fleshed pumpkin, peeled, seeded and cut into ½-inch dice
1½ pints chicken stock
A 1-lb. can of green pigeon peas (*gandules*) with their liquid
Salt
Freshly ground black pepper

These three steaming soups are almost meals in themselves. Jamaican callaloo, with crabmeat, is on the top left and centre right. *Saucochi di gallinja*, a chicken and vegetable soup from Aruba, is on the top right and centre left. Cuban black bean soup is in the middle.

To serve 6 to 8

A 5- to 5½-lb. boiling chicken, trimmed of excess fat and cut into 8 to 12 serving pieces

1 fresh pig's trotter (about 8 oz.)

3¼ pints water

1½ teaspoons salt

3 lb. boneless fresh shoulder of pork, or lean boneless beef, cut into 2-inch cubes

6 tablespoons cassareep (*Recipe Index*)

1 large onion, peeled and cut crosswise into ¼-inch-thick slices

1½ tablespoons dark pieces sugar

2 whole fresh hot chillies (*caution: see "How to Handle Chillies"*)

A 2-inch piece of stick cinnamon

4 whole cloves

¼ tablespoon crumbled dried thyme

2½ teaspoons malt vinegar

Pepper Pot (*Trinidad*)

CHICKEN AND PORK STEW

Put the chicken and the pig's trotter into a large, heavy pan and pour the water over them. The water should cover them by about 1 inch; add more if necessary. Add the salt and bring to the boil over a high heat, skimming off the foam and scum as they rise to the surface. Reduce the heat to low, partly cover the pan and simmer for about 1 hour, until the bird is almost tender and shows only the slightest resistance when pierced with the point of a small, sharp knife.

Skim as much fat as possible from the surface of the soup using a large spoon. Stir in the pork cubes, cassareep, onion, brown sugar, chillies, cinnamon, cloves and thyme. Bring to the boil over a high heat, reduce the heat to moderate and cook partly covered for about 30 minutes longer, stirring occasionally, until the chicken and pork are tender. Remove the chillies, cinnamon and cloves with a perforated spoon and discard them. Stir in the vinegar and taste for seasoning.

Heap up the pieces of pork, pig's trotter and the chicken attractively on a deep heated dish and pour the sauce remaining in the casserole over them. Serve the pepper-pot at once, accompanied, if you like, by boiled potatoes, yams or cassava biscuits (*Recipe Index*).

44

Callaloo (Barbados)

CRAB AND GREENS SOUP

To serve 4 to 6

Wash the callaloo greens (or spinach or seakale beet leaves) under cold running water and discard any discoloured leaves. Leave the callaloo greens whole but, if you are using spinach or beetroot, bunch the leaves together and shred them into fine strips.

Melt the butter over a moderate heat in a large, heavy pan. Add the onions and garlic and cook for 5 minutes, stirring frequently, until they are soft and transparent but not brown. Add the greens and turn them about with a spoon for 4 to 5 minutes, until they glisten with butter and become somewhat limp.

Stir in the stock, coconut milk, salt and a few grindings of pepper. Bring to the boil over a high heat, reduce the heat to low, and simmer uncovered for about 10 minutes, until the greens are tender. Add the crabmeat and A-1 or Pickapeppa sauce, and stir for 2 to 3 minutes to heat the crab through.

Taste for seasoning and serve at once, from a heated tureen or in individual soup plates.

8 oz. callaloo greens (dasheen or Chinese spinach, *see Glossary*), or substitute fresh spinach or seakale beet leaves
1½ oz. butter
2 oz. finely chopped onions
¼ teaspoon finely chopped garlic
1¼ pints chicken stock
6 tablespoons coconut milk (*see "Notes on Caribbean Cooking"*)
1 teaspoon salt
Freshly ground black pepper
8 oz. fresh, canned or frozen crabmeat, picked clean of all bits of shell and cartilage
A dash of A-1 or Pickapeppa sauce

Cassareep

To make about 6 tablespoons

Peel the brown fibrous bark off the white flesh of the cassava root with a small, sharp knife or swivel-bladed vegetable parer. Cut the cassava root in half and finely grate one half of it with a stand-up hand grater into a deep bowl lined with a double thickness of damp cheesecloth. Bring the ends of the cheesecloth together to enclose the pulp, and wring the cloth vigorously to squeeze the cassava juice into the bowl. Discard the pulp (or use in cassava biscuits or *brazo gitano, Recipe Index*). Grate and squeeze the rest of the cassava in the same way.

Transfer the entire contents of the bowl to a small, heavy frying-pan. Cook over a moderate heat for about 1 minute, stirring constantly, until the cassareep is smooth and thick enough to hold its shape almost solidly in the spoon.

NOTE: The amount of liquid in the cassava may vary, depending on the age and quality of the roots available. If there are any small dark flecks or spots of mould in the flesh of the cassava, the root is old and will yield little if any juice.

1 medium-sized (about 2 lb.) young cassava root

Saucochi di Gallinja (Aruba)

CHICKEN AND VEGETABLE SOUP

To serve 6 to 8 as a main course

Put the chicken and the fresh stock—or canned beefstock and water—into a large, heavy casserole and bring to the boil over a high heat. Skim off the foam and scum as they rise to the surface with a large spoon. Reduce the heat to low, partly cover the casserole, and simmer for 45 minutes.

Skim as much fat from the soup as possible, then add the tomatoes, corn, yams, boiling potatoes, pumpkin, peas, chillies, salt and pepper. Bring the *saucochi* to the boil again, reduce the heat and simmer partly covered for about 20 minutes longer, until the chicken and vegetables are tender but still intact.

Taste the soup for seasoning and stir in the chives. Serve at once from a heated tureen or individual soup plates.

A 3- to 3½-lb. chicken, cut into 6 to 8 serving pieces
5 pints freshly made beef stock or 2½ pints canned beef broth mixed with 2½ pints water
4 large tomatoes, peeled, seeded and coarsely chopped (*see sopa de gandules, Recipe Index*), or two 1-lb. cans chopped drained tomatoes
2 medium-sized ears fresh or frozen corn, cut into 3-inch rounds
2 medium-sized yams (about 1 lb.), peeled and cut crosswise into ½-inch-thick slices
2 small potatoes, peeled and cut into ½-inch-thick rounds
4 oz. West Indian pumpkin or substitute firm-fleshed pumpkin, peeled and cut into ½-inch dice
3 oz. fresh or frozen green peas
2 small fresh hot chillies, stalks removed, seeded and thinly sliced (*caution: see "How to Handle Chillies"*)
2½ teaspoons salt
Freshly ground black pepper
1½ tablespoons finely chopped fresh chives

How to Handle Chillies

Hot peppers, or chillies, require special handling. Their volatile oils may burn your skin and make your eyes smart. Wear rubber gloves if you can, and be careful not to touch your face or eyes while working with chillies.

To prepare chillies, rinse them clean and pull out the stalks under cold running water. Break or cut the pods in half, and brush out the seeds with your fingers. In most cases the ribs inside the pods are thin and may be left intact, but if they seem fleshy, cut them out with a small, sharp knife. The chillies may be used at once or soaked in cold, salted water for an hour or so to make them less hot. After handling hot chillies, it is advisable to wash your hands thoroughly with soap and warm water.

The hot chilli pepper that adds so much pungency to Caribbean cooking is part of a large and wonderfully diverse family called *Capsicum*. The plant, not the least of Columbus' discoveries in the New World, now grows all over the world. Its innumerable varieties range from the familiar sweet red peppers to the fiery little *habaneros* shown being picked here, and others so hot that their oil is literally lethal.

All pepper sauces contain chillies, but the other ingredients for recipes like those on these pages may vary every time a cook makes a new supply. In the islands pepper sauce is universally served as a condiment with boiled, grilled or roasted meats, poultry and seafood.

To make about 6 tablespoons

2½ teaspoons finely chopped fresh hot chillies (*caution: see "How to Handle Chillies"*)
1½ tablespoons finely chopped onions
½ teaspoon finely chopped garlic
2½ tablespoons malt vinegar
3 tablespoons water
½ teaspoon salt
2½ teaspoons olive oil

Saba Pepper Sauce

Put the chillies, onions and garlic into a small bowl. Bring the vinegar, water and salt to the boil in a small enamel, stainless-steel or glass saucepan and pour them over the chilli mixture, stirring constantly. Pour the oil over the top.

The Saba pepper sauce can be kept safely for about 3 to 4 weeks if tightly covered and refrigerated.

To make about ⅜ pint

6 oz. finely chopped onions
9 tablespoons strained fresh lime juice
1 oz. butter
1½ teaspoons finely chopped fresh hot chillies (*caution: see "How to Handle Chillies"*)
1 scant teaspoon finely chopped garlic
1½ teaspoons salt

Sauce Ti-Malice (*Haiti*)
CHILLI, ONION AND LIME JUICE SAUCE

Drop the onions into a small bowl, stir the lime juice into them, and marinate at room temperature for at least 30 minutes. Drain the onions in a fine sieve set over a bowl, tossing them with a fork to remove as much liquid as possible. Reserve the marinade.

Melt the butter over a moderate heat in a heavy, medium-sized frying-pan. When the foam begins to subside, add the onions and cook for 5 minutes, stirring frequently, until they are soft and transparent but not brown. Watch carefully for any sign of burning and adjust the heat accordingly.

Stir in the chopped chillies and the garlic, reduce the heat to low, cover the pan tightly, and cook for about 10 minutes, until the chillies are tender. Stir in the reserved marinade and the salt off the heat. Cool to room temperature before serving.

Sauce Ti-Malice can be kept safely for about 5 to 7 days if it is covered tightly and refrigerated.

Pepper Wine

Wash the chillies under cold running water and pat them completely dry with kitchen paper. Place the whole chillies in a 1½-pint bottle or jar and pour the rum over them. Cover tightly and marinate at room temperature for at least 10 days before using.

A drop or two of pepper wine is a fiery flavouring for such soups as callaloo and *saucochi di gallinja* (*Recipe Index*).

To make ⅜ pint

3 whole fresh hot chillies, each about 3 inches long (*caution: see "How to Handle Chillies"*)

⅜ pint light rum, or substitute pale dry sherry

Mrs. Bessie Byam's Mango Relish (Trinidad)

Peel the mangoes with a small, sharp knife and cut the flesh away from the stone. Discard the seeds and chop the fruit as finely as possible. Put the mangoes, chillies, garlic and salt into a deep bowl and turn them over and over with a spoon until thoroughly mixed.

Ladle the relish into a serving bowl or a clean jar, and trickle the oil over the top so that it floats on the surface. Cover tightly with a sheet of plastic until ready to serve.

The mango relish can be kept safely for about 4 to 6 weeks if it is covered and refrigerated.

To make about ¾ pint

2 large (about 1 lb. each) unripe mangoes (*see "A Note about Mangoes and Pawpaws"*)

5 teaspoons finely chopped fresh hot chillies (*caution: see "How to Handle Chillies"*)

1½ teaspoons finely chopped garlic

1 teaspoon salt

2½ teaspoons olive oil

Sauce Créole (Martinique)

Put the tomato purée, lime juice, onions, celery, chillies, salt and a few grindings of pepper into a deep bowl, and stir until they are thoroughly blended. Then stir in the sliced olives.

Serve at once, or cover the bowl tightly with a sheet of plastic and refrigerate it until ready to use. The sauce can be safely kept in the refrigerator for about 5 to 7 days.

Sauce créole is traditionally served as an accompaniment to seafood dishes, such as grilled lobster and *pescado asado* (*Recipe Index*).

To make about ¾ pint

An 8-oz. can tomato purée

3 tablespoons strained fresh lime juice

4 oz. finely chopped onions

2½ teaspoons finely chopped celery

1 scant teaspoon finely chopped fresh hot chillies (*caution: see "How to Handle Chillies"*)

1 teaspoon salt

Freshly ground black pepper

3 pimiento-stuffed olives, drained and cut crosswise into paper-thin slices

III

The Labourer's Life: Magic from the Soil

The vegetables that are the staple ingredients of the Caribbean cuisine, the spices that enliven it and the fruits that dress it up all grow easily in the verdant hills of Grenada. Everything in this basket, posed against the sweep of the Grand Anse Beach, was purchased in the Market Square in St. George's, the capital of the island (*pages 18, 19*).

Throughout the Caribbean there are still villages so primitive, so untouched by the modern world that one thinks on seeing them, "This could be Africa", or, "This could be 100 years ago." And both are true. One such village I visited is near St. Anne on the southern coast of Martinique. It was Sunday but the men were at work mending fishing nets laid out upon the ground. The women were chatting in front of their houses, or cooking the Sunday meal—also in front of their houses. One woman sat cross-legged before an outdoor fire, stirring a thick, leafy garden of a soup. Another was preparing tiny round flour dumplings, called *dombé*, to add to the pot of peppery black-eyed peas already simmering on her one-burner paraffin stove. The houses were wooden shacks, windowless and bare. There were no cars in the village; there were not even any streets. On wooden platforms, sardines lay drying for tomorrow's bait. A few chickens and an occasional skinny pig— *cochon planche*, the Martinicans say, to distinguish it from fatter, rounder pigs—rooted about in the sandy yards.

Children played among the fishing boats lined up on shore, the boys pretending to fish, the girls playing house. In one boat six little girls, with calabash bowls and stirring-twigs in hand, were feeding two fair-haired dolls. I stopped to talk to them and they asked me where I came from—France? The United States, I said. One of them had heard of my country and she asked me about the snow: "Does it hurt when it falls on you?" I tried to explain that it was like rain. "Does the rain hurt?" But she didn't believe me. Then I asked them what they were feeding their dolls. One answered, "*Farine*", which is what the Martinicans call cassava flour, "and then she'll have rice, this one. And this one fish if

West Indian Stand-bys: Squashes and Roots

The quintet of vegetables below may look unfamiliar to many cooks on the mainland but all of them are staple foods in a Caribbean kitchen. Left to right:

CALABAZA, OR WEST INDIAN PUMPKIN
Though their shapes and colours vary, large squashes like the one on the left are called calabaza. Usually boiled, they have firm, delicately flavoured flesh rather like that of a butternut or Hubbard squash.

CHRISTOPHENE
This small, pale pear-shaped vegetable, which varies from white to yellow and green, is also a kind of squash. It is cooked, and tastes, like a tender young courgette.

TARO ROOT
Under its brown skin, the flesh of the taro is white but may turn grey, green or violet when boiled. Whatever the colour, it has a faintly nutty taste.

CASSAVA ROOT
This all-purpose vegetable with its bark-like skin and starchy white flesh is not only boiled as a vegetable, but is also used for the cassareep in a Trinidad pepper-pot (*Recipe Index*) and for manioc meal and tapioca.

YAM
This tropical tuber—not the familiar orange sweet potato often confused with it—is the genuine yam. Its skin is tough and thick; its flesh may be white, yellow or, in some roots, red.

The doll's menu and the children's menu are the same. It is not so very different from what was eaten in this village and villages like it 100 or even 200 years ago. During the two centuries when the majority of people in the islands were enslaved, they ate what the plantation owners found economical. This almost never included meat and rarely included fresh fish. One early traveller to the Caribbean noted that, although the islands lie surrounded by the sea and its wealth of fish, the planters "tend their profits so much they will not spare a Negro's absence so long as to go to the Bridge and fetch it." Dried salt fish—mackerel or cod—was more convenient. It was cheap, it did not spoil in the tropical heat, and it came down from New England in the same ships that carried the islands' rum and molasses back to America. The salt fish sent to the West Indies was generally of second quality—the finest product of the Yankee fisheries went to European markets—but it was consumed in great quantities in the islands and was the main source of protein for generations of slaves. Otherwise the vast majority of the people of the Caribbean got along—and rather well you discover when you taste their dishes—on vegetables, usually starchy ones rich in carbohydrates.

This emphasis on vegetable cooking was strengthened in the 19th century when slavery ended and labourers from India and China were brought over to work the fields as indentured servants. They were almost as poor as the African slaves had been, and many observed religious restrictions in what they ate. So they, too, made their meals chiefly of local vegetables.

Soul food? Yes. Like American soul food, the food of most Caribbean islanders, like the food of the poor the world over, was composed of cheap, starchy and filling ingredients. Despite these limitations, and perhaps because of them, the islanders learned to make superb dishes that were cleverly flavoured with herbs and tingling with spices. Even today, when meat and fish are available, the islanders continue to lavish their attention and imagination on soups and vegetable dishes.

It was a meal in Guadeloupe that first made me realize that meat or fresh fish was not essential to a satisfying dinner. My husband and I have a French friend there, a man who loves and understands island food. After he had taken us to several of the small, red-tableclothed restaurants in the island to eat sea eggs and land crab and conch, he announced on our last night, "Now you are ready for the true Creole food." There was something a bit ominous in what he said. Was it to be the mucilaginous Caribbean cactus soup I had read about? No, that was from Curaçao. Or would it be *vers-palmiste*, the palm-tree caterpillar some islanders particularly relish when roasted? But no, it was vegetables he meant. And salt fish. There was a restaurant of which he was very fond, owned by an old Guadeloupian lady who in his opinion served the finest callaloo and the best vegetables in the islands.

The restaurant turned out to be the narrow veranda of an old wooden house. Several bare tables, a few wire-backed chairs and a single fluorescent light were the only furnishings. But Madame Touchin, a strikingly beautiful woman who greeted us at the foot of the steps of her porch, waved us graciously up the stairs. Eighty years old or more, she was dressed in the splendid costume—a blend of Africa and 18th-century France—that only a generation or two ago distinguished all the women of the French islands. Today only the very old still wear it, and Madame carried it off magnificently. Her dress was a floor-length printed cotton, from under which peeped her petticoats, one of lace, another of silk. Around her shoulders was a vivid red and purple and yellow silk scarf, fastened with a big gold pin whose glitter matched her long, dangling earrings and the bangles on her arms. Crowning all was her madwas, a bright Madras turban stiffly tied with four extended points. The protruding points of a French Creole's Madras were once a semaphore of love: If a girl displayed only one point, it meant, "I am free"; two points signified, "My heart is already taken"; three points said, "I am happily married"; four points meant, "Although that may be the case, there may yet be a place for you."

At Madame Touchin's there is no menu. One calls in to plan a dinner menu a day ahead because Madame must rise early to go to market. Our friend had discussed the meal with her, and she had decided to prepare what she would like to prepare. We would have callaloo to start with, of course. The principal ingredients of her callaloo are taro leaves and okra, which came to the islands from Africa. Taro leaves look like green elephant ears and grow on a bush whose edible root is called dasheen; sometimes, however, taro leaves are called callaloo after the soup made from them. Taro is not so well known in Britain as okra, but it is available in West Indian and Eastern shops and markets though it may confusingly sometimes be called dasheen, leaves and all. If you want to try callaloo you can avoid the problem by substituting spinach for the taro leaves.

Callaloo is eaten throughout the Caribbean, but the people of the French islands are especially fond of it. Listen to this from a Guadeloupian cookery book: "To relish and appreciate the subtlety and refinement of this preparation, one must be on the shaded shore of one of our beautiful rivers . . . sitting on a stone, feet in the water, or plunged up to the shoulders in a blue basin, the plate in one's hand and the soul impregnated with sun and euphoria."

We waited for the soup on the dimly lit porch, the palms around us scarcely stirring in the dense, hot August night. Soon a barefoot girl appeared with a big earthenware tureen from which she began to ladle for each of us an almost overflowing bowl. The colour of the soup was exactly the same deep forest green as the leaf-laden soup I had seen cooking out-of-doors in the little fishing village in Martinique, but Madame had mashed the leaves by twirling and twirling them with her *baton lélé*—the African wooden swizzle-stick that Caribbean cooks use as a whisk—until the soup was smooth.

In my first spoonful I tasted peppers, cloves and the pungent sharpness of the taro leaves. But our friend advised me to wait—there was more to come. The girl reappeared with a dish of marinated slivers of salt fish, onions and bright red peppers. She scooped spoonfuls of each into our soup bowls, and then left us to our meal. The soup was as softly fragrant as a somnolent tropical forest, yet it tingled with vinegary, peppery onions and salt fish. Marinated salt fish, in soup or by itself, is perhaps the most popular of the dozens of fascinating ways in which the islanders use salt cod. They always soak it first to soften it and reduce its saltiness. The Spanish-speaking islanders serve marinated salt fish with sweet peppers and call it *serenata*; the French make it with hot peppers and call it *féroce*.

Later we had more of Madame's repertoire of vegetables: bread-fruit cooked in two different ways, plantains and a variety of roots. All the vegetables were put on our plates at once, but they were so varied in texture and flavour that they in no way resembled one another. It was easy to taste the differences between the various roots, all steamed and buttered: nut-like yams, sugary sweet potatoes and delicate malanga, mealy and mild like a floury potato. One helping of the bread-fruit was creamy; it had been mashed up with chives, thyme, parsley, garlic and bacon fat. It bore little resemblance to bread-fruit served in another guise: fried *beignets* (fritters) that were puffy and light. The plantains, my own favourite, had been sautéed in such a way that they were crusty outside, but as soft as baby food inside.

Madame came and stood in the doorway of the porch. I smiled at her and she at me, and she said something in the Creole patois that I could not understand and I said something in my French that she could not understand. But we were communicating: I our pleasure in her food, she her pleasure in our pleasure. She stood for a while, proudly watching us eat, and when she was satisfied she withdrew into her house.

The dessert she sent out to us, a cake poetically called "the torments of love", was rich and chewy with coconut. It originated in the near-by islands called Les Saintes, and only a few old women remember how to make it. Madame Touchin was justly proud of her version, as she had been of her soup and vegetables, but we had eaten so well that we could not finish it.

Root vegetables such as cassava and yams existed in the islands when Columbus discovered them, but many others that are now important in Caribbean cooking came from the Old World. For a long time it has been believed that this was true of one of the region's most useful vegetables, the plantain, the cousin of the banana. Although it is really a fruit, the plantain must be cooked to be palatable and is therefore usually considered a vegetable. The plantain had reached Southern Europe via Africa in the caravans of Arab traders who had discovered it growing in India; when a Spanish friar called Tomás de Berlanga went as a missionary to the New World in 1516 he took plantain shoots with him, thinking that they would do well in the tropics. Berlanga's plantains did indeed thrive in the Caribbean, but it is now believed that his botanical experiment was unnecessary. Many experts think that plantains were already growing on some of the islands when the Spanish arrived, since research shows they were growing at the time in Peru, Mexico and other parts of Central America.

Whatever their origin, plantains now grow throughout the islands; they are also becoming increasingly available in the United States and

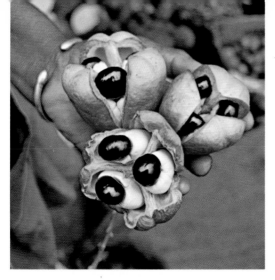

Akee (*left*), one of the Caribbean fruits treated as a vegetable, grows to about the size of a peach. When ripe, its woody shell bursts, revealing shiny black seeds and three segments of edible flesh. In the Jamaican salt fish and akee shown below, the bland scrambled-eggs flavour of the fruit is contrasted with the cod, onions and peppers.

in West Indian shops and markets in Britain, and Americans, in particular, are beginning to show the same sort of enthusiasm for them that turned bananas, in the course of the last 50 years, into one of the country's biggest fruit imports.

Plantains, though less sweet than bananas, are more versatile. They can be cooked and eaten at various stages of ripeness, and each stage has its own taste and treatment. Green or unripe plantains, which are almost as hard as potatoes, are often simply boiled in salted water and served with meat, as we serve boiled potatoes. They taste starchier than potatoes, however, and to be really appetizing should be accompanied by a lot of pepper and onion and spices or made into a casserole or a hot salad. They are also good cut into slivers, deep-fried and served as crisps (*Recipe Index*); they make an interesting change from potato crisps at parties.

The half-ripe plantain is the main ingredient in a superb Puerto Rican appetizer, *mofongo*. Not yet sweet but no longer merely bland and starchy, the plantain is fried, then mashed up with pork cracklings and garlic to a delicious avocado-like creaminess and can be served on bread.

But it is when the plantain is fully ripe that it is at its most glorious. It is served most often as Madame Touchin served it, sliced into rounds and sautéed in butter, crisp outside and soft inside. Its mild but definite sweetness blends magnificently with pork or chicken and it makes beef more interesting, too. Chopped beef and ripe plantains are, in fact, the basis of another special Puerto Rican dish, *piononos*. In this ingenious creation, ripe plantains, which have been sliced, fried and wrapped round a mixture of meat and cheese, are dipped into beaten egg and refried until the plantains taste flaky and sweet as pastry (*Recipe Index*).

It is easy to be enthusiastic about plantains, but bread-fruit, the Caribbean's next most important vegetable, takes some getting used to. It has a bland stand-offish personality and must be carefully handled if it is to be seen at its best. The first time I ate it boiled, which is the way it is most frequently served; it seemed completely flavourless. But when one gets to know the bread-fruit and to explore its possibilities, it becomes more interesting. French fried, made into crisps, roasted with butter, served cold with mayonnaise, onions and sweet peppers as a salad, it is versatile and friendly and goes well with everything. It is at its most enticing when it is scraped from its skin, boiled, then stuffed back into its own prickly green round vase-like shell with onions, spices and salt fish, and is frequently the centre-piece of Caribbean buffets, the most handsome dish at the party.

The history of the bread-fruit is entangled with some of the most dramatic incidents of 18th-century exploration—and has played a central role in some. It first came to the attention of Europeans when Captain Cook encountered it on Tahiti, where it was a staple food. He himself did not care for its flavour, "as disagreeable as that of a pickled olive generally is the first time it is eaten". But the botanist who accompanied him on the voyage did like it and wrote that the rest of the crew agreed with him; they ate it for several months on the return voyage to England as a substitute for bread and found it consistently tasty and nourishing. Perhaps the cook on that first voyage knew the bread-fruit's shy secrets. In any case, the botanist wrote, "No one of the whole ship's Company complained when served with bread-fruit in lieu of biscuit;

and from the health and strength of whole nations, whose principal food it is, I do not scruple to call it one of the most useful vegetables in the world." A humanitarian, he urged that no expense be spared in attempting to grow bread-fruit in other tropical regions where hunger was a problem.

The West Indian planters, always on the look-out for filling foods that would grow with a minimum of care and demand as little of their valuable sugar land as possible, were intrigued with his description. One Jamaican landowner travelled to England especially to petition King George III to dispatch an expedition to the South Seas to carry bread-fruit to the Caribbean. The King was amenable, and in 1787 Captain William Bligh was chosen to lead the expedition. His ship was H.M.S. *Bounty*.

His crew's famous mutiny is a familiar story, but less well known is the fact that one of the chief causes of the men's hatred for their captain was his devotion to bread-fruit. First he delayed too long in the South Seas in his efforts to gather perfect and well-established bread-fruit saplings. Then, during the homeward voyage he denied water to his crew in order to keep the precious bread-fruit alive. The story of what Bligh did after he was cast overboard by the mutineers and made his way thousands of miles to safety in an open boat is also little known. Almost as soon as he got back to England he set out once again to fulfill his mission. This time he succeeded. In 1793 he sailed into Port Royal Harbour in Jamaica with a ship so crowded with beautiful leafy saplings that the Jamaicans rowed out to the ship to inspect with the greatest enthusiasm this "floating forest", "the ship that have the bush".

The bread-fruit tree is one of the most attractive in the Caribbean, tall and crowned with intensely dark green leaves; it took root and spread miraculously. Now it is found on virtually every Caribbean island; its sustaining qualities are so highly thought of that the men in St. Vincent have a saying, "Give me a good working woman and a bread-fruit tree and I need never work again."

The saying is somewhat fanciful because bread-fruit is not, on its own, nourishing enough to keep a man fat and lazy. But the islanders have a whole spectrum of other vegetables to fill out their menu. Among them corn and okra are particularly popular. Corn was indigenous to some of the islands; Columbus saw it growing in Hispaniola and early Spanish writers described how it was boiled and then fried into cakes, one sort for the common Indians, another for their chiefs. Today it is often prepared as a peppery companion to soups or stews. In this form it is called funchi or fungee; both names are African, although the dish closely resembles polenta, the cornmeal pudding of Italy.

HOW TO PEEL A GREEN PLANTAIN
Ripe plantains can be peeled as easily as bananas. But the green ones used for plantain chips or for *banane pesé* (*Recipe Index*) require special handling, since the thick skin clings tightly to the fruit and tends to break off in little pieces. The diagram below illustrates an efficient—and unfrustrating—way of removing the peel. With a sharp knife, slice off the ends and cut the plantain in half. Make four evenly spaced lengthways slits in the skin of each half, cutting through to the flesh from one end to the other. Then, starting at the corner edge of one slit, lift the skin away a strip at a time—pulling it off crosswise rather than lengthways.

In Curaçao, funchi and fish chowder inevitably go together. In a country restaurant where my husband and I sat on a patio at a big rough-hewn table shaded only by an awning made of fish nets, we sampled funchi at its best. The restaurateur, Janchi, would not even begin to make the dish until we were ready to eat. "It has to be springy and soft," he said, "and it grows hard if it waits for you. You must wait for it." We did, sipping rum and contemplating the fierce cactus, the *cadushi*, that grows in quantity in Curaçao and makes a meal for those too poor to eat funchi and chowder. The funchi finally arrived, pale yellow and as puffy as a pillow. We cut into its steaming centre, dunked great chunks of it in a savoury snapper-filled chowder and discovered its earthy moistness. Sometime later I read an 18th-century poem in which a slave whose wife has deserted him mourns her absence. He complains, "My fungee, alas! is unboil'd . . .," and I felt sympathy for him. No doubt he missed his wife, but I could see that it might be easy to miss fungee more.

Okra, though now as prevalent as sweet corn, was not indigenous to the Caribbean; it came over with the slaves from Africa. It is often combined with funchi to make a dish known as coo-coo. Or it is cooked into a soft pudding of mashed plantains called foo-foo, which, in the words of a song sung by the Jamaican folk-singer Louise Bennett, is a very good dish "for when you lose your teeth". Funchi, coo-coo and foo-foo all entered the Caribbean cuisine from Africa, and are found on all the islands regardless of their colonial background; they offer fascinating evidence of the basic homogeneity of the islands' cuisine. Curiously, their names in the original African usage referred to their texture rather than to their ingredients. Funchi is from a word that means mush or meal, while foo-foo described the paleness of pounded, doughy food. Duckunoo is another Caribbean dish of African descent, which can be made from any of several vegetables, as long as they are grated, then wrapped up for steaming in a banana or plantain leaf; it may be spicy and eaten with meat or soup or it may be sweetened with coconut, sugar and vanilla and eaten as a dessert.

Also from Africa came the most exotic among those Caribbean fruits that, like the plantain, masquerade as vegetables. This is the akee, which a friend of mine once described as looking "like a one-pot meal". Split, its yellow flesh resembles a plateful of scrambled eggs, its seeds a garnish of shiny black olives and its mottled red skin a glazed pottery casserole; its texture is soft and its flavour mild. It first crossed the Atlantic in slave ships bound for Jamaica, and was undoubtedly carried along by Africans anxious to take with them some familiar taste of home with which to face the unknown.

Strangely enough, akee never caught on anywhere in the Caribbean except Jamaica. "Akee, rice, salt fish are nice," goes a verse in the song "Jamaica Farewell," "And the rum is fine any time of year." All the islands have fine rum, but only Jamaica has akee and salt fish; which, as any Jamaican will tell you, is one of the best dishes anywhere in the Caribbean. The cod is soaked overnight to reduce its saltiness; then it is boiled and shredded. A sauce of sautéed garlic, onions, sweet or hot peppers and bits of bacon punctuates the mildness of the akee. But stubbornly, the fish stays salty and the akee stays mild, and the combination is so felicitous that they seem an ideally married pair, able to adapt itself to any course that follows.

Opposite: These Moslem women, who live in Port of Spain, Trinidad, have gathered for a lunch of some of the traditional Indian dishes that are gradually becoming part of the cookery of the Caribbean. Among the foods being offered here are chicken *biriani* (*foreground*), a kind of saffron-coloured chicken *pelau* served with hard-boiled eggs; *polouri*, deep-fried balls of chick-pea meal, and curried prawns with tomato (*centre*).

It was long believed that akee was poisonous if not picked at a precise stage of ripeness and then boiled for many hours. This view, which may account for its absence on the other islands, is contested by agricultural researchers at the University of the West Indies in Kingston; they claim that the idea is pure superstition. Nevertheless, the belief is still widely held and no one will eat raw akee or pick it before the fruit has begun to split and show its shining seeds. Fortunately cooks in Great Britain do not have to worry about the problem, since only canned akee is available here.

Akee, bread-fruit and plantain, however familiar in the islands, all seem a bit exotic to Americans and Europeans; but there is another classic Caribbean vegetable dish that is a good deal more humble in our eyes: beans and rice. Each large island has its own favourite version of this combination, and each version, far from being humble, is memorable.

In Jamaica, the dish is known as rice and peas—what the Jamaicans call peas, we know as beans; in this dish they are either red kidney beans or the small red beans native to the island. (Throughout the islands the words pea and bean are often used interchangeably.) Jamaican rice and peas is always made with coconut milk, but beyond that every cook is on her own; there are countless variations. Some call for sweet peppers and tomatoes, some for bacon, some for soup beef or stewing beef, some for onions or chives or hot peppers, some for any combination of these (*Recipe Index*).

I became a devotee of Jamaican rice and peas the very first time I tasted it. It was in New York. My daughter had just been born, and I was feeling weak, nervous about this first baby, and determined to have for a while no other responsibilities. So we engaged a young Jamaican nurse-housekeeper. I planned that I would feed the baby and Vivian would feed my husband and me. She could do a little American cooking, she said, so my husband obligingly went to the supermarket and bought easy things, steaks and a joint. But after three days he began to complain and after the fourth he was miserable. The steaks were always too well done; the roast beef was garlicky. And Vivian herself looked disdainfully at her own handiwork and would not eat it.

So I pleaded with her: "Vivian, make something you enjoy making. If you make something you like I'm sure we'll like it too." "Oh, no," Vivian insisted. "Americans don't like West Indian food." "What is it?" I asked weakly. "Well, it's rice and peas." I told her to make it, whatever it was, tottered off to bed, and dozed self-indulgently while Vivian went out shopping. She came back laden with chunks of beef, spring onions, sweet peppers, red kidney beans and a hairy coconut. From my bedroom I heard her banging at the coconut with my husband's hammer, and I went into the kitchen to see what was happening. The red beans had been put on to simmer with the beef; the coconut was split open, and Vivian began grating it on a small hand grater. Then she squeezed what she had grated between her fingers, picking up lump after lump of coconut, moistening it with water, and pressing and struggling with it until its juices flowed and a white milk was obtained. It seemed terribly slow and painstaking to me, but I could tell she was absorbed in a way she had not been by the dishes I had asked her to cook. As I saw how involved she was in her work, my own interest in cooking revived and for the first time since my daughter's birth I became curious about something apart from myself and the baby.

Ultimately, Vivian threw away the coconut mash and used only the liquid she had so patiently squeezed from it, which she called coconut cream. She poured this into the beans and beef mixture when the water had boiled down, and followed it with the onions and peppers that she had prepared separately, and finally with the rice. That night we sampled the dish. The rice came out of the pot fluffy, but dappled with the beans' earthy redness; in each hearty forkful there was the barest hint of coconut, a sweet tropical teasing. "We love it," we told Vivian. And she smiled and said, incomprehensibly, "I knew you would".

Another Jamaican favourite—a partiality shared also by the inhabitants of Trinidad—is rice and pigeon peas, small yellow peas that came originally from Africa and are known in the Caribbean by names, Congo or goongoo peas, that point to this origin. Jamaicans cook the goongoo peas either with rice or into dumplings; they also sing about them, as they so often sing about food in their folk songs. Indeed, love and food receive almost equal emphasis in the hauntingly sad Jamaican songs of deprivation. "Catch up the fire, Martha; pass me the goongoo peas. Rub up the flour, Sarah. Lord, feel the evening breeze!" sings a field worker in "Evening Time", expressing his relief that at last at the day's end he may return home to the good things of life, "to go walk on the mountain side" and "to eat sing, dance and play".

In Cuba black beans are the speciality. These are to my mind the heartiest and meatiest of beans. Usually they are not cooked with rice but they are served with it, and one shovels great coal-dark scoops of the beans on top of the soft snowy rice. One without the other is a disappointment. There is also a Cuban dish in which the beans and rice are cooked together and this black and white combination is known colloquially as *Moros y Cristianos*.

Haiti too has its own distinctive rice and bean dish, rice *djon djon*, a dish made nowhere else in the Caribbean because it calls for an ingredient found only on Haiti—black mushrooms. Haitian black mushrooms are quite small, and only their earthy-tasting caps are edible. But the stems make a deep-black dye; they are used to colour the water in which the rice is cooked, then discarded. The caps are added to the rice and so are lima beans. European dried mushrooms have virtually the same taste as the Haitian ones, but they do not lend such an interesting colour to the dish.

The ubiquitous bean appears often in another universal Caribbean speciality: soup. There are dozens of rich, vegetable and bean laden brews to tempt the traveller from one end of the Caribbean to the other. They are almost always hot, both in temperature and in taste, for islanders believe that a hot soup, because it causes one to perspire, is a healthful and cooling dish. One feels warmer while eating it, but cooler afterwards; the bland, chilled concoctions that tourists prefer may whet the appetite but they merely postpone the cooling off.

The opulent *soupe à Congo* of Martinique starts with a large assortment of mixed local beans or peas and is then laden with aubergine, yams, green beans, cabbage, avocado, carrots and okra, and flavoured with garlic, onion, cloves, hot pepper, a single sweet potato and a pig's tail. Jamaica has red-pea soup, deliciously flavoured with salt pork. But it is the black bean soup of Cuba that I find most memorable of all. Thick and dark and highly spiced, the beans as satisfying as any meat, it is usually served with side dishes of rice and chopped raw onion; you

Continued on page 66

59

Carnival Capers in Port of Spain

For complexity and sheer spectacle, even Rio de Janeiro would be hard put to equal the pre-Lenten carnival in Port of Spain, Trinidad. For two days thousands of masked and costumed revellers surge through the streets, miming, singing, making music, joking and soliciting tips from the onlookers. The marchers are organized into groups, or bands, each representing a specific theme that is either traditional (Bad Behaviour Sailors, Red Dragoons) or topical (a local murder case, a new film). Carrying on all round the clock, the celebrants replenish their energies at food stalls that spring up all over town to serve them.

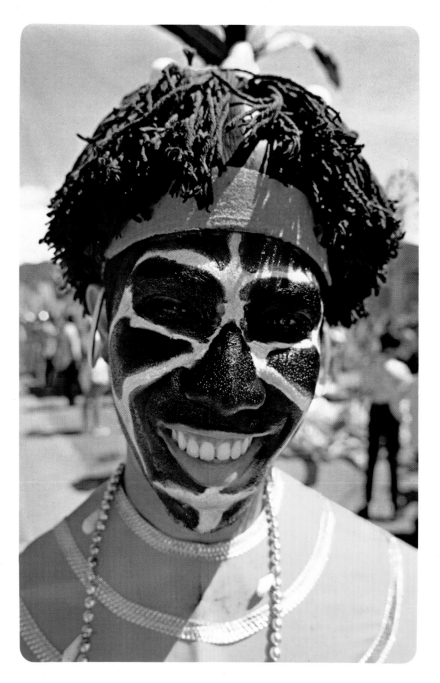

Expert carnival goers can distinguish the many different bands that march through the streets by their costumes and antics. The fearsome wig and face paint on the masker on the left identify him as one of the African Warriors. The brilliantly costumed marchers on the right all belong to a vast carnival band with 1,200 members called Psychedelic Latin America, which came third in the 1969 band-of-the-year competition. The Tambourine Dancers are on the right in the picture, and the Magnificent Matadors are on the left. Maskers' outfits are generally elaborate and expensive, but a way has been found to ease the financial strain: after the carnival is over the participants can often sell their costumes to tourists as souvenirs.

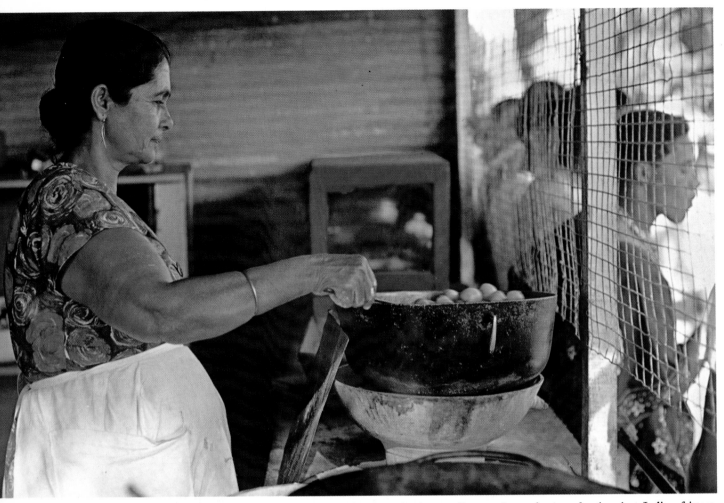

At carnival time in Port of Spain, Mrs. Sookday Maharaj works in a stall preparing *polouris* and other hot Indian fritters.

To make *sabinas*, her favourite fritters, Mrs. Maharaj spreads taro leaves with batter, then stacks, rolls, slices and fries' them.

Indian fritters, shown in the making on the opposite page and on the left, have been adopted as a carnival treat by the people of Trinidad. Three varieties displayed in the wooden tray above are, from the left, *polouris*, small balls of split pea meal; *sahinas*, made of a batter of ground split peas and saffron; and *kachouris*.

Overleaf: Dozens of food stalls like Mrs. Maharaj's ring the savannah in Port of Spain during carnival, and do a brisk business among the marchers and dancers who fill the central square of the town to overflowing with gaiety, movement and colour.

Kachouris are chick-pea fritters flavoured with spring onions and served with pepper sauce.

thicken the soup to suit yourself by ladling in rice and sharpen it to your taste by sprinkling in the onions.

Pervasive as the African influence is throughout the islands, it is not everywhere supreme. In some areas the culinary effects of the oriental influx of the 19th century are also strongly felt. To the beans and starchy vegetables basic to the cooking of African peoples, the Indians and Chinese added a taste for leafy and green vegetables. The Orientals have long been recognized as the finest gardeners in the islands, and in many places they supply the demand they created for lettuce, cabbage, cucumber and green beans by cultivating and selling them. Trinidad, where nearly all the commercial gardeners are Indian, has the most verdant vegetable markets in the Caribbean. In Kingston, Jamaica, if one wants really fine vegetables one goes to the Chinese traders in Barry Street. Sitting on folding chairs in the street, their wares displayed beside them, they boast as great a variety as can be found in the city's big covered market-places; and the green of their lettuces and extra-long Chinese string beans is dazzling.

Apart from their magic with vegetables, the Chinese have affected the culinary habits of the islanders chiefly through the proliferation of Chinese restaurants all over the region. Virtually every island has at least one, simple or grand. In Cuba, where the Chinese have intermarried with the rest of the population, Chinese food became so popular that an entirely new fashion in restaurants has developed: Cuban-Chinese restaurants specializing equally in standard Cuban dishes and standard Chinese dishes. Now, run by émigrés, they have mushroomed all over New York City and Florida.

But even more than the Chinese, the Indians have had a deep effect upon the Caribbean cuisine, primarily through their enthusiasm for curry, which is becoming as much a part of Caribbean as of Indian cooking. The method is different: the islanders do not mix a curry paste for themselves as the Indians do, but always use prepared curry powder. But in many parts of the area, curry is regularly used to flavour chicken, meats, potatoes, even the African akee. Indeed, in Jamaica, the national party dish, eaten whenever there is something special to celebrate or just to be happy about, is curried goat. In Trinidad *pelau* has the status of a national dish, and many people claim it was popularized by the Indians. Like pigeon peas and rice. Trinidad's *pelau* also contains chicken or meat and can be embellished with saffron and raisins and tomatoes.

The Indian influence on the cuisine of the Caribbean is a quite recent development, and its impact is steadily spreading. Usually the study of how one people's food affects another's is a study of the past, but in the Caribbean the process is going on now. I saw convincing evidence of this influence at work in Port of Spain, Trinidad, during a recent carnival week.

Carnival is celebrated all through the islands, though nowhere more exuberantly than in Trinidad. It began as a French Catholic custom, an indulgent celebration before the strict fasting required during Lent. The colonialists attended lavish parties and wore masks and finery; the slaves celebrated with mimicking versions of the festivity back in their own quarters. After emancipation the Africans began to participate in the carnival openly and their mimicry became public. They donned home-made papier mâché masks and, too poor for fine robes, whatever costumes they could devise, and they paraded and cavorted, reciting witty satires in which a man's or woman's most embarrassing foibles were pointed out. Some of the costumed figures became traditional, and they can still be seen in today's carnival—some French, like Pierrot Granad, a pompous grandee in tattered robes, and some straight out of African mythology, like Moko Jumby, a witch doctor on stilts, or the Shango men with nut and seed necklaces about their necks. Now, however, the festivities are organized on a far grander scale, with expensive costumes and elaborate, carefully rehearsed presentations.

The essence of carnival is embodied in the celebrants' ecstatic, rapturous dancing and their spirit of joyous self-expression. Carnival is a time for the assertion of freedom, for giving free flow to primitive urges. At the carnival no one complains about drunkenness, exhibitionism, or even fighting, and every November, nine months later, there seems to be a sudden increase in the number of babies born in the islands.

Yet one basic urge, eating, was long neglected at the carnival. Only now is it becoming an exciting part of the event, and this is because of the Indians. They participate in only a limited way in the actual pageantry of the carnival; but they come to the savannah, the central park in Port of Spain where the carnival shows take place, and there they set up rough wooden stalls with grand names like Taj Mahal and Ali's Caribbean Restaurant, from which they dispense sustenance to the carnival players. Although traditional Creole food is sold all round the savannah, it is the wares of the Indian food sellers that seem especially suited to the enthusiasm for the exotic that *is* carnival.

On Tuesday of the carnival week I spent in Port of Spain, when it seemed to me that the entire population of the city had been either making music or dancing to it non-stop for more than 30 hours, I went to the savannah to watch the climax of the festivities, the masqueraders' grand, marathon march. For months before they had been rehearsing for this final parade. Now the singers, bandsmen and masqueraders came pouring into the savannah in a whirl of silks, feathers and sequins. Renaissance princes, cruel pirates, African warriors and fierce mythical animals swarmed in exuberant conviviality. And when they were not dancing, they besieged the Indian food sellers behind their counter fortresses that ringed the savannah. The Indians met the onslaught bravely with trays of triangular meat pies and stacks of *roti*, the flat Indian bread. Beef stewed in tomatoes, chicken caramelized with brown sugar and fragrant with lime, steaming split-pea purée and chunky potato curry were packed into the *rotis* as fast as agile hands could work. At the sweet stalls there were crowds of children reaching up for cakes and candies that were spiky with coconut, sandy with sugar and dripping with honey.

But the crowds were thickest at the stalls serving Indian vegetable fritters: golden balls of ivory-smooth chick-pea batter, sparkling with oil and studded with little emerald treasures of split peas and spinach.

I spent an hour that morning watching one Indian woman, Mrs. Sookday Maharaj, deftly squeeze and roll, pet and pat an endless flow of fritters through her fingers. Like many of the food sellers, Mrs. Maharaj lives in the country and comes to Port of Spain only for special events like carnival or the horse races held in June and December. Her husband drives a taxi in their country village, an occupation that does not pay very well; but at the races and carnival, the Maharaj family, feeding the throngs with the same dishes that they enjoy at home, makes enough money to assure a fairly comfortable life. There are 12 children, and all, except one son who had emigrated to London, were helping out. The teenage sons took charge of the soda and beer, and laboriously peeled and diced potatoes for the curry and green mangoes for the mango pickle. The daughters, under their mother's fierce tutelage, mixed the batter for the fritters and did the selling. Mrs. Maharaj herself did all the frying, though, for the secret of her fritters is to keep the oil at exactly the right temperature and to remove the fritters at exactly the right moment. When she was talking to me at one point, her teenage daughter, fearing that her mother was being distracted and that the fritters might get too dark, made a movement towards the red-clay cooking stove. Mrs. Maharaj saw it all from the corner of her eye and uttered a resounding, "Nah, nah, nah! Only I will take them out".

She and the other Indian women who do the cooking in the savanna in their sandals, earrings and golden arm bands are very proud of their work. The most popular fritter is *polouri*, made of preground split-pea meal, flour, baking powder, salt and saffron. These are sold by the bagful, and it is rare that the sellers can keep up with the demand. Equally good are *kachouri*, fritters made of hand-ground chick-pea meal, flour, salt and spring onions. *Kachouri* are meant to be spicy, but Mrs. Maharaj does not put hot pepper into her *kachouri* batter at the stand as she does at home—she hand-mixes so much batter in the course of a day that a peppery mixture would burn her skin. Instead the spiciness is supplied separately by pepper sauce. She also makes *bara*, similar to *polouri* but shaped differently, and *baigani*, made of aubergines.

Her own favourite fritter is *sahina*, made from taro leaves. She and her children pick them—the plant seems to grow wild on much of the island—and set them to dry on the roof of the stall. When the leaves have turned slightly brown, they are spread individually with a batter of split peas, flour, baking powder, salt and saffron and stacked on top of one another. When the stack is a few inches thick, it is rolled up like a Swiss roll, and then it is spread with batter and sliced crosswise. The slices are fried and produce the most exquisite of all her fritters. I bought a collection of Mrs. Maharaj's fritters, but when she was filling my bag with *sahina* she said sharply, "These you must eat yourself. Don't give any away. Even to your daughter."

I hurried away with my treasures, pushing through the throng of dancers to find somewhere to stop and taste them. Watching her cook and all the celebrants dance had made me extremely hungry. I found some unoccupied grass and eagerly opened my brown paper bag. I was not disappointed: The *polouri* was soft within, the batter airy and sweet; the *kachouri* had a more assertive taste, nut-like and salty; but the *sahina*, as Mrs. Maharaj had promised, was the best. With each bite, it was at once pungent and sweet, chewy and crisp. Its many-layered texture reminded me of when I was a child, and used to go to my grandmother's for nut strudel, when it seemed that counting all the thicknesses of that flaky delicacy would have meant counting higher than I could add.

Indians form only a tiny percentage of the Caribbean population, of course, and the legacy from Africa will always predominate. But those ebullient crowds of carnival dancers swarming round the Indians' food stalls made me realize how dynamic the Caribbean cuisine is, and how it continues to expand and grow more exciting as it draws upon the culinary imagination of all who come to the islands.

Opposite: A Christmas favourite in the English-speaking islands of the Caribbean: the refreshing drink called sorrel is made not from the pot herb of the same name but from a member of the hibiscus family. Parts of the blossoms, seen behind the jug, are mixed with various flavourings and steeped in water for a day or two to produce a spicy, rather tart drink. In Trinidad, it is lightly fermented and rum is added to produce a headier concoction.

68

To serve 4

2 large ripe plantains (about 1 lb. each)

1½ oz. butter

2½ teaspoons vegetable oil

2½ tablespoons vegetable oil mixed with 1 teaspoon liquid annatto

1 lb. lean minced beef, preferably minced topside

2 oz. finely chopped onions

1 oz. finely chopped green pepper

2½ teaspoons finely chopped fresh hot chillies (*caution: see "How to Handle Chillies"*)

1 scant teaspoon finely chopped garlic

¼ oz. plain flour

4 oz. boiled ham, cut into ¼-inch dice

3 medium-sized firm ripe tomatoes, peeled, seeded and finely chopped (*see sopa de granules, Recipe Index*), or substitute a 1 lb. can chopped drained tomatoes

3 tablespoons water

1 teaspoon salt

Freshly ground black pepper

3 large pimiento-stuffed olives, thoroughly drained and finely chopped

2½ teaspoons finely chopped capers

5 teaspoons malt vinegar

Vegetable oil for deep frying

4 eggs

Piononos (*Puerto Rico*)

DEEP-FRIED PLANTAIN RINGS WITH SPICED MINCED BEEF FILLING

Peel the plantains and cut each one lengthways into 4 thick strips. Melt the butter in 2½ teaspoons of vegetable oil in a large, heavy frying-pan. When the foam begins to subside, add the plantain. Cook them for about 4 minutes on each side, turning the strips over with a perforated fish slice until golden brown. Transfer the strips to kitchen paper to drain and cool.

Heat the annatto-flavoured oil in the same pan over a moderate heat until a light haze forms above it. Drop in the beef and cook until all traces of pink disappear, mashing it up constantly with the back of a spoon to break up any lumps. Add the onions, green pepper, chillies, and garlic and cook for 5 minutes, stirring frequently, until the vegetables are soft but not brown. Add the flour, and stir for 3 to 4 minutes to remove any taste of raw flour. Stir in the ham, tomatoes, water, salt and a few grindings of black pepper. Cook briskly, stirring occasionally, until most of the liquid in the pan evaporates and the mixture thickens enough to hold its shape lightly in the spoon. Stir in the olives, capers and vinegar off the heat, and taste for seasoning.

To make the *piononos*, shape each strip of plantain into a ring about 3 inches in diameter, overlapping the ends by about ½ inch and securing them with a wooden toothpick inserted lengthways. Lay the rings side by side and spoon about 4 tablespoons of the beef mixture into the centre of each one. Pat the meat firmly into place and gently press the top as flat as possible.

Fill a deep-frying pan or large saucepan with vegetable oil to a depth of 2 to 3 inches and heat the oil to a temperature of 350° F. on a deep-frying thermometer.

Beat the eggs in a small, shallow bowl with a fork or whisk until they are thoroughly blended. Place the filled plantain rings on a perforated fish slice, one at a time, and dip them into the eggs, coating them completely. Immediately slide each ring into the hot oil and deep-fry it for about 3 minutes, gently turning it over with a spoon until golden brown on both sides. Transfer the rings to kitchen paper to drain as they brown. Serve at once with *riz et pois* or *riz au djon djon* (*Recipe Index*).

Sautéed plantains are curved into rings and filled with meat (*below, left*), then coated with egg and deep-fried to produce the crusty Puerto Rican favourite *piononos*, shown opposite arranged round a heap of red beans and rice and accompanied by beer.

To serve 6

¾ oz. dried Haitian *djon djon*
   mushrooms (*see Glossary*), with
   stalks removed, or dried black
   European mushrooms
¾ pint boiling water
2½ teaspoons vegetable oil
1 oz. salt pork, cut into ¼-inch
   dice
1 oz. finely chopped green pepper
3 tablespoons finely chopped fresh
   parsley
1 tablespoon finely chopped
   spring onions, including 1 inch of
   the green tops
1 teaspoon finely chopped garlic
6½ oz. uncooked long-grain white
   rice
¼ teaspoon crumbled dried thyme
A pinch of ground cloves
1 teaspoon salt

To serve 4

6 tablespoons vegetable oil
2 medium-sized green plantains,
   peeled (*see "How to Peel a Green
   Plantain"*) and cut crosswise
   into ½-inch-thick slices

To make about 20 two-inch round cakes

1 lb. fresh yams, *not* sweet
   potatoes (*see Glossary*), peeled and
   finely grated
½ oz. butter, melted and cooled
2½ teaspoons finely grated onion
1 tablespoon finely chopped fresh
   parsley
1¼ teaspoons salt
Freshly ground black pepper
2 egg yolks
3 tablespoons vegetable oil

Riz au Djon Djon (*Haiti*)
SAUTÉED RICE WITH DRIED BLACK MUSHROOMS

Put the mushrooms into a small enamel, stainless-steel or glass saucepan and pour in ¾ pint of boiling water. Let the mushrooms soak for 30 minutes, then bring them to the boil over a high heat. Reduce the heat to low and simmer uncovered for 15 minutes. Drain the mushrooms in a sieve set over a bowl, and measure and reserve the cooking liquid. If you are using European mushrooms chop them coarsely; Haitian mushrooms are left whole.

Heat the oil over a moderate heat in a large, heavy saucepan until a light haze forms above it. Fry the pork in the oil, turning the pieces over with a spoon until they are crisp and brown and have rendered all their fat. Transfer the pork to kitchen paper to drain with a perforated spoon. Add the green pepper, parsley, spring onions and garlic to the fat remaining in the pan and stir for about 2 minutes, until the vegetables are soft but not brown.

Add the rice and stir constantly for 2 to 3 minutes, until the grains begin to turn milky and opaque. Do not let them brown. Mix the reserved mushroom cooking liquid with enough boiling water to make ¾ pint and pour the mixture over the rice. Stir in the mushrooms, pork, thyme, cloves and salt, and bring to the boil over a high heat. Reduce the heat to low, cover tightly, and simmer for about 20 minutes, until the rice has absorbed all the liquid in the pan and become a rich walnut-brown colour. Taste for seasoning, fluff the rice with a fork, and serve at once.

Banane Pèsé (*Haiti*)
TWICE-FRIED PLANTAIN SLICES

Heat the oil in a large, heavy frying-pan over a moderate heat until a light haze forms above it. Add as many plantain slices as you can without crowding the pan, and brown them for about 2 minutes on each side. Transfer them to kitchen paper to drain as they brown. Press each slice into a flat round about ¼ inch thick and 2 inches in diameter on a board, using a broad solid palette knife. Heat the oil and fry the rounds again for about 1 minute on each side. Drain on kitchen paper and serve at once. Traditionally, *banane pèsé* is served as an accompaniment to *griots* (*Recipe Index*).

Frituras de Name (*Dominican Republic*)
FRIED YAM CAKES

Put the yams, butter, onion, parsley, salt and a liberal grinding of pepper into a deep bowl, and mix well. Drop in the egg yolks and beat vigorously with a wooden spoon until the mixture is fairly smooth and thick enough to come away from the sides of the bowl in an almost solid mass.

Line a large shallow baking dish with kitchen paper and put it in the oven. Preheat the oven to the lowest setting. Heat the oil over a moderate heat in a large, heavy frying-pan until a light haze forms above it. For each cake, drop about a tablespoon of yam mixture into the hot oil. Cook 4 or 5 at a time, leaving enough space between them for them to spread into 2- to 2½-inch rounds. Fry the cakes for about 4 minutes on each side, until golden and crisp around the edges. Transfer the *frituras de ñame* to the lined dish to drain as they brown, and keep warm. Serve at once.

Riz et Pois (Haiti)
RED BEANS AND RICE

Wash the beans under running water in a large sieve or colander until the draining water runs clear. Transfer them to a large, heavy saucepan, add ¼ teaspoon of the salt and a few grindings of pepper, and pour in 2½ pints of water. Bring to the boil over a high heat; reduce the heat to low, and simmer partly covered for about 1½ hours, until the beans are tender but still intact. Drain in a sieve set over a deep bowl and put the beans aside. Measure the cooking liquid and add enough water to make 1½ pints.

Melt ½ ounce of the lard over a moderate heat in a heavy, medium-sized saucepan. When it is very hot but not smoking, add the rice and stir for 1 to 2 minutes, until the grains begin to turn milky and opaque.

Stir in the 1½ pints of reserved liquid and water, the remaining teaspoon of salt and a liberal grinding of pepper, cover tightly, and reduce the heat to the lowest possible point. Simmer undisturbed for about 20 minutes, until the rice is tender and has absorbed all the liquid. Taste for seasoning and set aside off the heat, partly covered to keep the rice warm.

Melt the remaining ounce of lard in a heavy, medium-sized frying-pan, working quickly. Drop in the beans and stir until they are heated through. Watch carefully for any sign of burning and adjust the heat accordingly.

Fluff the rice with a fork, heap it up on a heated dish and surround it or top it with the beans. Serve at once.

To serve 6

6 oz. dried red kidney beans
1¼ teaspoons salt
2½ pints freshly ground black pepper
2½ to 3¼ pints water
1½ oz. lard
13 oz. uncooked long-grain white rice

Moros y Cristianos (Cuba)
BLACK BEANS AND RICE

Wash the beans under cold running water in a large sieve or colander, until the draining water runs clear. Transfer the beans to a large, heavy saucepan, pour in 2¾ pints of water, and bring to the boil over a high heat. Reduce the heat to low and simmer partly covered for about 2½ to 3 hours, until the beans are tender but still intact. When the beans are done, almost all the cooking liquid should have cooked away; if the liquid seems to be evaporating too quickly, add more boiling water when necessary.

Drain the beans in a sieve or colander. Mash 1½ tablespoons of them to a smooth paste with a pestle and mortar or in a small bowl with the back of a fork. Set the beans and bean paste aside.

Heat the oil over a moderate heat in a large, heavy frying-pan until a light haze forms above it. Fry the pork in the oil, turning the dice over with a spoon until they are crisp and brown and have rendered all their fat. Remove them from the pan with a perforated spoon and drain on kitchen paper.

Add the garlic, onions and green pepper to the fat in the pan. Cook for about 5 minutes, stirring frequently, until the vegetables are soft but not brown. Watch carefully for any sign of burning and adjust the heat accordingly. Stir in the bean paste, then add the beans and the pork dice, reduce the heat to low, and simmer uncovered for 10 minutes.

Return the entire contents of the frying-pan to the saucepan and add the rice, salt and ¾ pint of water. Bring to the boil over a high heat, stirring constantly. Reduce the heat to low, cover tightly, and simmer for about 20 minutes, until the rice is tender and all the liquid has been absorbed. Taste and season with salt and a few grindings of pepper. Serve at once.

To serve 6 to 8

6 oz. dried black beans
3½ to 4 pints water
3 tablespoons vegetable oil
1 oz. lean salt pork, cut into ¼-inch dice
2 oz. finely chopped onions
1 oz. finely chopped green pepper
1 teaspoon finely chopped garlic
9¾ oz. uncooked long-grain white rice
1¼ teaspoons salt
Freshly ground black pepper

Salt Fish and Akee (Jamaica)

To serve 4

1 lb. salt cod
4 oz. salt pork, cut into ¼-
    inch dice
4 oz. finely chopped onions
1 scant teaspoon finely chopped
    fresh hot chillies (*caution: see "How
    to Handle Chillies"*)
A 1-lb. 2-oz. can of akee,
    thoroughly drained (*see Glossary*)
A pinch of crumbled dried thyme
Freshly ground black pepper
1 firm ripe tomato, cut lengthways
    into 8 wedges

Starting a day in advance, place the cod in a glass, enamel or stainless-steel pan or bowl, cover it with cold water, and soak for at least 12 hours, changing the water 3 or 4 times.

Drain the cod, rinse under cold running water, place it in a saucepan, and add enough fresh water to cover the fish by 1 inch. Bring to the boil over a high heat. (Taste the water. If it seems excessively salty, drain, cover with fresh water, and bring to the boil again.)

Reduce the heat to low and simmer uncovered for about 20 minutes, until the fish flakes easily when prodded gently with a fork. Drain thoroughly. Remove and discard any skin and bones using a small knife, and separate the fish into coarse flakes. Set aside.

Fry the salt pork over a moderate heat in a heavy, medium-sized frying-pan, turning the dice over with a spoon until they are crisp and brown and have rendered all their fat. Discard the pork.

Add the onions and chillies to the rendered fat in the pan and cook for about 5 minutes, stirring frequently, until they are soft but not brown. Watch carefully for any sign of burning and adjust the heat accordingly. Add the flaked cod, akee, thyme and a few grindings of pepper, and cook for a minute or two to heat them through.

To serve, transfer the entire contents of the pan to a heated dish and garnish with the wedges of tomato.

Akee Soufflé (Jamaica)

To serve 4

A 1-lb. 2-oz. can of akee
    thoroughly drained (*see Glossary*)
1½ oz. butter, plus ½ oz. butter,
    softened
¾ oz. flour
⅜ pint milk
1 teaspoon Worcestershire sauce
½ teaspoon salt
¼ teaspoon white pepper
4 egg yolks
5 egg whites

Drop the akee into a small frying-pan or saucepan and slide the pan gently backwards and forwards over a moderate heat for about 5 minutes, until all the liquid has evaporated. Force the akee through a fine sieve set over a deep mixing bowl with the back of a wooden spoon or purée it in a food mill. Set the akee aside.

Melt 1½ ounces of the butter over a moderate heat in a heavy, medium-sized saucepan. When the foam begins to subside, stir in the flour and mix thoroughly. Pour in the milk and cook over a high heat, stirring constantly with a whisk, until the mixture thickens heavily and comes to the boil. Reduce the heat to low and simmer for about 3 minutes to remove any taste of raw flour. Stir in the Worcestershire sauce, salt and white pepper.

Remove the pan from the heat and beat in the egg yolks, one at a time. Stir in the akee and cool the mixture to room temperature.

Preheat the oven to Mark 5: 375° F. Spread the ½ ounce of softened butter evenly over the bottom and sides of a 2½-pint soufflé dish, using a pastry brush.

Beat the egg whites in a deep bowl with a whisk or a rotary egg beater until they are stiff enough to stand in unwavering peaks on the whisk when it is lifted from the bowl. Stir about a quarter of the whites into the akee mixture, then pour it over the rest of the egg whites. Thoroughly but gently, fold them together with a rubber spatula, using an over and under cutting motion rather than a stirring motion.

Pour the soufflé mixture into the prepared dish and lightly smooth the top with the spatula. Bake in the middle of the oven for about 35 minutes, until the soufflé puffs above the rim of the dish and the top is lightly browned. Serve at once.

Bakes (Trinidad)

FRIED BISCUITS

Sift the flour, baking powder and salt together into a deep bowl and drop in the lard. Rub the flour and fat together, working quickly and using your finger-tips, until they look like fine breadcrumbs. Pour in the sugar and water mixture all at once, toss together, and gather the dough into a ball. If the dough crumbles, add a little more cold water, a teaspoon or so at a time, until the particles adhere. Pinch off about $1\frac{1}{2}$ tablespoons of dough for each biscuit, and pat it into a ball. Roll each ball into a round about 3 inches in diameter and $\frac{1}{4}$ inch thick on a lightly floured surface.

Pour oil into a large, heavy frying-pan to a depth of about $\frac{1}{4}$ inch and heat until it is hot but not smoking. Fry the biscuits, four or five at a time, for about 3 minutes on each side, turning them over with a perforated spoon and adjusting the heat so that they brown richly and evenly without burning. Transfer them to kitchen paper to drain as they brown. Serve warm, or at room temperature, with butter or cheese.

To make about 9 three-inch round biscuits

8 oz. plain flour
$1\frac{1}{2}$ teaspoons baking powder
1 teaspoon salt
1 oz. lard, chilled and cut into $\frac{1}{4}$-inch dice
$1\frac{1}{2}$ teaspoons sugar dissolved in 3 tablespoons cold water
Vegetable oil for frying

Cassava Biscuits (Barbados)

Preheat the oven to Mark 6: 400° F. Peel the brown bark-like skin from the cassava, using a sharp knife, then grate it finely on a hand grater. Wrap the grated root in a double thickness of cheesecloth and squeeze hard to extract its liquid. It may be used in pepper-pot (*Recipe Index*).

Cream the butter, lard and sugar together in a deep bowl, beating and mashing them against the sides of the bowl with a wooden spoon until the mixture is light and fluffy. Beat in the egg, cassava and coconut.

Mix the flour and baking powder, and sift them onto a sheet of greaseproof paper. Add about 2 ounces at a time to the creamed mixture, beating well after each addition. The dough should be firm enough to be gathered into a compact ball; if necessary, add a little more flour a tablespoon at a time. When the dough becomes too stiff to stir, knead in the rest of the flour with your hands.

Knead the dough for 2 to 3 minutes on a lightly floured surface, pushing it down with the heels of your hands, pressing it forwards, and folding it back on itself. Then roll it into a circle about $\frac{1}{4}$ inch thick. Cut the dough into 2-inch rounds, using a biscuit cutter or the rim of a glass. Gather the scraps into a ball, roll it out into another circle, and cut out rounds as before.

Place the rounds about 1 inch apart on one or two large ungreased baking sheets and bake in the middle of the oven for 20 minutes, until the biscuits are firm to the touch and golden brown. Serve at once.

To make about 2 dozen two-inch round biscuits

1 lb. sweet cassava, or yuca (*see Glossary*)
2 oz. butter, softened
2 oz. lard
$3\frac{1}{2}$ oz. castor sugar
1 egg
$5\frac{1}{2}$ oz. finely grated fresh coconut
8 oz. plain flour
1 teaspoon baking powder

Sorrel Drink (Trinidad)

Place the sorrel sepals, cinnamon stick, orange rind, whole cloves and sugar in a large jar or crock and pour the boiling water over them. Cool, cover with foil or a sheet of plastic, and set aside at room temperature for 2 or 3 days. Strain the liquid through a fine sieve, return it to the jar, and stir in the rum, ground cinnamon and ground cloves.

Let the liquid stand at room temperature for another 2 or 3 days. Then strain it through a fine sieve lined with cheesecloth and refrigerate until thoroughly chilled. Serve in chilled glasses with or without ice.

To make about $3\frac{1}{4}$ pints

1 oz. dried Jamaica sorrel, or roselle, sepals (*see Glossary*)
A 3-inch piece of cinnamon stick
A 3-by-1-inch strip of fresh orange rind
3 whole cloves
12 oz. sugar
$3\frac{1}{4}$ pints boiling water
3 tablespoons medium-dark rum
$\frac{1}{2}$ teaspoon ground cinnamon
$\frac{1}{4}$ teaspoon ground cloves

IV

The Planter's Life: Rich, Plentiful Fare

The colonial era of the Caribbean was a time of contrast. While those who worked in the fields lived on vegetables, the planters who owned the fields enjoyed a way of life as elegant as any back home in Europe. Their plantations had huge kitchens and a large household staff, and they combined the culinary traditions of the Old World with the New World's plenty to produce legendary meals. They served all the vegetables that their lands produced, but the keystones of their generous cuisine were the meat from the animals and poultry bred on the plantations. And today, long after that opulent era has gone, there remains a tradition of good eating and a treasury of imaginative meat recipes.

I first sensed the richness of this heritage at a farm in Jamaica. A friend had invited me to visit a family in a remote area of the island, two hours from Montego Bay along treacherous winding roads. Now I was seeing the variety of terrain that makes Jamaica different from many of the smaller islands. They are, at best, counties; Jamaica is a *country*, a collection of disparate elements. It has dozens of beaches, coral-reefed and silver-sanded, as well as palm trees that grow as high as 20 feet in five years. But Jamaica also has a dramatic interior—mountains and hills, fertile upland valleys with precariously perched villages. Here is the heart of the country and it dominates whatever occurs along its shores, from politics to weather.

We set out for the farm in daylight, but drove along roads so closely hemmed in by huge ferns and trees that we seemed to ride through dimly lit tunnels. Then the cane-scented tropical darkness descended quite as abruptly as the travel books say it does. The road got rougher and the houses further apart, and soon the only lights to be seen were those of

At one time only the rich families in the great houses of the islands could afford meat, and the cooks devised many imaginative dishes to treat tropical foods in a Continental style. One favourite dish is baked pawpaw with a spicy beef filling, here shown next to a salad of watercress and onion rings.

occasional roadside stalls. We stopped to treat ourselves to a polismun, as the Jamaican Red Stripe beer is called, after the red stripe on the uniforms of the island's police. Soon there were no longer any stalls nor many people along the roads. For we had come to duppy country—ghost country—where many people still believe that the human personality is divided threefold into body, soul and shadow, and the shadow rises after death and wanders forth to terrify the living. Duppies do their wandering at night, so people stay at home, and all the houses we passed were tightly shuttered against ghosts.

When we finally reached the farm it was too dark to see the land and, surprisingly to me, too chilly up there in the hills to want to stay outside. The farmhouse was inviting, its paraffin lamps flickering defiance at the night and the duppies. Our hosts gave us some home-made sweet-potato wine, thick and warming, with a faint flavour of the raisins that had steeped in it. The potion soon warmed us, and we toured the house, which turned out to be stuffed with the furniture of another era, when human beings liked to be dwarfed by their possessions. There were chairs in which I got lost and armoires that threatened me with their height, and an island-made table of mahogany, a grandiose four-footed creation, that took up the entire dining-room. I wondered what my hostess could put upon it to fill all that space; for this was a table worthy of the massive silverware that was found everywhere in Jamaica in the days of piracy. One Frenchman of the time suggested that his countrymen would do better to plunder the tables of the English than the galleons of the Spanish silver fleet.

But when dinner came I understood why such gigantic tables are still used in so many island homes; whenever I sat down at one afterwards, whether on a plantation, a small farm like this one or even, once in the town house of a Trinidad family who had once been farmers, I knew that its entire surface would soon be covered with an astonishing array of dishes.

The display was one that spoke of the generosity of both the farmer and his fields. We began that night with Jamaican pepper-pot soup, thick and green with the farm's cultivated spinach and okra and the leaves of the prickly susumber bush that grows wild where other things will not. When the soup was cleared away, my hostess and the woman who helped her with the cooking, and who had worked in this house for 40 years, carried in from the outside kitchen dish after dish of farm produce. There were vegetables in profusion, of course: roasted white yams; tender boiled chocho, a member of the squash family that combines the flavours of courgettes and cucumbers, vivid orange carrots to complement the pallor of the chochos; tomatoes; fried white bread-fruit slices; baked plantains golden with butter.

But it was the meat dishes that were the most exciting. In the centre of the table, confusing me by an embarrassment of riches, were a plump roasted chicken, a baked loin of pork and a high-heaped casserole of goat. The chicken had been imaginatively stuffed with mashed bananas (*Recipe Index*), the pork was glazed with brown sugar (*Recipe Index*), and the goat, cut into cubes, had been curried.

I could not decide where to begin my meal or what combination of foods to put on my plate: The pork and plantains went together naturally, I knew, but what else? The chicken with chochos and carrots? The goat with the rice and bread-fruit? My hostess solved the problem

78

for me—there was no beginning; everything must be sampled, and all together. This is usual in many island houses, and at first I found it as disconcerting as the traditional Oriental way of ending a meal with soup. There is no arbitrary separation of courses in the Caribbean. I have had fish and meat on my plate at once, bananas between them and vegetables all round. One keeps the tastes separate by following one's own order; it is the heaped-up plate that is the ideal.

My plate certainly achieved the ideal that night. From among the wealth of tastes offered by the feast, the one that intrigued me most was the goat. I had never eaten it before and, like many Americans, expected it to be stringy and gamy. I was wrong. First of all, the meat was incredibly tender—partly because, I discovered later, the cook had softened it in the old country fashion, rubbing it with green pawpaw, which has tenderizing juices. As for the flavour, I have since confirmed what I then suspected through the dominant curry, that goat tastes mild and rather like lamb. In fact, as goat is hard to get in Britain and the United States, lamb makes a good substitute for it in curried goat (*Recipe Index*). For this dish, with its coconut-flavoured curry, is too good to miss for lack of a goat. The real thing is best, of course; but you are not likely to get it in Jamaica unless you leave the beaten tourist path. By all means do so—but be warned that the meat is sometimes less than carefully prepared and you are likely to encounter some bones.

The venerable ancestry of many farm dishes is documented in a remarkable treasure that belongs to one of the oldest English families in Jamaica, the Pringles. It is an unpublished collection of recipes going back almost two centuries, compiled by a Pringle lady in the 1840s from the many instructions and scraps of paper she had inherited from aunts and grandmothers. The recipes—still being used by Pringle descendants—reveal how much attention and imagination the colonial planters' wives brought to bear on their unfamiliar surroundings. Ways of enhancing local foods share a place with ways of adapting favourite European dishes. There is one recipe for squab pie so charming that I have long admired its unknown inventor. It is, she notes, a Devonshire dish, a chicken pie cooked with apples. But she is forced to "rearrange" it, substituting pork for the squab and chochos for the apples. Undaunted, she still calls it squab pie.

This antique collection also contains warnings that are clearly as valuable a contribution as the recipes themselves, about what *not* to eat. A note with the recipe for mutton with guinea-hen weed reads: "Avoid this altogether. The people soak the meat in vinegar which they fondly hope destroys the detestable taste of the weed; but it cannot do so completely and once smelt and tasted it cannot be mistaken. Sometimes beef tastes and smells of it too. Avoid that also."

Mutton with guinea-hen weed was presumably not on the menu at the plantation dinners enjoyed by Lady Janet Schaw, a Scottish lady who visited Jamaica and other islands in 1774. She was so impressed by her first plantation meal that she wrote, "In England it might figure in a newspaper, as if it were given by a Lord Mayor or the first Duke in the kingdom," but on her host's plantation it was merely "a family dinner." She was at first critical of such extravagance, but she concluded, "Why should we blame these people for their luxury? Since nature holds out her lap, filled with everything that is in her power to bestow, it were sinful in them not to be luxurious."

Continued on page 82

A Substantial Jamaican Favourite

The culinary influence of India on the Caribbean has produced one dish that is an island-wide party speciality in Jamaica: curried kid. In countries where goat meat is a rarity, the curry may be made with lamb, as shown on the left (*Recipe Index*). With curry, islanders often serve (*counter-clockwise from bottom right*) grated fresh coconut, fried plantains (*Recipe Index*), saffron rice and fresh pineapple.

In Lady Janet's day the expression "as rich as a Creole" was as common as "as rich as a Rockefeller" is in our own time. Mansions, called great houses, that rivalled in size and furnishings the finest houses in Europe were built in the Caribbean, and even kings were awed by the wealth of their West Indian subjects. King George III once had his afternoon drive in London spoiled because he saw a coach more magnificent than his own. Learning it was the property of a Caribbean planter, he grumbled, "Sugar, eh?" and then, with jealousy, "All *that* from sugar?"

Unfortunately for the Caribbean planters, in the mid-18th century a German scientist succeeded in making a loaf of sugar from beetroot. The Chinese had made a crude sugar from beetroot juice for centuries, but Europe and America had relied on sugar-cane. By the end of the century many European countries had begun to manufacture their own sugar at home. This, combined with the anti-slavery movement and the growing import duties on Caribbean sugar, began to undermine the wealth of the planters.

So in the early decades of the 19th century a period of decline set in and most of the Caribbean became, until after World War II, a sleepy and forgotten region. Small farmers once again obtained a foothold on many islands, as they had done before the great days of sugar. While they were not so rich as the estate owners, they nevertheless retained many of the traditions of the landowners of the past. My host's farm in the Jamaican hills had been in his family a hundred years. Once productive commercial acreage, it now provides only vegetables for local sale and enough meat for the family. It is neither a plantation nor even a very profitable farm, yet I found there pleasurable proof that dinner in such island households is still a momentous affair.

Unlike vegetables, which are generally prepared, cooked and eaten in much the same way in all the islands, meats have come to be handled quite differently in different groups of islands. Indeed, it is in the meat dishes that the Caribbean cuisine best reflects the different geographic and cultural forces that have shaped the various islands. Because some islands are damp and some are arid, some hilly and some flat, and because some were owned by Spain and some by France, some by England and some by Holland during colonial times, important individual characteristics have developed.

The Spanish, the earliest colonizers in the Caribbean, thought of their new possessions—once it was apparent that no gold was to be had from them—as supply houses from which to feed the busy conquistadors on the mainland. And so from the beginning of their settlement on Hispaniola they imported cattle, pigs, sheep and horses from Spain. So great was their success with livestock that as early as 1503 Hispaniola became self-sufficient, and by 1521 Jamaica, then a Spanish possession, was supplying not only enough meat for its own needs but also for those of the new colony of Panama. The Spanish continued to maintain diversified farming on their islands, including Cuba and Puerto Rico, producing proportionally less sugar and using fewer slaves than did the French and English. These powers entered the Caribbean later, at the time of Northern Europe's commercial interest in sugar-cane. They went all out for the profit yielded by sugar and put almost all their land under cane, neglecting livestock in areas where herds could flourish.

Thus to this day there are more beef dishes on the Spanish-speaking islands than on the others. Many are Caribbean translations of recipes from Spain, but like all translations they take on a character of their own, changing the original in subtle but important ways. Cuba's popular *picadillo* (*Recipe Index*), made of chopped or shredded beef, is clearly descended from an old Moorish dish cooked with olives and raisins, but it also contains the tomatoes and peppers of the New World—which in turn the modern Spanish have since adopted. *Ropa vieja* (*Recipe Index*), which means old clothes, differs from its Spanish ancestor in having tomatoes and peppers and a handsome orange colour derived from the annatto seeds used in its preparation.

Also found on all the Spanish-speaking islands is *sancocho*, a stew that can be made with anything from goat and chicken to pork and beef. I once helped a friend from the Dominican Republic to shop in New York for the ingredients she needed for *sancocho*. It took us all day. We went to the Puerto Rican market in Spanish Harlem on a cold snowy Saturday, wearing boots and furs and scarves, and I had to pause several times to buy hot coffee while waiting for Ilka to find what she had told me were "just a few essentials". These turned out to be plantains and chilli peppers, cassava roots, sweet potatoes, yams and *lerenes*, a small tuber that looks like a new potato but has the crunchiness of a water chestnut. Her *sancocho*, which we ate next day—after it had simmered for almost 3 hours—was superb. Its beef chunks and thick broth, almost imperceptibly sweetened with coconut were the foreground of a tropical still life, a garden of roots and tubers. I forgot completely that we had nearly frozen the day before while she rummaged through the market's vegetable stalls seeking the perfect accompaniments for the meat.

The Spanish-speaking islands have also contributed excellent poultry and pork recipes to the Caribbean cuisine. *Lechon asado*, whole spit-roasted young pig, and *chicharrones*, crisp tasty pork cracklings, are good examples. Less well known is *chicharrones de pollo*, small bits of crisply fried chicken, a speciality of Cuba and the Dominican Republic. The chicken is chopped into perhaps 20 small pieces, marinated in lime juice and soy sauce, then dipped into flour and quickly deep-fried. It is succulent within, crusty without, and it is less messy to eat with the fingers than American fried chicken.

When a whole bird—a turkey, for instance—is roasted in the Spanish islands it is usually stuffed with an intriguing combination of chopped pork, ham or beef, olives, raisins and peppers, a kind of *picadillo*, a recipe within a recipe (*Recipe Index*); in Puerto Rico, where the American custom of serving turkey at Thanksgiving has caught on, the ceremonial bird is always filled with a Spanish stuffing—a culinary demonstration of the two distinct cultural ties that pull at the island.

A number of different meats—chopped pork, ham and beef—mixed with raisins, olives, capers, almonds and various other flavourings form the stuffing of another holiday favourite in Puerto Rico, *pasteles*. The meat mixture is placed on a plantain leaf spread with a combination of mashed plantains, green bananas and starchy roots or pumpkin. Then the leaf is folded to make an envelope and the whole thing is steamed. The slightly sweet fragrance of the plantain leaf gives *pasteles* a more enticing flavour than the cornhusks that often envelop the similar Mexican tamales possess. Although *pasteles* can be eaten all year round, they are essential at Christmas time. In the country, carollers go from house to house, starting their rounds in the dead of *Continued on page 88*

Elegance Paid For by Sugar-Cane and Slavery

For the most part only the legends remain. The balls, the splendid dinners, the clothes and furniture and paintings brought at vast expense from Europe are no more. The legions of servants are gone. The great houses that were a sign of the wealth of 18th-century planters have nearly all succumbed to hurricanes, termites and the inexorable pressures of modern economics. One of the few left is Whim Great House (*above*), now restored as a museum, standing much as it did when it was erected about 1790 on the outskirts of Frederiksted on St. Croix in what was then the Danish Virgin Islands. The U.S. bought the islands in 1917. Relatively small and gem-like, the house was built in the neo-classical style with a surrounding moat that allowed light to reach the cellar. Reputedly, the original owner was a Dane with the un-Danish name of McEvoy —a rather mysterious figure, but obviously, since the place was built to order, a man of refined and expensive tastes. Not every great house can have been as exquisite as Whim, because not every owner shared its builder's sophistication. But it survives with some of its out-buildings (*left*) as a testament to the kind of life that sugar-cane and slavery once provided for a favoured few.

While the great house served as a show place, the real business of the estate went on elsewhere—in the fields, the chimneyed boiling houses and the cane-crushing windmills (*opposite*). Even the cooking for the master's meals was usually done in a separate kitchen building (*above*) equipped with a large stove and brick ovens. Here, using utensils like those on the table in the foreground, slaves prepared the food that was enjoyed in the stately dining-room shown below.

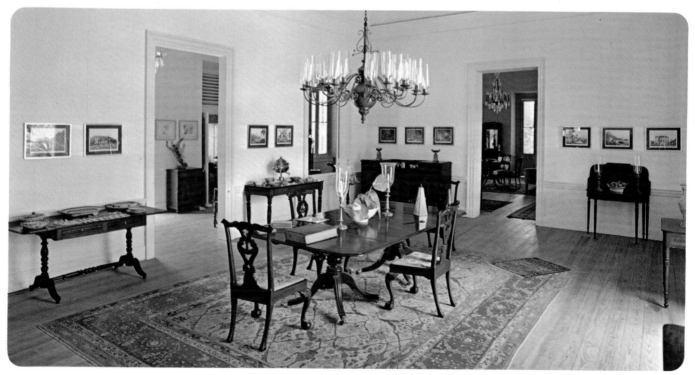

A 19th-Century Guide to the Laborious Business of Supplying the Old World with Sugar

Planting the cane in sections diked to hold rain water.

Cutting the tall cane and loading it on carts.

In 1823 an Englishman called William Clark published a handsome volume entitled *Ten Views in the Island of Antigua, in Which Are Represented the Process of Sugar Making, and the Employment of the Negroes, in the Field, Boiling House and Distillery.* Clark's pictures, five of which are reproduced here, illustrate the basic steps in the production of sugar in the Caribbean 150 years ago. They also show the essential role played by slaves in the West Indian economy of the time. Large numbers of workers were needed at every stage of the operation, from the hand planting of cane to the production of raw sugar. One contemporary observer reckoned that to run the smallest possible plantation profitably required a minimum of 250 slaves.

Boiling down the juice. At one stage of the process a skimmer (left) ladles liquid sugar out of a vat.

86

Squeezing juice from the cane in a wind-powered mill. Two crushing rollers can be seen in the mill.

Rolling hogsheads of dry sugar into boats—a tricky manoeuvre—for loading on to bigger vessels and eventual shipment abroad.

Whipping up the master's omelette was made easier for the 18th-century cook who was equipped with this wooden egg beater. Pushing and pulling the notched, horizontal rod makes the beater, bristling with pegs, revolve rapidly.

Another piece of 18th-century kitchen equipment on display—like the egg beater in the top picture—in the Whim Great House kitchen is this herb mill. Fresh or dried herbs were placed in the vessel, then pulverized by the toothed wooden disc.

night and singing hopefully at each stop, "Esta casa tiene puertas de acero, pero el que vive en ella es un caballero"—"This house has doors of steel but he who lives within is a gentleman." If he is, he opens his doors to the carollers and rewards them with a *concoco*, rum with coconut water, or a *conlimon*, rum with lime juice, and a heaped plate of *pasteles*. These must be hot even though it is the middle of the night, for another Puerto Rican folk-song warns the host, "If you give me *pasteles* give me hot ones, for cold *pasteles* cause indigestion." When served piping hot, the little packages of highly seasoned meat are indeed like Christmas gifts themselves.

Further down the Caribbean chain from the main Spanish-speaking islands lie the French jewels, Guadeloupe and Martinique where the early planters, rich in sugar and rum and proud of their ties with the cultural centre of Europe, lived in a cosmopolitan comfort that in many cases has lasted to this day. Here the lovely land seems to have a particular affinity with the sea; the low curving hills, called *mornes*, succeed one another like the gentle waves of the water beyond. And dotting the *mornes* like the white foam on the waves the sheep that make so important a contribution to the cuisine of the French islands.

A modern Martinican cookery book still gives an 18th-century recipe for barbecued sheep stuffed with onions, spices, orange juice, wild ducks, sandpipers, and other small birds, and pit-roasted. More practical and familiar today is *mechoui*, spit-roasted sheep, which the islanders borrowed from their colonial cousins in Algeria. Their own unique contribution is, however, a lamb or mutton dish called *pâté en pot*.

It was the highlight of a meal I had during a visit to a Martinican plantation house. My host, Charles Clément, the owner of a cane and banana plantation and a distillery that produces one of the finest Caribbean rums, belongs to a distinguished Creole family long prominent in Martinique. With the enthusiasm for their island's history that distinguishes the French Creoles, he took me early one morning to see the ruins of St. Pierre, the New World Pompeii. Once the most elegant city in the Caribbean, it was destroyed on the 2nd of May 1902 when the volcano Mont Pelée erupted and destroyed the town and its inhabitants. The jumbled remains—broad, curving staircases that go nowhere, carved stone arches decorated with fleurs-de-lis, fragments of exquisite French floor tiles, a marble nude—are fascinating to explore; but I left depressed. So little in the Caribbean seems to last, I thought. Tiny destroyers like termites and vast ones like volcanoes, yearly hurricanes and the occasional uprisings of people too long oppressed demolish the old before the new can take hold. But back in my host's house, called Acajou, there was a sense of a past still vibrant. The building is 200 years old. Its floors are made of delicately tinted pale blue, grey and yellow tiles brought as ballast in French sailing ships. Its crystal chandeliers, gilt-edged mirrors and velvet chairs were carefully chosen in Paris by people who meant to make their mark on Martinique, to stay and last out the violence of the tropics.

We sat on the red-bricked porch, surrounded by ferns and flowers, drinking a pre-lunch punch made with M. Clément's fine fragrant rum. It was 1 o'clock, not the best time for a hot meal, I thought; surely stuffed avocados or an iced bread-fruit vichyssoise would have been better. But my host had made a special point of inviting me to taste *pâté*

88

en pot, so I dutifully accompanied him to the mahogany-panelled din-ing-room.

From the kitchen building came the cook carrying her offering in a huge china tureen. Soup? Well, yes, but also more than soup. *Pâté en pot* is made from many parts of a sheep or lamb—tripe, heart, belly, lungs and the meat from the feet and head, all finely chopped. It is one of the thickest soups I know. But it is not quite a stew; nor is it a pâté as we have come to use the word. Probably the name of the dish comes from another form of the word, *pâtée*, which denotes a pulpy consistency, a mash; to confuse things further, one French island gourmet suggests that the name is a corruption of the word *patte*, which means paw. The confusion extends, in a delightful way, to the taste of the concoction. Mingling in fascinating complexity with the meat are cloves, garlic, hot pepper, thyme, bay leaf and celery, a kaleidoscope of textures and flavours changing with every spoonful. In my enjoyment of the *pâté en pot* I stopped worrying about the origin of its name and forgot that it was a hot day in the tropics.

I did not have time to think about that anyway, for the soup bowls were quickly followed by thick slices of a roast lamb that was as rare and juicy as any *gigot* I have eaten in Paris. The rest of the meal con-tinued to mingle France and the Caribbean: The lamb was accompanied by a kind of plantain pudding; we then had coconut ice-cream escorted by *petites madeleines* imported from France and followed by a tray of French blue and Camembert cheeses that we ate with sweet slabs of guava jelly. The conversation, too, was cosmopolitan. M. Clément had met Franklin Roosevelt and had also known many of the Caribbean independence leaders, Cheddi Jagan of Guyana and Bustamante of Jamaica among them. But like most of the French Creoles, he was in favour of continuing the close ties of the French West Indies with their mother country; he quoted a favourite French proverb: "God, I don't ask you to make me a rich man, but merely to keep me close to one."

After lunch we sat in the parlour with its many remembrances of Madame Clément, my host's wife, who had died a few years before, but whose presence still seemed to dominate the house. As a tribute to her, because she loved flowers, the room is filled each day with hibiscus blossoms carefully perched upon slender reed stalks. French in his romanticism, my host showed me his wife's photograph, a beautiful dark-eyed woman in a white ruffled gown. "Like Josephine," he said, for all the Martinicans often talk of Napoleon's adored Empress, Josephine, who was born in this island.

We drank what my host called a shrub, sometimes known as shrob, a home-made liqueur, bitter-sweet with the flavour of bitter oranges; then when the sun had lost its midday fierceness, we set off to view the ruins of Josephine's home. Only the foundation stones remain of La Pagerie, as the house was called. It was destroyed by a hurricane in 1766, when the future empress was a small girl. Later her father, a pros-perous sugar planter, built a second, smaller house. Part of this house still stands, but it is the gardens, beautifully re-created, that best evoke the atmosphere of Josephine's girlhood. Resplendent with red and white bougainvillea, climbing oleander bushes and pink amaryllis, they evoke an image of the future empress running barefooted and free across the grass. She admired the countryside of Martinique and once wrote with a burst of poetic enthusiasm, "Nature, rich and sumptuous, has

Continued on page 92

Now Cattle, Not Sugar, Bring Wealth to the Land

About 40 per cent of Jamaica's arable land is still part of privately-owned estates, a legacy of the colonial past. But sugar is no longer the keystone of the plantation economy. Estate Braco, owned by V. C. Parnell, comprises 1,800 acres of rolling pastures, orchards and scrub woods in the north-east corner of the island. Stock-breeding is now the big money earner; 600 head of cattle are sold from the ranch annually. And although this restored plantation house is not quite as grand as the great houses of the past—it was originally built for the estate overseer—its graciousness proves that some of the old traditions of wealth from the land still live on.

Parnell and his wife entertain guests from England in the dining-room at Braco with a meal planned round beef reared on the estate. Most of the furniture is Jamaican mahogany, but the silver is antique English. Judging by the date of an overseer's journal found during renovations, the Parnells believe that the house was built about 1790.

Most of Val Parnell's 900 head of cattle are Jamaican Brahmans, a hardy breed first brought to Jamaica from India in the early 19th century to haul sugar-cane. On the left, Parnell (*standing*) inspects part of his Brahman herd with head cattleman Percy Johnson. Nestled against the hill beyond them is the Braco Great House and, on the far left, an old sugar works now being used to distil allspice oil. Parnell also breeds Aberdeen Angus (*below*) that have been "tropicalized" by cross-breeding with the Brahman strain.

covered our fields with a carpeting . . . I love to hide myself in the green woods that skirt our dwelling place."

I asked the director of the restoration whether Josephine had served any favourite Martinican dishes when she was empress. He did not know, he said, but he did claim that when Napoleon was exiled on St. Helena, the one dish that gave him an appetite was a fritter made of bananas marinated in rum—a story I had not heard before. Perhaps, said the director, it was because it reminded Napoleon of his lost empress. She had retained throughout her days in Europe a lifelong passion for Martinican fruits and when she was living in Paris wrote home to ask her mother for supplies of guavas, mangoes, oranges and bananas.

Josephine was not the only princess the island produced. Madame de Maintenon, who became the last wife of Louis XIV in 1684 and died in the palace of Versailles, was brought up on one of the tiniest, sleepiest islands in the Caribbean, Marie Galante. Throughout Europe, in fact, the women of the rich island families were thought to possess an un-equalled languid grace. "Beautiful as a Creole" and "rich as a Creole" were common expressions. It was undoubtedly the slow pace of their lives that gave them the time to develop a feminine elegance. Many were surrounded by slaves and had little work to do, and sometimes 18th-century artists poked fun at their lazy lives. One print shows a planter's wife demanding of her slave, "Mimbo, tell Quashebah to tell Dido to tell Sue to come and pick up my needle." The slave replies, "But Quashebah is gone to market and won't be back for three hours—and Sue is scratching the master's legs for two." "Oh, dear me," is the reply, "one must have the patience of Job to live in this world with any comfort. Here I must wait two hours for my needle."

Certainly there were women like that in the islands, but the satirists overlooked many others who were industrious and self-reliant. They not only took a keen interest in running their houses and kitchens, but were adventurous souls ready for disasters of weather, war or sea. Père Labat, the French priest who lived in and wrote about Martinique, tells a delightful story about two planters' wives he encountered under try-ing circumstances. He was on his way from Martinique to St. Thomas, sailing, of all things, aboard a pirate vessel, when bad weather blew the ship off course, forcing it to put in for repairs at a tiny desert island in the eastern Caribbean. He was amazed to discover that another ship, beset while *en route* to Antigua, had abandoned two Barbadian ladies and their servants on the same island.

The priest and the ladies spent several days in each others' company and they indulged in the favourite sport permitted to Labat: eating. Exchanging recipes, the ladies taught Labat how to cook brisket of Irish beef, pâtés, turtle steaks and ragouts, and he taught them various methods of boucaning, or barbecuing, meats and in particular how to boucan a turtle. "Our two ladies took charge of everything in connec-tion with the culinary department and performed wonders," Labat wrote admiringly, after the ship was repaired and the pirates had dropped the ladies off at Antigua. "I could write a volume on the subject," he declared, "telling how to serve 125 dishes at no cost on a desert island in magnificent style."

One recipe the two ladies may have taught the priest is for conkies, a very old speciality of Barbados. Conkies are little banana-leaf envelopes filled with cornmeal, chopped meat, raisins and coconut, very like the *pasteles* of the Spanish-speaking islands. Traditionally they were served in Barbados to celebrate that most English of holidays, Guy Fawkes Day. The island's post-colonial government, anxious to be independent of England in all ways, stopped the celebration of Guy Fawkes Day; but conkies have not gone out of favour, and they are served today for any special occasion in Barbados.

Barbados was in many ways the most aristocratic of the islands, for it was here that sugar-cane was first planted and that the greatest sugar fortunes were made. The island was often called Little England, because of the stuffy determination of its colonists to maintain their native customs and because the landscape of Barbados bears an odd resemblance to England. Neat and tranquil, the Barbadian cane fields are set out remarkably like English wheat fields; manor houses dot the countryside, completing the illusion. It is only when you notice that the trees dividing the fields are tall palms that you remember that this island is a tropical one.

Here, in placid surroundings, the planters lived the most luxurious life in the islands. In 1700 a visitor wrote, "The opulence and good taste of the inhabitants may be remarked in their furniture, which is magnificent, and in their silver, which they have in considerable quantities . . . They eat much meat and little bread, and their tables are well served. They have excellent cooks and very fine linen and much order and cleanliness . . . Their houses are well-stocked with every kind of wine and liqueur and they are delighted if their guests are hard put to it to find their way home."

Today's traveller finds many reminders of this way of life on Barbados. Every mile or so the sugar-cane is interrupted by an arcade of trees leading to a graceful manor house with an impressive double staircase and pillared porticoes. Within, carefully carved doorways open into spacious, cool rooms with furniture in the style of Sheraton and Hepplewhite, beautifully copied by Barbadian craftsmen in local lignum vitae, mahogany and cordia.

I stopped one afternoon to visit a family in one of these houses, not to eat but just to talk. The house looked much as it must have looked when it was built in 1840, shortly after a hurricane had destroyed all the really old houses in the island and virtually all its trees. Delightful touches of the past were to be seen everywhere. The kitchen tables still have little cups of water at their feet to drown any ants ambitious enough to attempt to climb the table legs. The water container once found in all the island houses but rarely seen now was still in use, a large, porous limestone vat through which rain water slowly seeped into a handsome pottery jug. And the native mahogany table inlaid with whalebone was set with delicate china and massive silver for dinner that evening. I asked what would be served and was told that the meal was to be a traditional plantation one, like the one I had eaten in Jamaica. There would be pepper-pot, lots of farm vegetables, glazed roast pork and—a Barbadian speciality at the turn of the century—duck with tomatoes, chives, thyme and garlic, all simmered in local rum.

While planters in the English and French colonies of the 18th century were cultivating their sugar crops and grooming their plantations, quite a different, though still prosperous way of life was developing on the various Dutch-owned islands. Small and few in number, they had an economic and culinary effect on the Caribbean area out of all propor-

Radial steps lead gracefully to the entrance of Acajou, paternal home of the Clément family in Martinique. *Acajou* means mahogany, a tree that grows in abundance locally. The Clément plantation produces bananas and several of Martinique's splendid rums; it exports the bananas and much of the rum to Europe.

tion to their size. Here there was never a strong plantation tradition. When the Dutch entered the scramble for Caribbean territory they were not looking for agricultural lands but for salt for their North Sea fisheries and, being already a mercantile people, bases from which they could trade. They established commercial ports on Statia in the northeast corner of the Caribbean, and Curaçao in the south, and both islands soon became very rich, handling large numbers of slaves and European goods. Statia was destroyed by the British in 1781 and never recovered its prosperity, but Curaçao remained the key trading island in the Caribbean for three centuries. The capital, Willemstad, with its Dutch-style gabled buildings painted in picturesque pastel shades, became the most European-looking city in the Caribbean.

The prominent Curaçaoans even today are merchants. The ancestors of many of them were Sephardic Jews who went to the island in the early 1600s, fleeing the Inquisition that had driven them from Spain and Portugal. Deeply rooted in the island's history, they are secure and generous and their life goes on at a placid pace. Because there was considerable wealth on the tiny island for centuries and little opportunity to spend it, people had to rely on one another for diversion. Two social customs connected with food resulted from this. One is the birthday reception, an open house held from dawn to dusk and attended by everyone who knows the person whose birthday it is, however slight the acquaintance. The other social event, tea-time, has become less important now than it was 50 years ago, when society was smaller and everyone knew everyone. In those days tea-time was known as the

94

gossip hour by the maids of the well-to-do, and tea itself in the Papiamento dialect was called *awa di redu*, gossip water.

Papiamento, a second language spoken everywhere in the Dutch islands, is a combination of Spanish, Dutch and English, with a smattering of Portuguese, French and African words. But if one knows Dutch and English and has no Spanish, Papiamento is hard to understand, while if one knows Spanish and not the other two there is little difficulty. Similarly, the cooking of Curaçao, although a mixture, is more Spanish than anything else, largely because Spain held the islands for more than a century before the Dutch took over in 1634. I was invited one afternoon to the gossip hour at the house of a merchant in Curaçao. My hostess' friends had helped to prepare the typical tea-time treats. These were flaky, buttery little pastries and little leaf-wrapped parcels containing meat, fish or cheese. The cheese-filled *pastechi*, the chopped beef, banana-leaf-wrapped *ayacas* and the cornmeal and beef *cachapas* that we ate at tea-time differed little from the *pasteles* of Puerto Rico and the *hallacas* and *arequipas* of the mainland.

My hostess' house, built in the fashion favoured in Curaçao, was three-sided, with a large inner garden providing access to all rooms. Curaçao has so little rainfall that its people use their gardens as integral parts of their living quarters. The gardens are difficult to keep green, however, and the only time a Curaçaoan lady loses her temper is when one of the hundreds of goats that roam the island gets into her garden to gorge on the carefully nurtured grass. There is, my hostess told me, a constant battle in the local newspaper between the garden-minded who want the goats restricted and the tourist-minded who claim that being able to take pictures of the goats is a major attraction for visitors. All of which is beside the point, she said, for without the goats the local inhabitants would be deprived of one of their favourite dishes, *stobá*.

This complex stew has been immortalized in a folk-song as common among the children of the island as "Mary Had a Little Lamb" is among ours. It sings the praises of a certain Alberta, the cook of Shon (Madame) Rica Tutuchi:

Alberta of Shon Rica Tutuchi
Only has one eye
One eye alone has she.
But with that eye she sees the onions
Sees the tomatoes
Sees all the seasonings
to throw into stobá.

And, as one of the guests said, seeing all the seasonings for *stobá* is no easy matter, even with two eyes, for the stew has in it capers, cumin, celery, garlic, ginger, olives, limes, sweet peppers, hot peppers, cucumbers and shallots, as well as goat or lamb.

I sat all the afternoon in the garden, listening fascinated to the stories about Curaçao, and when the day had grown cool we went into the town. It was late afternoon and the Dutch houses were daintily pink and blue and yellow in the waning sunlight. My hostess explained the reason why the houses are painted in pastel colours. An early Dutch governor of the island suffered from severe headaches and, deciding they were caused by the strong sunlight glaring on white houses, issued a decree forbidding the use of white paint. The results of this auto-

With the wealth amassed throughout several centuries as the foremost traders of the Caribbean, the burghers of Willemstad, Curaçao, built these shops and houses, whose Dutch-style façades might well grace a canal in Amsterdam. They stand in the Punda Quarter of the city, overlooking St. Anna Bay. On the right is the Queen Emma pontoon bridge, which opens at least 30 times a day to let ships pass through on their way to or from the sea.

cratic fiat are lovely, and they form a delicate background for the dazzling goods displayed in the Willemstad shops, which are as sumptuously stocked as the finest stores in New York and Paris. Whether I was overstuffed with *pastechi* and *cachapas*, or merely held by the fascination all shoppers feel in Curaçao, I was reluctant when my hostess told me that it would soon be time for dinner. I felt rather like a visitor to the islands of many years ago, a Lady Nugent, who, overfed on exotic foods, complained, "I am doomed to go to dinner".

Yet I made a remarkable recovery that night when I was introduced to what is perhaps the Caribbean's most unusual and exciting dish, *keshy yena (Recipe Index)*. The name is Papiamento and very like the Spanish words *queso* (cheese) and *llena* (filled). I thought it was a pale-yellow casserole that my hostess was carrying to the table, but it turned out to be a huge Edam cheese that had just spent almost an hour baking in the oven and yet had retained its firm roundness. The top of the cheese had been sliced off to be used as a cover and the inside had been hollowed out as one scoops out a pumpkin, then mixed with chopped beef, olives, tomatoes and onions and put back inside the cheese.

My hostess set the cheese before me and asked me to lift the cover. An entrancing aroma leapt out, and the taste of melted cheese and meat within was even better. I decided then and there to try to make *keshy yena* when I returned to New York, and eventually I did so, but I adapted the Curaçaoan method by baking a small cheese for each guest, so that all could have that enchanted moment of surprise, when the lid is lifted to let the genie of delicious smells escape. I worked for a long time over the small Edams, peeling the wax off and hollowing them out

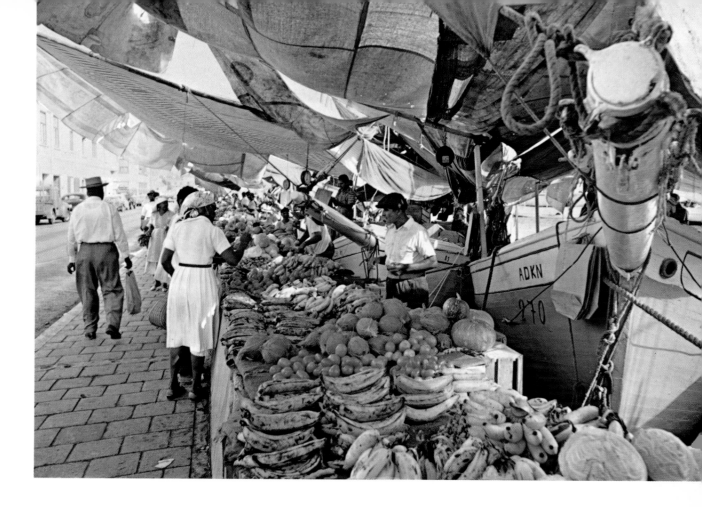

to a thickness of half an inch. But it was fun, reminding me of the childhood pleasure of modelling bowls of clay to be fired in the oven. When you make *keshy yena*, I thought, you really make something. The cheese and meat filling is very savoury—and may be interestingly varied to include prawns, fish or chicken instead of meat—but the thrill of this dish lies in its appearance as much as in its flavour. Unfortunately this advantage is lost when *keshy yena* is served in another way that is rather quicker and more practical: with the meat filling surrounded by slices of Edam, rather like a giant cheeseburger. This version *is* quicker, perhaps, and more convenient, but it seems to me rather like giving someone a Christmas present that has not been gift-wrapped.

My own *keshy yena* was a success, but there was one thing I could not give my guests at home that was given to me in Curaçao. That was my host's entertaining tale of life on Curaçao when he was a boy, when the tram went into town only once a day and when the island's one telephone operator listened in on everyone's calls so that she could serve as a central source of news about everyone's health or whereabouts.

In fact, wherever I have been in the islands, nostalgic stories and the foods and flavours of the past were on everybody's tongue. Perhaps in this part of the world, which is changing every day, the past serves as source of personal and even social stability. New governments, new industries are dramatically altering the Caribbean scene and much that is connected with the past is disappearing. But when it comes to food, dishes that were once enjoyed only by the very rich are not disappearing, but are being revived, gradually forming a heritage for all who live in the islands.

Being semi-arid, Curaçao must depend on its neighbours for fresh fruits and vegetables. Fortunately its neighbours—Venezuela and the islands of Aruba and Bonaire—are well able to meet the need. At the schooner market along the Ruyterkade in Willemstad the trading vessels put up canvas awnings for shade, and sell their cargoes—which also include groceries—directly to shopkeepers and housewives.

CHAPTER IV RECIPES

Roast Pork Calypso (Jamaica)

Preheat the oven to Mark 4: 350° F. Lightly score the pork loin by making diagonal cuts ¼ inch deep at 1-inch intervals on the fat with a sharp knife. Place the pork scored side up in a shallow roasting tin just large enough to hold it comfortably. (If you prefer to use a meat thermometer, insert it into the loin after you have scored the fat. Be sure the tip of the thermometer does not touch any fat or bone.) Roast the loin in the middle of the oven for about 1 hour, until the pork is golden brown. Remove the tin from the heat and transfer the loin to a cutting board or dish. Skim the fat from the juices in the tin, pour in the stock, and set the tin and its liquid aside.

Mash the pieces sugar, 1½ tablespoons of dark rum, the garlic, ginger, cloves, bay leaf, salt and pepper to a smooth paste with a large pestle and mortar or in a small bowl with the back of a spoon. Spread the paste evenly over the scored pork fat with a palette knife or your finger-tips. Return the loin to the tin fat side up, and roast in the middle of the oven for another 30 minutes, until the surface is crusty and brown. (The thermometer should reach a temperature of 160° to 165° F.)

Transfer the loin to a heated dish and let it rest for 10 minutes for easier carving. Meanwhile, warm the 3 tablespoons of rum in a small pan over a low heat. Set light to the rum with a match, off the heat, then slide the pan gently backwards and forwards until the flames die out.

Bring the liquid remaining in the roasting tin to the boil over a high heat. Give the arrowroot and water mixture a quick stir to blend it again and add it to the pan. Cook briskly, stirring constantly, until the sauce thickens enough to coat the spoon thickly. Remove the tin from the heat and stir in the flamed rum and the lime juice. Taste for seasoning and pour the sauce into a heated bowl or sauceboat. Serve accompanied by cornmeal coo-coo or *christophene au gratin* (*Recipe Index*).

To serve 6 to 8

A 5- to 6-lb. lean pork loin, preferably centre cut
¾ pint chicken stock
7 oz. light pieces sugar
1½ tablespoons dark rum
1½ teaspoons finely chopped garlic
1½ teaspoons ground ginger
⅛ teaspoon ground cloves
1 medium-sized bay leaf, crumbled
1 teaspoon salt
¼ teaspoon freshly ground black pepper
3 tablespoons light rum
1½ teaspoons arrowroot blended with 2½ teaspoons cold water
2½ tablespoons strained fresh lime juice

Cornmeal Coo-Coo (Barbados)

FLAT CORNMEAL AND OKRA CAKE

Wash the okra under cold running water and scrape the skin lightly to remove any surface fuzz, using a small, sharp knife. Cut ⅛ inch off the stalk at the narrow end of each pod, and slice the okra crosswise into ¼-inch-thick rounds. Put the okra, water and salt into a heavy, medium-sized saucepan, and bring to the boil over a high heat. Reduce the heat to low, cover tightly, and simmer for 10 minutes, until the okra is tender but still intact.

Pour in the cornmeal in a slow thin stream, stirring constantly. Cook over a moderate heat, still stirring, for about 5 minutes, until the mixture is thick enough to leave the bottom and sides of the pan in a solid mass.

Spoon the mixture on to a heated serving plate and shape it into a round cake about 1 inch thick and 8 inches across with a palette knife. Spread the top with the softened butter and serve at once. Cornmeal coo-coo is a traditional accompaniment to meat dishes such as roast pork calypso, *chicharrones de pollo*, or *pollo a lo agridulce* (*Recipe Index*).

To serve 4 to 6

½ lb. fresh okra
¾ pint water
1 teaspoon salt
4½ oz. yellow cornmeal
1 oz. butter, softened

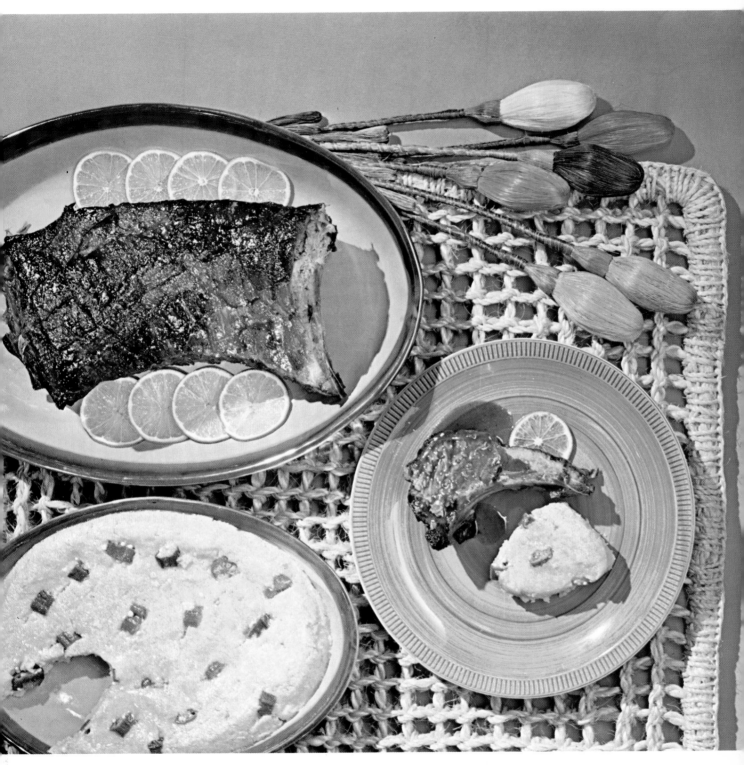

Jamaica's roast pork calypso, shown on the top, is a succulent pork loin coated with a crunchy glaze of pieces sugar, rum, garlic and ginger, garnished with slices of fresh lime and served (*right*) with a spoonful of lime and rum sauce. Balancing the spiciness of the pork is a mild coo-coo from Barbados, a cornmeal cake studded with okra and brushed with butter.

To serve 6

3 lb. lean boneless shoulder of
    lamb, trimmed of excess fat and
    cut into 1½-inch cubes
2 oz. butter
1½ tablespoons vegetable oil
12 oz. finely chopped onions
2½ tablespoons curry powder
2½ teaspoons finely chopped fresh
    hot chillies (*caution: see "How to
    Handle Chillies"*)
½ teaspoon ground allspice
1½ teaspoons salt
Freshly ground black pepper
⅜ pint coconut milk made from
    4 oz. coarsely chopped fresh
    coconut and milk (*see Notes on
    Caribbean cooking*)
⅜ pint chicken stock
1 medium-sized bay leaf
1½ tablespoons strained fresh lime
    juice

To serve 4

A 1½- to 2-lb. flank steak,
    trimmed of excess fat
1 large onion, peeled and coarsely
    chopped
1 medium-sized bay leaf
2½ teaspoons salt
Freshly ground black pepper
3¼ pints water
2½ tablespoons vegetable oil mixed
    with 1 teaspoon liquid annatto
6 oz. finely chopped onions
1 teaspoon finely chopped garlic
4 oz. finely chopped green pepper
½ teaspoon finely chopped fresh hot
    chillies (*caution: see "How to Handle
    Chillies"*)
1 large carrot, scraped and finely
    chopped
6 medium-sized firm ripe tomatoes,
    peeled, seeded and finely chopped
    (*see sopa de gandules, Recipe Index*), or
    substitute two 1-lb. cans chopped
    drained tomatoes
⅛ teaspoon ground cinnamon
⅛ teaspoon ground cloves
2½ teaspoons capers, washed and
    drained
1 whole canned pimiento, drained
    and finely chopped

Curried Lamb (*Jamaica*)

Pat the lamb cubes completely dry with kitchen paper. Melt 1 ounce of the butter in the oil over a moderate heat in a large, heavy frying-pan. When the foam begins to subside, drop 6 or 7 cubes of lamb into the hot oil. Turn them over with a spoon until the cubes are brown on all sides, adjusting the heat so that they brown richly and evenly without burning. Transfer the cubes to a plate as they brown, and brown the rest of the lamb in the same way.

Melt the rest of the butter in the pan, add the onions and cook for about 5 minutes, stirring frequently, until they are soft and transparent but not brown. Add the curry, chillies, allspice, salt and a few grindings of pepper and simmer for 2 to 3 minutes, stirring constantly.

Return the lamb and the juices that have accumulated round it to the pan, stir in the coconut milk, stock and bay leaf, and bring to the boil over a high heat. Reduce the heat to low, cover tightly, and simmer for about 1¼ hours, until the lamb shows no resistance when pierced with the point of a sharp knife. Remove the bay leaf and stir in the lime juice. Taste for seasoning.

To serve, heap up the lamb on a deep, heated dish or in a heated bowl and pour the sauce over it. Curried lamb is traditionally accompanied by plain boiled or saffron rice and mango chutney (*Recipe Index*).

NOTE: In Jamaica, this curry is prepared with goat meat rather than lamb—and you can substitute kid or goat if it is available.

Ropa Vieja (*Cuba*)
SPICED SHREDDED FLANK STEAK

Place the flank steak in a large, heavy casserole, add the coarsely chopped onion, 1 bay leaf, 1½ teaspoons of the salt and a few grindings of pepper, and pour in the water. The water should cover the steak by at least 2 inches; if necessary, add more water. Bring to the boil over a high heat, reduce the heat to low, partly cover the casserole, and simmer for about 1½ hours, until the meat shows no resistance when pierced with the point of a sharp knife.

Transfer the steak to a plate to cool. Strain the cooking liquid through a fine sieve set over a bowl, and discard the onion and bay leaf. When the steak is cool enough to handle, cut it along the grain into ¼-inch-wide strips and slice the strips crosswise into pieces 2 inches long. Set the meat and the cooking liquid aside.

Pour the annatto-flavoured oil into the casserole and heat it over a moderate heat until a light haze forms above it. Drop in the 6 ounces of finely chopped onions and the garlic, green pepper, chillies and carrot. Cook for about 5 minutes, stirring frequently, until the vegetables are soft but not brown. Watch carefully for any sign of burning and adjust the heat accordingly.

Stir in the tomatoes, cinnamon, cloves, the remaining teaspoon of salt and a few grindings of pepper, and cook briskly until most of the liquid in the pan has evaporated and the mixture is thick enough to hold its shape lightly on the spoon. Return the meat to the casserole, add ⅝ pint of the reserved stock, and the capers. Cook for 2 to 3 minutes to heat the meat through, stirring constantly, taste for seasoning.

To serve, transfer the entire contents of the casserole to a heated dish or serving bowl and sprinkle the pimiento on top. Serve with fried plantains or *riz et pois* (*Recipe Index*).

100

Sancocho (Trinidad)

BEEF AND VEGETABLE STEW

To serve 6 to 8

Place the salt beef in a heavy, medium-sized saucepan and add enough cold water to cover it by about 2 inches. Bring to the boil over a high heat, reduce the heat to low, and simmer partly covered for 1 hour. Drain thoroughly and cut the salt beef into 1-inch cubes.

Meanwhile, lay the plantains in a large, heavy frying-pan, pour in enough water to cover them completely, and bring to the boil over a high heat. Cook briskly for 30 minutes, then drain, peel and cut the plantains crosswise into slices an inch thick. Set them aside.

Fry the pork over a moderate heat in a large, heavy saucepan, turning the dice over with a spoon until they are crisp and brown and have rendered all their fat. Discard the pork and drop the beef and the salt beef into the hot fat. Brown the cubes of meat, turning them over frequently and adjusting the heat so that they brown richly and evenly without burning. Transfer them to a plate with a perforated spoon.

Add the onions to the fat remaining in the pan and cook for 5 minutes, stirring frequently, until they are soft and transparent but not brown. Watch carefully for any sign of burning and adjust the heat accordingly. Return the meat to the pan, add the split peas, stock, salt and a liberal grinding of pepper. Bring to the boil over a high heat, then reduce the heat to low, cover tightly, and simmer for one hour.

Add the white potatoes, sweet potatoes, dasheen, cassava, yams, chilli and coconut cream. Cover and simmer for about 15 minutes, until the meat and vegetables are tender but not falling apart. Add the cornmeal dumplings and simmer partly covered for 15 minutes, until they puff up and rise to the surface. Then gently stir the reserved plantain slices into the stew, and simmer for 5 minutes longer to heat them through.

Serve at once, straight from the casserole or from a large heated tureen.

Ingredients

- ½ lb. lean salt beef
- 2 large green plantains, washed but not peeled
- 4 oz. salt pork, finely diced
- 2 lb. lean, boneless beef, preferably beef chuck, trimmed of excess fat and cut into 1-inch cubes
- 8 oz. finely chopped onions
- 1 oz. dried yellow split peas
- 5 pints freshly made beef stock, or 2½ pints concentrated canned beef stock mixed with 2½ pints water
- 1½ teaspoons salt
- Freshly ground black pepper
- 1 lb. potatoes, peeled and cut into 1-inch slices
- 1 lb. sweet potatoes, peeled and cut into 1-inch slices
- 8 oz. dasheen (taro root), peeled and cut into 1-inch slices
- 8 oz. cassava root, peeled and cut into 1-inch slices
- 8 oz. yams, peeled and cut into 1-inch slices
- 1 fresh red or green hot chilli, about 3 inches long, washed but left intact with stalk attached (*caution: see "How to Handle Chillies"*)
- ⅜ pint coconut cream made from 4 oz. coarsely chopped fresh coconut and ⅜ pint double cream (*see "Notes on Caribbean Cooking"*)
- Cornmeal dumplings (*Recipe Booklet*)

Cocido de Riñoes (Puerto Rico)

KIDNEY STEW

To serve 4

Heat 2½ tablespoons of the olive oil over a moderate heat in a heavy, medium-sized frying-pan until a light haze forms above it. Add the onions and garlic and cook for about 5 minutes, stirring frequently, until they are soft and transparent but not brown. Watch carefully for any sign of burning and adjust the heat accordingly.

Add the tomatoes and vinegar and cook briskly, still stirring, until most of the liquid in the pan has evaporated and the mixture is thick enough to hold its shape lightly in the spoon. This mixture is called a *sofrito*. Remove the pan from the heat.

Heat the rest of the olive oil in a large, heavy frying-pan. Pat the pieces of kidney completely dry with kitchen paper and sprinkle them with salt and a few grindings of pepper. Drop the kidneys into the hot oil and cook for about 4 to 6 minutes, turning them frequently, until they are firm and lightly browned on all sides. Pour the *sofrito* over the kidneys and cook for a minute or two to heat the *sofrito* through, stirring constantly.

Taste for seasoning and serve at once from a heated dish or a bowl with plain boiled rice.

Ingredients

- 6 tablespoons olive oil
- 2 oz. finely chopped onions
- 1 teaspoon finely chopped garlic
- 3 medium-sized firm ripe tomatoes, peeled, seeded and finely chopped (*see sopa de gandules, Recipe Index*), or substitute a 1-lb. can chopped drained tomatoes
- 2½ teaspoons malt vinegar
- 1½ lb. lamb kidneys, trimmed of excess fat, and cut into quarters
- ½ teaspoon salt
- Freshly ground black pepper

The Cuban *brazo gitano*—a baked cassava roll with salt beef filling—is named after a Spanish cake that is rolled the same way.

Baked Pawpaw with Meat Filling (Jamaica)

To serve 6 to 8

A 5- to 6-lb. green pawpaw (*see* "*A Note about Mangoes and Pawpaws*") cut lengthways into halves and seeded

2½ tablespoons vegetable oil

2 oz. finely chopped onions

½ teaspoon finely chopped garlic

1 lb. lean minced beef

4 medium-sized firm ripe tomatoes, peeled, seeded and finely chopped (*see sopa de gandules, Recipe Index*), or substitute three 8 oz. cans chopped drained tomatoes

1 teaspoon finely chopped fresh hot chillies (*caution: "How to Handle Chillies"*)

1 teaspoon salt

Freshly ground black pepper

3 tablespoons freshly grated Parmesan cheese

Preheat the oven to Mark 4: 350° F. Heat the oil over a moderate heat in a large, heavy frying-pan until a light haze forms above it. Drop in the onions and garlic and cook for about 5 minutes, stirring frequently, until they are soft and transparent but not brown. Stir in the beef and cook until all traces of pink disappear, mashing it up with a spoon to break up any lumps. Add the tomatoes, chillies, salt and a few grindings of pepper. Cook briskly, stirring occasionally, until most of the liquid in the pan has evaporated and the mixture is thick enough to hold its shape almost solidly in the spoon. Taste for seasoning.

Spoon the meat mixture into the pawpaw shells, spreading out and smoothing the filling with a fish slice. Place the shells side by side in a shallow roasting tin. Set the tin in the middle of the oven and pour in enough boiling water to come about 1 inch up the sides of the pawpaw. Bake for 1 hour. Then sprinkle each shell with 2½ teaspoons of the cheese, and bake for about 30-minutes, until the pawpaw shows no resistance when pierced with the point of a small knife and the top is delicately browned.

To serve, transfer the pawpaw shells to a large heated dish and sprinkle them with the rest of the cheese.

Brazo Gitano (Cuba)
BAKED CASSAVA ROLL WITH SALT BEEF FILLING

Place the salt beef in a large saucepan or casserole and add enough cold water to cover the meat by about 2 inches. Bring to the boil over a high heat, reduce the heat to low, and simmer partly covered for about 2½ to 3 hours, until the salt beef is tender and shows no resistance when pierced with the point of a sharp knife.

Drain the salt beef thoroughly and, when it is cool enough to handle, trim off and discard all its fat. Cut the meat into strips about ⅛ inch wide and 1 to 1½ inches long using a small, sharp knife, and set it aside.

Meanwhile, drop the cassava slices into enough lightly salted boiling water to cover them completely. Reduce the heat to moderate and cook partly covered for about 1 hour, until the cassava is tender but still intact. Drain the cassava in a sieve or colander, return the slices to the pan and slide it backwards and forwards over a moderate heat for 10 to 15 seconds, until the cassava is completely dry.

Force the cassava through a ricer set over a deep bowl, or mash it thoroughly with a fork. Then beat in 2 ounces of the softened butter, 2 of the eggs, one at a time, 6 ounces of flour, about 2 ounces at a time, and 1 teaspoon of the salt.

Continue to beat until the cassava mixture is smooth and dense enough to hold its shape almost solidly in a spoon. (If the mixture seems too fluid, beat in the rest of the flour, a tablespoon at a time.) Cover the bowl tightly with a sheet of plastic and set aside.

Preheat the oven to Mark 4: 350° F. Coat a large baking sheet with the rest of the softened butter, using a pastry brush.

Melt 1 ounce of butter over a moderate heat in a large, heavy frying-pan. When the foam begins to subside, add the onions and garlic and cook for about 5 minutes, stirring frequently, until they are soft and transparent but not brown. Watch carefully for any sign of burning and adjust the heat accordingly.

Stir in the tomatoes, chillies, the rest of the salt and a few grindings of pepper. Cook briskly, still stirring, until most of the liquid in the pan has evaporated and the mixture is thick enough to hold its shape. Stir in the salt beef off the heat and taste for seasoning.

Gather the cassava dough into a ball, place it on a lightly floured sheet of greaseproof paper, and pat it into a thick rectangle. Roll the dough into a rectangle about 12 inches wide, 18 inches long and ½ inch thick with a floured pin. Dust the top from time to time with a little flour to prevent it from sticking to the pin.

Spread the meat mixture evenly over the surface of the dough, to within about 1½ inches of the outside edges. Lift the greaseproof paper, starting with the long side of the dough and roll the dough lengthways into a thick, compact cylinder using the paper for support.

Transfer the *brazo gitano* to the baking sheet using 2 large fish slices. Beat the third egg with a whisk or fork until it is light and lemon coloured, then brush it over the top and sides of the roll. Bake in the middle of the oven for about 1 hour, until the crust is golden brown.

Transfer the roll to a heated dish, cut it crosswise into 3-inch-thick slices, and serve the *brazo gitano* at once.

To serve 6

1 lb. lean salt beef
2 lb. fresh cassava root, peeled and cut crosswise into ½-inch-thick slices
2½ oz. butter, softened, plus 1 oz. butter
3 eggs
6 to 8 oz. plain flour
1½ teaspoons salt
4 oz. finely chopped onions
1 teaspoon finely chopped garlic
6 medium-sized ripe tomatoes, peeled, seeded and finely chopped (*see sopa de gandules, Recipe Index*), or substitute two 1-lb. cans chopped drained tomatoes
1½ teaspoons finely chopped fresh hot chillies (*caution: see "How to Handle Chillies"*)
Freshly ground black pepper

The *poulet rôti à la créole* of Haiti is a double-stuffed roast chicken, with banana stuffing in the breast cavity and a breadcrumb mixture in the neck. The stuffing ingredients include (*from left*) garlic, pieces sugar, bananas, toasted crumbs, rum, lime and nutmeg.

To serve 4

3 tablespoons dark rum

3 tablespoons soya sauce, preferably the Japanese type

3 tablespoons strained fresh lime juice

A 3½- to 4-lb. chicken, chopped into 16 small pieces by dividing the wings, thighs, drumsticks and breasts into halves

¾ pint vegetable oil

½ teaspoon salt

Freshly ground black pepper

4 oz. plain flour

Chicharrones de Pollo (*Dominican Republic*)

MARINATED FRIED CHICKEN

Warm the rum in a small pan over a low heat. Set light to the rum with a match off the heat, and gently shake the pan backwards and forwards until the flame dies. Add the soya sauce and lime juice to the rum. Place the chicken in a deep bowl and pour in the rum mixture, turning the pieces over with a spoon to coat them evenly. Marinate at room temperature for about 2 hours, or in the refrigerator for at least 4 hours, turning over the chicken pieces occasionally.

Preheat the oven to the lowest setting and line a large shallow baking dish with a double thickness of kitchen paper. Heat the oil over a high heat in a large, heavy frying-pan until it is very hot but not smoking. Pat the pieces of chicken completely dry with kitchen paper and season them with salt and a few grindings of pepper. Dip them in the flour and shake vigorously to remove the excess.

Fry 5 or 6 pieces of chicken at a time for about 6 minutes on each side, turning them with a perforated spoon and regulating the heat so that they brown richly and evenly without burning. Transfer the pieces to the lined baking dish as they brown, and keep them warm in the oven.

Serve the chicken as soon as all the pieces are cooked, accompanied, if you like, with hot boiled rice.

Poulet Rôti à la Créole *(Haiti)*
ROAST CHICKEN WITH TWO STUFFINGS

To serve 6

Preheat the oven to Mark 4: 350° F. Melt 1½ ounces of butter over a moderate heat in a small, heavy frying-pan. When the foam begins to subside, drop in the garlic and stir for 10 to 15 seconds. Remove and discard the garlic; add the breadcrumbs and stir until they are crisp and brown. Stir in 2½ tablespoons of the lime juice, the lime rind, 1 tablespoon of the rum, the pieces sugar, nutmeg, cayenne pepper, 1 teaspoon of the salt and a few grindings of pepper off the heat, and taste for seasoning. Set the stuffing aside.

Peel and chop the bananas finely, and drop them into a small bowl. Add the rest of the lime juice, 1 teaspoon of the rum, the rest of the salt, and a few grindings of pepper, and turn the ingredients over and over with a spoon to mix them thoroughly.

Pat the chicken completely dry inside and out with kitchen paper. Fill the breast cavity with the banana stuffing and close the opening by lacing it with skewers or sewing it with a large needle and thick white thread. Fill the smaller neck cavity with the breadcrumb stuffing and skewer or sew the opening shut. Truss the chicken securely and coat it thoroughly with the 2 ounces of softened butter using a pastry brush.

Place the bird on a rack in a shallow roasting tin just large enough to hold it comfortably and roast in the middle of the oven for about 1½ hours, basting occasionally with the juices as they accumulate in the tin. To test for doneness, pierce the thigh of the bird with the point of a small, sharp knife. The juice that trickles out should be pale yellow; if it is tinged with pink, roast the chicken for another 5 to 10 minutes.

Transfer the bird to a large, heated dish, cut off and discard the trussing strings, and let the chicken rest for about 5 minutes for easier carving. Meanwhile, skim the fat from the juices in the tin and pour in the stock. Bring to the boil over a high heat, stirring and scraping in any brown particles clinging to the bottom of the tin. Cook the sauce briskly for 2 to 3 minutes, taste for seasoning, and pour it into a small bowl or sauceboat. Just before serving, warm the remaining 2 tablespoons of rum in a small pan over a low heat. Set light to the rum with a match and pour it flaming over the chicken.

1½ oz. butter, plus 2 oz. butter, softened
1 small whole garlic clove, peeled
1 oz. soft fresh crumbs made from white bread trimmed of crusts and prepared in a blender or finely shredded with a fork
3 tablespoons strained fresh lime juice
2½ teaspoons finely grated fresh lime rind
3 tablespoons plus 1 teaspoon dark rum
1 teaspoon dark pieces sugar
¼ teaspoon ground nutmeg
¼ teaspoon cayenne pepper
1¼ teaspoons salt
Freshly ground black pepper
3 medium-sized ripe bananas
A 3½- to 4-lb. whole roasting chicken
⅜ pint chicken stock

Fried Ripe Plantains

To serve 3 or 4

Peel the plantains, using a small, sharp knife, following the diagram (*see Banana Pese, Recipe Index*). Cut each plantain segment in half lengthways after peeling, or, if you prefer, slice them crosswise on the diagonal to make ovals, ¼-inch-thick.

Heat the oil over a moderate heat in a heavy, medium-sized frying-pan until a light haze forms above it. Fry the plantains in the hot oil for about 4 minutes on each side, turning them with a perforated fish slice and adjusting the heat so that they brown richly and evenly without burning. Transfer the plantains to kitchen paper to drain and serve at once from a heated dish.

2 large very ripe plantains
3 tablespoons ground nut or vegetable oil

V

The Abundant Fruits of Eden

This fairytale fruit tree
was devised by Jasmin
Joseph, a young Haitian artist.
It shows some of the island's
best-known fruits, as well as a
few known only to Haiti.

1 Mango
2 Star apple
3 Shaddock
4 Orange
5 Apple
6 Mamey apple
7 Apple
8 Melon de France
9 Star apple
10 Mango
11 Fig
12 Star apple
13 Melon
14 Pawpaw
15 Pepper
16 Melon de France
17 Pomegranate
18 Corn
19 Cashew
20 Mamey apple
21 Star apple
22 Plantain
23 Sour-sop
24 Star apple

Christopher Columbus was the first to compare the Caribbean islands to the Garden of Eden—and he was convinced that they were
literally one and the same place. Sailing past Trinidad on his third
voyage to the New World, he was deeply moved by the sight of shores
"so fair and so verdant and full of trees and palms," where "every tree
. . . is pleasant to the sight and good for food". Since the authorities of
his day placed the Garden of Eden in Eastern Asia, which is where
Columbus thought he was when he reached Trinidad, his mistaking the
island for Paradise is understandable.

Though the authorities of my own day know better, I confess that
there are times when I agree with Columbus. The stately palms and
graceful ferns, the bamboo thickets and trails of creepers, the cascading
purple and scarlet and yellow flowers, and especially the fantastically
fruitful trees of the Caribbean islands, all fit perfectly my image of Eden.

Some of the trees in this garden are bizarre, like the jack-fruit, which
bears gross, malodorous fruits weighing 30 to 40 pounds and sometimes as much as 70 pounds. Some of the trees are deadly, like the
manchineel, whose deceptively sweet-smelling apples contain a milky
juice that can be fatal and was used, in fact, by the Carib Indians to
poison their enemies. But most of the trees of the Caribbean are beautiful, the bearers of beneficent fruits and nuts, and prolific in their uses
for men. The stately tamarind not only bears a fruit that makes a sugary,
spicy candy and an aromatic drink, but it also provides protection from
hurricanes to islanders who plant it beside their houses as a wind-break.
The cashew tree provides its crisp nut as well as a fruit that, though
tart, can be eaten raw or made into sweet wines and syrupy liqueurs.

The pineapple that Columbus saw for the first time in the West Indies has by now spread all over the world. Special water-storing tissues allow it to grow in dry climates as well as wet. But it still flourishes in the Caribbean, and is Puerto Rico's largest export fruit crop. The plant above is seen in bud (*top*) and then in flower. The blossoms live only a day; when they wither they leave behind the spots that will become the eyes of the mature pineapple.

Over all presides the coconut, the tree that most strongly evokes the lost Eden—a noble palm that gracefully bends and withstands hurricane winds, gives shelter on sun-beaten beaches, and provides a constant supply of food and drink everywhere. The almost clear liquid inside the immature, or green, coconut, called coconut water, is sometimes easier to come by than fresh water in the Caribbean; always pure in its sturdy container, always sweet and cool, the drink could claim to be, as one Caribbean explorer put it, "the nectar of the gods". When the coconut is still young its meat is like jelly, with a fresh, fruity flavour, and is eaten with a spoon, as we might eat a melon. When the coconut matures, the meat dries out and, when shredded, has endless uses in such enticing confections as Barbados' chewy coconut custard pie, Puerto Rico's *tembleque*, a trembling coconut flan, or Jamaica's *gisada*, a little coconut tart heady with rum.

It is in the astonishing variety of fruits growing in the islands that nature most conspicuously manifests her bounty, and a visit to a well-supplied Caribbean fruit market confirms the impression that here indeed is Paradise. The fruits displayed are overwhelming in their extravagant colours and exotic textures. To the traveller from the north some of the fruits are familiar: mounds of prickly-skinned pineapples, a few cut open to show off their juicy yellow inner secrets; stalks, as tall as a boy, of tiny sweet bananas; great pyramids of oranges and limes so fragrant that peeling one of them perfumes the hands for the rest of the day; piles of pawpaw and many varieties of mangoes, mottled red and green and yellow like the brilliant birds of the tropics.

There are dozens of other fruits encountered only in the islands themselves. A visitor finds their shapes odd and their names even stranger. Fruit sellers called higglers in the English-speaking islands walk about the streets carrying baskets on their heads and chanting the names of their wares like a musical pagan litany: "Cherimoya, carambola, mamey, sapote, monstera, mangosteen, loquat." There are smooth fruits, nobbly ones, delicate and coarse, sweet-smelling and foul. Some have short seasons, some are picked all the year round, but there is always a profusion to choose from.

Tropical fruits spoil easily and often do not travel well, and Caribbean fruit-growers are poorly organized, so a comparatively small selection of the island fruit delicacies is available elsewhere. But these few are sufficient to give outsiders a taste of the islands, and a chance to produce in their houses some of the exotic desserts found there.

Of the Caribbean fruits available in the United States I think the mango is the most exquisite, although I find its flavour, which seems to combine so many tantalizing, hints of other fruits, almost impossible to describe. People always seem able to agree on the flavour of exotic meat; whether it be monkey, iguana or agouti, explorers invariably exclaim, "Hmm . . . tastes amazingly like veal." But when it comes to tropical fruits, and especially to mangoes, all attempts at definition fail. It is not for lack of trying, though I have listened to dozens of firm and assertive opinions about what the mango tastes like—all different.

A Haitian friend insisted that I describe it as "a combination between a pear and an apricot". A friend in St. Kitts said just as positively, "It's like a melon mixed with a pineapple". A Puerto Rican woman told me. "It has the flavour of an apricot and a texture between that of an avocado and a cassava melon," while her husband contended, "It's a cross between a peach, a melon and a banana." The man who best described its essence was a Jamaican, who said with the poetic turn of speech typical of his people, "You can't describe a mango. Unless you say that it's a delicious, nourishing, breast-shaped delicacy that grown men may nibble in public. It's God's way of making every man outgrow his mother".

One reason it is so difficult to define the mango's taste is that there are so many kinds of mangoes. Hundreds of varieties grow in the islands, and they range in size from that of a small plum to that of a big honey-dew melon, in form from round to kidney-shaped and in colour, when ripe, from pale yellow to scarlet. My supermarket in New York carries only Haitian mangoes; they weigh about half a pound and are kidney-shaped and green. And the shop assistant often fails to tell buyers what they should know—that a green mango is unripe. A mango can be bought green but it must be put on the window-sill to ripen. It should not be eaten until it blushes pink or yellow and, as with bananas, until it is flecked with brown or black. Green mangoes are used to make mango chutney, a popular accompaniment to curries, but they are picked weeks before they are ripe.

How to cut a mango is a problem as much debated as its taste. It is an extremely juicy fruit, and when one bites into it or cuts it and applies pressure in the wrong places the juice tends to spray out. It has often been called a fruit to be eaten in the bath. Furthermore, most varieties of mango have a flat stone that, unlike that of a freestone peach, does not come away cleanly from the flesh, but clings with stringy tenaciousness. So getting all the flesh off while staying dry is something of an achievement.

I learned about the many opinions on how best to do this at a meal in Trinidad where I, as guest of honour, was given the last ripe mango my hostess had been able to find in the market. She, her husband and each of their two daughters had a favourite way of eating the fruit. One said peel some of the skin away and suck the fruit; another recommended peeling and eating it with a spoon; the others had intricate systems of cutting and slicing. I ended up cutting off two slabs from the flattish sides of the mango and eating them with a spoon, as you do a melon, and then tackling the rest with knife and fork and, finally, my fingers. Eventually I was covered with juice anyway—and did not mind a bit, because I found the taste so compelling that I ceased to care about anything but eating it. And, of course, I know exactly what it tastes like: mostly peach-like, with hints of banana, melon, apricot and pineapple, and with a little bit of plum.

Another Caribbean fruit that only recently has begun to claim the attention of Americans is the pawpaw. Like the pineapple it is a truly New World fruit, one of the first to catch Columbus' interest. In his journal he wrote that the natives of the islands were "very strong and live largely on a tree melon called 'the fruit of the angels'. "It seems an apt name for this sweet, musky fruit. Pawpaw grows on what looks like a tall tree—15 to 20 feet high—that is really not a tree at all but the woody stalk of a giant plant. This stalk has no branches and at its top is a burst of leaves, a crown carrying the heavy dark-green fruits like jewels.

The pawpaw has many names in the islands. The Spanish explorers evolved the word pawpaw from the Carib Indian language, and it came directly into English. But most often in the Spanish-speaking islands today the fruit is called either *lechosa* or *fruta bomba* because in

Seven months after budding, the pineapple is ripe and ready for harvesting. This is done either by breaking it free with a twist of gloved hands, or by slicing it off with a machete, the technique being used here. The golden blush of these pineapples—of the Red Spanish variety—shows that they are too ripe to be shipped whole for any distance: they will either be sold in local markets or processed for canning in a Puerto Rican plant.

109

On hot days in the Dominican Republic—that is, most of the time —a favourite and inexpensive cooler is a *frio-frio* (*frio* is Spanish for cold). Made by pouring a dollop of fruit syrup over a paper cupful of crushed ice, *frio-frio* goes down especially well with children. These pictures were taken as they were coming out of school in Santo Domingo, but the same refreshments are found in other islands too—Jamaicans, for instance, call them snow cones or snowballs.

its small varieties it looks like a hand grenade; in the English-speaking islands it is called pawpaw. And the pawpaw has even more uses than names. Its leaves and fruit contain a valuable enzyme, papain, which breaks down protein tissue in the same way as the digestive juices of the stomach. This makes it a natural meat tenderizer. For centuries the islanders have wrapped meat in pawpaw leaves or rubbed it with a raw young fruit to make it tender, and in recent years the enzyme, has been isolated and put into commercial preparations that are widely used round the world. The leaves of the pawpaw can be boiled and served as a green vegetable, with a delicate, slightly bitter flavour that is reminiscent of dandelion leaves. When the fruit itself is not yet ripe, it too is treated as a vegetable that is very popular throughout the islands. It is usually split in half and baked with butter or stuffed (*Recipe Index*), and it has the appearance and flavour of a mild, sweet squash. But pawpaw is at its best when it is ripe, a juicy, fragrant breakfast or dessert fruit. It is served sliced like a melon, its shiny black seeds clinging decoratively to its firm orange or pink flesh.

Both the mango and the pawpaw are so good eaten raw that at first I wondered why anyone did anything else with them. But I have learned to love the many other ways the islanders use them for desserts. They make mango pie, mango brown Betty, mango mousse (*Recipe Index*); they are fond of pawpaw ices and of a confection of baked crushed pawpaw cooked with vanilla and sprinkled with cinnamon. The Cubans use either mango or pawpaw in an ambrosial concoction that I find irresistible. The raw fruit is put into a blender with milk and ice and is pulverized to produce a tropical milk shake called a *refresco de papaya*, or, simply, a *batido* (*Recipe Index*). I often order one at Victor's Café, my favourite Cuban restaurant in New York, even after a generous meal of lobster and black beans and fried plantains, and even though I have reached a stage at which I try hard to avoid desserts altogether. I order guiltily, feeling as if I were 14 again and back in the innocent days when the only thing adolescents were hooked on was milk shakes; and I drink it, my husband says, with a faraway look on my face.

Mangoes and pawpaw are still rare enough outside the tropics to be considered exotic delicacies, but it may not be long before they become familiar fruits, if we can judge from the history of the banana and the pineapple which were virtually unheard of in the United States or in Europe a century ago.

During the days of the American Civil War, sailing vessels from the West Indies occasionally reached an American port with a few bunches of blackened bananas left over from the crew's food stores; and sometimes these would be sold in port. Now and then some bananas reached New Orleans from Central America; shipped north to New England, a single piece of fruit gaily wrapped in tinfoil commanded a price equivalent to one dollar today. Then, in 1870, a Cape Cod sea captain named Lorenzo Baker, who sailed regularly to the islands, received two big bunches of bananas as a parting gift from a Jamaican plantation owner. When Baker's schooner reached Boston the bananas were still in good condition, and he discovered a ready market for the exotic fruit. He began bringing bananas back with him regularly from the West Indies, and 15 years later formed the Boston Fruit Company to import the fruit on a large scale. Just before the turn of the century his company merged with that of a railway entrepreneur in Costa Rica to form the

110

United Fruit Company. By the mid-1920s, with the development of refrigerated ships and rail transport, bananas were to be found in stores all across the country.

The pineapple, too, was a curiosity to most Americans until the 20th century, despite its popularity with the Caribbean Indians and their European conquerors. While it was grown under glass as a botanical hobby for gentlemen farmers—a pastime introduced into England in 1690 by the Earl of Portland—few people except those in the upper crust of society or those who travelled to the islands were ever able to taste the fruit. George Washington sampled the pineapple on a trip to Barbados in 1751 with his brother Lawrence, who was ill and needed to recuperate in a warm climate. In his diary, Washington listed all the fruits he was served, which included such rarities as sapodilla, forbidden fruit and guavas, but only when it came to the pineapple did he become expansive: "None pleases my taste as do's the pine."

Lady Janet Schaw, travelling in the West Indies at about the same time, described an occasion when she was served 32 tropical fruits for dessert, and she too wrote that she was most pleased by the pineapple. She had tasted pineapple before, the hot-house variety raised by friends. But apparently a hot-house pineapple was so precious that one ate every bit of it, including the hard centre. Lady Janet wrote of Antigua: "When I first came here I could not bear to see so much of a pine apple thrown away. They cut off a deep paring, then cut out the firm part of the heart, which takes away not much less than half the pine apple." But she soon grew accustomed to this wasteful luxury. In fact, like the princess who slept on the pea, Lady Janet became finicky. "Only observe how easy it is to become extravagant," she wrote. "I can now feel if the least bit of rind remains; and as to the heart, heavens! who would eat the nasty heart of a pine apple."

In the islands today both the banana and the pineapple are essential culinary ingredients. Pineapple accompanies poultry and pork dishes and is made into cakes, pies and pancakes. Once I had it baked in its shell, sprinkled with rum and cinnamon, and flamed, the most flamboyant tropical dessert I have come across. Bananas are used in the same ways as pineapple, but there are even more banana recipes: fried bananas, baked and flamed bananas (*Recipe Index*), banana pancakes, sweet banana omelettes. Many of these are beginning to become popular in Europe. Once at a picnic on Jamaica I had a banana dessert that was so superbly innocent that I was astonished that the idea had never occurred to me. My friends roasted unpeeled bananas in the ashes of a fire for about half an hour until the skins turned very black. Then we opened the bananas, sprinkled them with sugar and a touch of lime juice, and ate the pudding-like sweet with spoons.

There is another group of fruits, the citrus family, whose absence would change the entire landscape of the Caribbean and the taste of its cuisine. Citrus groves bloom and bear fruit all the year round from Cuba to Trinidad. Yet they are not native to the region. It was Columbus himself who brought the first citrus plants to the New World, oranges from the Grand Canary Island, which he planted in Hispaniola in 1493. Indeed, according to John McPhee, author of a delightful and exhaustive book on the orange, the movement of the fruit from its origins near the South China Sea down into the Malay Archipelago, across the ocean to Africa and across the African deserts into the Mediterranean

Continued on page 116

The bright red fruity part of the cashew (*left*) is called a cashew apple, but is technically the pedicle, or base, of the cashew flower; it produces the nut. The unshelled nuts shown below have been separated from their ripened pedicles. The shelled cashew nut on the right is freshly picked; when it has been roasted, it will be the familiar tan colour, crisp and ready for eating.

From Curious Cashew to Ugly Ugli, The Yield Is Fruitful

Reina Reynoso adds to her family's income by selling cashew apples and nuts to motorists in the countryside near Santo Domingo in the Dominican Republic. The tart cashew apple can be eaten stewed, but it is usually made into jelly, wine or a liqueur.

In a way the cashew tree sums up both the magnanimity and the general unpredictability of nature in the Caribbean. While it is enough for most trees to produce either a fruit or a nut, the cashew bears both. But it also tempers its generosity; because it is botanically related to—of all things—poison ivy, one part of its nutshell will cause a rash. As a whole, the harvest of the groves, orchards and jungles of the Caribbean islands is more richly varied and more delectable than that of almost any other region on earth. Some fruits are well known—bananas, pineapples, certain citrus species. Others never go abroad, or so deteriorate in travelling that most foreigners can form little idea of their true quality. Part of the abundance antedates the coming of the Spanish galleons. Long before them the coconut palm, for example, was everywhere in the Caribbean. But settlers impressed by the climate and the soil introduced wholly new plants, such as bread-fruit, mango, orange and lime. Even today, as if in the vast hot-house of some super-botanist, spontaneous cross-breeding of plants keeps bringing fresh hybrids into existence—the tangelo, the tangor, and the splendidly named cross of grapefruit, orange and tangerine, the ugli.

Banana hands grow upwards. The dangling bud is eaten as a vegetable.

Green coconuts are filled with clear, sweet water and savoury jelly-like flesh.

The pawpaw may be cooked when green, or eaten raw when ripe.

Though lumpy and ill-favoured, the ugli, pronounced 'hoogly' in Jamaica, is sweeter than the grapefruit and nearly seedless.

The guava is botanically related to the clove. It may be sliced open and eaten raw or made into a rich sweet preserve, paste or jelly.

Despite its name, the starchy-fleshed bread-fruit is prepared as a vegetable.

The prickly sour-sop has a cottony consistency, and makes a tart drink.

The cacao tree yields cocoa, chocolate and cocoa butter from its pod-enclosed beans.

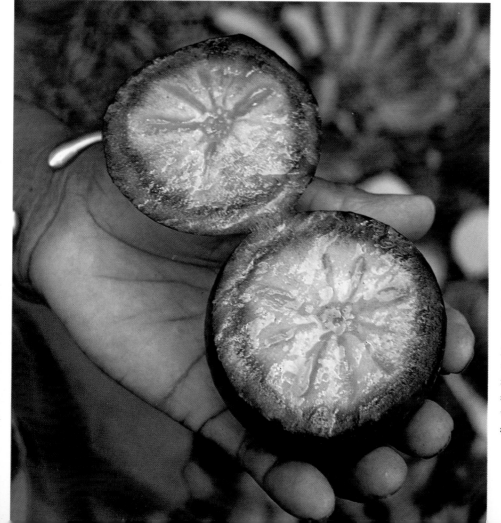

Many Caribbean fruits are unknown outside the islands, but the star apple in particular remains obscure. It is very sensitive to the cold, must be tree-ripened, and has such a short season that even the most determined tourist may never see or taste one. The fruit is about the size of an apple, and its name comes from the fact that the seeds are distributed in a handsome star-like pattern clearly visible when it is sliced open, as on the left. The flesh is slightly gelatinous, mild and sweet. It grows throughout the West Indies but is especially abundant in Jamaica and Haiti.

115

Opposite: A hospitable custom of the old-time Jamaican planter was the breakfast fruit bowl, an iced array of local fruits. A number of Jamaican hotels and resorts have revived the tradition, and a fortunate tourist may now wake to an inviting sight like this. It includes bananas, mango slices, black-seeded pawpaw, oranges, limes, grapefruit, pineapple and, in the centre, two naseberry halves.

and thence to the Americas "closely and sometimes exactly kept pace with the major journeys of civilization". Arab traders took it to Africa, Islamic warriors to Spain, and Spanish *conquistadores* to the New World. For centuries the orange was an expensive luxury in Europe; the demand for a new source of supply was great. By the beginning of the 16th century, orange trees were growing all across the Caribbean.

Most Caribbean oranges look very different from the smooth-skinned, bright-coloured product of South Africa, Spain and Israel. Some have bumpy skins, and most are lime green; colour is not an indication of the fruit's ripeness or sweetness, and a green orange may be perfectly ripe inside. However they look, Caribbean oranges are sweet and juicy, though some have a tartness that seems a natural antidote to the tropical sun. In Trinidad, oranges are sold on the street cut in half and sprinkled with salt. On many islands they are sold by street traders who use ingenious hand-turned peeling machines to cut off the skin in a long, thin spiral, leaving the fruit ready to eat then and there.

Lime trees were also planted by the early European settlers, and this fruit has become an ingredient that rivals the pepper in its importance to Caribbean cookery. The West Indian limes bear little relation to the smaller, less juicy specimens that find their way to European markets. Caribbean limes seem to be bigger and greener than any I have seen elsewhere. Fragrant and gloriously juicy, they are as much part of the Caribbean experience as sun and sea, and it is almost impossible to imagine island cooking without them. Lime juice is used in almost every Creole sauce, in countless fish, vegetable and poultry dishes; countless desserts are flavoured with lime, and, of course, it is the perfect companion to rum.

Grapefruit is less important to the Caribbean cuisine, but it deserves special attention because it is a West Indian creation. Grapefruit did not even exist before the 18th century. In the 17th century a British ship captain named Shaddock sailed into Jamaica, having brought from Polynesia a large citrus fruit with a thick rind and yellowish-red flesh that was aromatic but bitter. Planted in the West Indies, the fruit flourished, and came to be called shaddock, also known as pomelo. Some time later, a fruit began to appear in the islands that was either a natural mutation of the shaddock or the result of some botanist's attempt to cross it with a sweet orange. It resembled the shaddock but its skin was thinner, its flesh yellower, and its flavour sweeter. Thus, the grapefruit was born.

Other citrus fruits have been developed, as well. Among the hybrids recently evolved are the tangelo, a cross between the tangerine and the grapefruit, the tangor, a cross between the tangerine and the orange, and, most intriguing of all, the ugli, a cross between a grapefruit and an orange. The ugli got its name from its resemblance to a lumpy, misshapen orange. But the name is affectionately meant. Jamaicans, who developed the fruit and gave it its unflattering name, have nothing but praise for its inner beauty, its delicate, slightly tart flavour. Also grown on many islands is the citron, which has tough skin and a pulp too acid to eat, but which makes excellent candied peel, and a bitter orange that is also too sour to eat but is the basis used to flavour Curaçao's world-famous orange liqueur. The ancestors of these bitter oranges were probably Valencia oranges which were planted in the 17th century by a governor of Curaçao.

116

Mango chutney is a tart, gingery accompaniment for roast meat and poultry as well as for curries. Ingredients for the Jamaican version shown above include (*from the left*) fresh ginger root, malt vinegar, unripened mango, ground allspice, garlic, sugar, raisins, peppers, salt and dried tamarind.

From this array of citrus fruits the islanders make spectacular desserts. Cored oranges are stuffed with sugar and butter, and baked and served with cream. Or oranges are pulped, then mixed with dates and nuts and brown sugar, and the mixture is stuffed back into the orange rind and baked. They are then doused in rum and carried, flaming, to the table. Orange fritters, orange cakes, grapefruit mousse, grilled grapefruit topped with grapefruit marmalade, lime pie, spongy lime puddings— all are popular. Perhaps the most elegant Caribbean citrus dessert is lime soufflé, a fragrant creation whose airiness is punctuated with shredded coconut (*Recipe Index*).

The crowning Caribbean achievement with citrus fruits is the wedding cake made in all the English-speaking islands. When one says "wedding cake" in Jamaica or Barbados or Antigua, one means a dark fruit cake made with candied lime and orange and citron, and heavily steeped in rum. It is also known as Christmas cake, bride's cake and, most commonly, black cake. The shape of the cake may vary. Some-

118

times there are two—a small, round one for the bride and a tall one for the groom; sometimes there is a single three-tiered cake; sometimes it is in the shape of a garden or a house, and is a work of elaborate artistry that demands month-long attention and creativity on the part of the bride's female relations and friends. One woman I met described the wedding cake she and her friends had made for her niece the winter before. It was built in the shape of a church and, like an architect's model, was perfect in detail: Its roof was made with almond-flavoured icing tinted the reddish-brown colour of Spanish tiles, and its steeple actually contained a clock, the watch of one of the women working on the cake.

Whatever the design of the cake, it is made with citrus fruits and rum, and in its rich moistness is very similar to the kind of wedding cake that has been traditional in England since the 18th century. Comparing a contemporary Jamaican wedding-cake recipe with one in an English cookery book written in 1813, I found them almost identical. "Beat in your sugar a quarter of an hour" and the egg yolks, "half an hour at least," are the stern instructions given in the book. The other ingredients, almost all gifts of England's West Indian colonies, were candied orange, lemon and citron peel, mace, nutmeg and brandy. The hand beating and the ingredients are unchanged in the islands today, although local rum is now used instead of brandy. It is an interesting example of how the centuries of isolation in the islands have helped to preserve a tradition intact.

The islands are, of course, no longer isolated, and no doubt there will be increasing culinary interchanges. Certainly more and more of the exotic fruits of the Caribbean are finding their way on to North American and European tables. I hope this trend continues. But I have to admit that however quickly modern air traffic can whisk them from tropical tree to urban shop, many of the Caribbean fruits seem to taste best when eaten in the Eden where they grow. One of my greatest delights in visiting the islands is, in fact, to look for unfamiliar fruits, and I try to find a new one every time I go. It is not difficult. On one trip, in a Jamaican market, I discovered the sapodilla, dusty and brown on the outside but containing a sweet purplish jelly within. At a bar on a sandy beach in Dominica I first tasted passion fruit, a small yellow plum-shaped fruit with too many seeds to make chewing easy but delicious in a rum punch. Elsewhere I came to know genip, a pale-green grape-like fruit that grows in clusters and has pink flesh, sorrel, a flower that is used to make a deep-red aromatic drink (*Recipe Index*) that is traditional at Christmas in the English-speaking islands, sour-sop, a big bumpy-skinned fruit with juicy white flesh that is unrivalled for making drinks and sherbets; and the star apple, which, when cut horizontally, reveals a magical star of purple seeds in its white interior.

Perhaps my favourite of all is a fruit I found at a roadside stand in the mountains of Trinidad. They call it pomerac there and some other islands know it as Otaheite apple. It looks like a fruit from a fairy tale—waxy and bright red, shaped like a pear, with snow-white flesh that smells incredibly of roses. But the roster of fruits in the Caribbean seems to be endless; I have yet to try a sugar apple, a granadilla, a forbidden fruit, a cherimoya, a hog plum. I am sure I will find a new favourite the next time I go there.

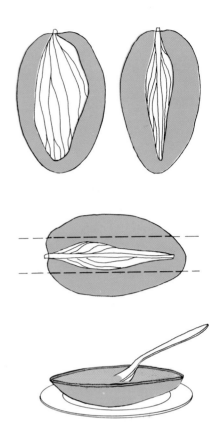

HOW TO TACKLE A RIPE MANGO
The stone inside a mango is almost flat and is generally found within the fruit as shown in the two cross sections at the top; the flesh clings to the stone and must be cut away. The simplest way to do this is to lay the mango on its flattest side and cut a thick slice off the top (*centre drawing*). Turn the fruit over and repeat the process. The two slices may be served like avocado halves and eaten with a spoon. The juicy flesh still attached to the stone can be cut off in chunks, or eaten—messily—straight from the stone.

119

As the nut ripens, its thick pericarp splits open.

The mature nutmeg is covered with scarlet mace.

Grenada's Marvellous Two-in-One Spice Kit

In 1843, an English sea captain homeward bound from the Spice Islands in the East Indies called at the Caribbean island of Grenada. He carried with him some small nutmeg trees and left them with his hosts when he sailed for England. Fifteen years later, Grenada marketed its first crop of nutmeg and mace. Today the island produces nearly 40 per cent of the world's supply.

Nutmeg and mace are different parts of the nut that grows on the 70 to 90 foot tall nutmeg tree. As the nut ripens, the spongy outer pericarp splits open and eventually gapes wide enough to allow the mace-covered nutmeg within to fall obligingly to the ground. Plantation workers pick up the nutmegs and strip away the still pliable mace. The mace is dried and graded (*opposite*) and the nutmegs are shelled and then sorted according to their size and oil content—the best being those that are round, oily and heavy. Most nutmegs are ground into powder or crushed for their oil; the most perfect are shipped whole to gourmet markets.

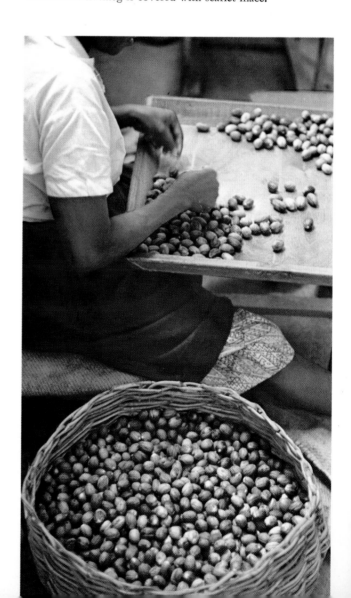

The mace webbing stripped from the nutmeg is valued and treated as a spice in its own right. It tastes something like nutmeg, but is stronger, more astringent and less sweet. About one pound of mace is produced for every six pounds of nutmeg. The woman on the left is sorting mace at the Gouyave processing station, one of three most important nutmeg co-operatives in Grenada. The mace is put through a curing process during which it turns yellow and golden. The best quality is called "whole pale" and has a high oil content, and a golden colour. In the picture below, this grade is at the bottom and on the top right is broken mace; the rest is fresh, uncured mace. The various grades of mace will be packaged and sold to spice jobbers.

Pineapple Fool (*Jamaica*)

Place the pineapple in a sieve or colander set over a bowl and let it drain for at least 10 minutes.

Whip the cream in a large chilled bowl with a whisk or a rotary egg beater until it is stiff enough to hold its shape softly. Taste the pineapple and sprinkle the cream with 1 to 3 tablespoons of icing sugar, depending upon its sweetness and your own taste. Add the vanilla and continue beating until the cream is stiff enough to form firm, unwavering peaks on the whisk when it is lifted from the bowl.

Chill the whipped cream and the pineapple separately until you are ready to serve them. Whipped cream can be kept for an hour or so if tightly covered with a sheet of plastic. Fold the pineapple into the cream with a rubber spatula at the last possible minute, blending them together thoroughly but gently. Spoon the fool into chilled individual bowls or sundae glasses and serve immediately.

NOTE: Mango can be substituted for the pineapple.

To serve 4

12 oz. finely chopped fresh pineapple (*see "How to Prepare Pineapple Wedges"*)
$\frac{3}{8}$ pint double cream
1 to 3 tablespoons icing sugar
$\frac{1}{2}$ teaspoon vanilla essence

Refresco de Coco y Piña (*Dominican Republic*)
CHILLED COCONUT MILK AND PINEAPPLE DRINK

Put the coconut milk, pineapple and sugar into the jar of an electric blender and blend at high speed for about 30 seconds, until the pineapple is completely pulped and the mixture is reduced to a smooth purée. Pour the entire contents of the blender jar into a fine sieve set over a deep bowl and lined with a double thickness of cheesecloth. Press down hard on the pineapple with the back of a spoon to extract all its juices before discarding the pulp.

(If you do not have a blender, rub the chopped pineapple through a fine sieve set over a deep bowl or force it through a food mill. Stir in the coconut milk and sugar.)

Taste the *refresco de coco y piña* and add more sugar and a drop or two of almond essence if desired. Cover tightly and refrigerate for at least 2 hours, until thoroughly chilled. To serve, pour the drink into tall tumblers with or without ice cubes.

To make about $1\frac{1}{4}$ pints

$\frac{3}{4}$ pint coconut milk, made from 8 oz. coarsely chopped fresh coconut and $\frac{3}{4}$ pint hot water (*see "Notes on Caribbean Cooking"*)
14 oz. coarsely chopped fresh pineapple (*see "How to Prepare Pineapple Wedges"*)
5 teaspoons sugar
Almond essence (optional)

Refresco de Papaya (*Dominican Republic*)
ICED MILK AND PAWPAW FRAPPÉ

Peel the pawpaw using a small, sharp knife or swivel-bladed vegetable parer. Cut it in half lengthways and scoop out the black seeds inside, then chop the pawpaw coarsely.

Place the pawpaw in the jar of an electric blender and add the milk, lime juice, lime rind, sugar, vanilla and crushed ice. Blend at high speed for 20 to 30 seconds, until the pawpaw is completely pulped and the mixture is smooth and thick.

Pour the *refresco de papaya* into tall chilled tumblers and serve at once, garnished if you like with thin slices of lime.

To make about $1\frac{1}{4}$ pints

1 medium-sized (about 12 oz.) firm ripe pawpaw (*see "A Note about Mangoes and Pawpaws"*)
6 tablespoons milk
$2\frac{1}{2}$ tablespoons strained fresh lime juice
$\frac{1}{2}$ teaspoon finely grated fresh lime rind
2 oz. sugar
$\frac{1}{4}$ teaspoon vanilla essence
6 tablespoons crushed ice or 4 ice cubes, wrapped in a tea towel and finely crushed with a mallet or heavy pan
Thin lime slices for garnish (optional)

Three fruit-laden Caribbean delights are *refresco de coco y piña (far left)* and *refresco de papaya,* both drinks; and pineapple fool, a sweet dish.

To serve 4

4 large ripe bananas
3 tablespoons light rum
2 oz. butter
3½ oz. dark pieces sugar
½ teaspoon ground allspice
3 tablespoons strained fresh lime
   juice

Baked Bananas Flambés (*Antigua*)

Preheat the oven to Mark 6: 400° F. Pierce the unpeeled bananas deeply in two or three places with the prongs of a long-handled fork. Lay them on a baking sheet and bake them in the middle of the oven for about 10 to 15 minutes, until the skins have darkened and the bananas feel tender when pressed gently between your thumb and forefinger.

Remove the bananas from the oven and slit their skins lengthways along their inside and outside curves using a small, sharp knife. Gently lift and peel off the top half of the skin, leaving the underside intact.

About 10 minutes before serving, warm the rum in a small pan over a low heat. Meanwhile, melt the butter in a large, heavy frying-pan over a moderate heat. When the foam begins to subside, add the sugar and allspice to the butter and stir until well mixed. Gently lay the bananas flesh side down in the pan, one at a time, and carefully lift and peel off the rest of the skin. Sprinkle the bananas with lime juice. Then set light to the rum with a match, and pour it flaming over the bananas a little at a time, shaking the pan gently to and fro until the flames die down. Spoon the sauce over the bananas and serve at once.

To make about 1½ pints

The meat of 1 medium-sized (about
   1½ lb.) fresh coconut (*see "Notes on
   Caribbean Cooking"*)
¾ pint warm milk
8 oz. sugar
3 tablespoons water
A pinch of cream of tartar
1 to 2 drops almond essence

Coconut-Milk Sorbet (*Barbados*)

Preheat the oven to Mark 3: 325° F. Pare off the brown outer skin from a piece of coconut meat about 4 inches square, using a swivel-bladed peeler or a small, sharp knife. (Set the rest of the coconut aside unpeeled.)

Grate the peeled piece coarsely with a hand grater and measure it. You should have about ⅜ pint. Spread the grated coconut in a thin layer in a large, shallow baking tin and toast it in the middle of the oven for about 15 to 20 minutes, stirring occasionally, until light brown. Remove the coconut from the oven and set it aside.

Meanwhile, following the directions in "*Notes on Caribbean Cooking*", make coconut milk with the rest of the coconut meat and ¾ pint of warm milk.

Bananas flamed with rum make a spectacular Antiguan sweet dish. To produce it without burning or bruising the fruit, bake the unpeeled bananas until their skins blacken. Slit the skin of each banana from end to end and gently peel off one half as shown in the photograph on the far left. The next step is to melt butter and brown sugar in a large frying-pan. Lay the bananas in the pan, one at a time, flesh side down, and carefully lift off the remaining skin (*centre*). To flame the bananas, pour flaming rum over them slowly, shaking the pan to and fro, all the time.

Bring the sugar, water and cream of tartar to the boil over a medium heat in a small, heavy saucepan, stirring until the sugar dissolves and the syrup becomes completely clear, about 5 minutes. Pour the syrup into a heatproof mixing bowl and let it cool to room temperature.

Stir the toasted coconut and the coconut milk into the cooled syrup and flavour the sorbet with a drop of the almond essence. Taste and add more of the essence if desired. Pour the mixture into 2 ice-cube trays from which the dividers have been removed.

Freeze the sorbet for 3 to 4 hours, stirring it every 30 minutes to break up the solid particles that will form on the bottom and sides of the tray. The finished sorbet should have a fine, snowy texture.

To serve, spoon it into sundae glasses or small bowls.

Mango Chutney *(Jamaica)*

To make about 2½ pints

Place the tamarind in a small bowl and pour the boiling water over it. Let the tamarind soak for about 1 hour, stirring and mashing occasionally with a spoon, until the pulp softens and breaks up in the water. Rub the tamarind and pour its soaking liquid through a fine sieve set over a bowl, pressing down hard with the back of a spoon before discarding the seeds and fibres.

Peel each mango, using a small, sharp knife, and cut the flesh away from the large, flat stone. Discard the seeds and cut the mangoes into 1-inch dice.

Put the mangoes and vinegar into a large, heavy enamel or stainless-steel pan. Bring to the boil over a high heat and cook briskly for 10 minutes, stirring occasionally. Stir in the sugar, raisins, ginger, garlic, chillies, allspice and salt, reduce the heat to low, and simmer uncovered for about 45 minutes, until the mango flesh is tender.

Remove the pan from the heat. Ladle the chutney immediately into hot sterilized preserving jars with a large spoon, filling them to within ⅛ inch of the top. Seal each jar quickly and tightly with sterilized rings and lids.

2 oz. dried tamarind (a piece approximately 2 by 2 by ¾ inches)
6 tablespoons boiling water
4 lb. medium-sized unripe mangoes (*see "A Note about Mangoes and Pawpaws"*)
¾ pint malt vinegar
8 oz. sugar
2½ oz. seedless raisins
2¼ oz. peeled, very finely chopped fresh ginger root
1 teaspoon finely chopped garlic
1 teaspoon finely chopped fresh hot chillies (*caution: see "How to Handle Chillies"*)
½ teaspoon ground allspice
5 teaspoons salt

125

Coconut bread (*left*) and banana bread are tea-time favourites in the islands; the iced tea is usually served with lime.

Violet Hurdle's Coconut Bread (Barbados)

Preheat the oven to Mark 4: 350° F. Spread ½ ounce of softened butter evenly over the bottom and sides of three 3½-by 7-inch bread tins, using a pastry brush. Sprinkle 2½ teaspoons of the flour into each tin and tip the tins from side to side to spread it evenly. Then invert the tins and rap the bottom sharply to remove any excess flour. Set aside.

Sift the remaining 1¼ pounds of flour, the sugar, baking powder, cinnamon, cloves and salt into a deep bowl. Add the grated coconut and mix all the ingredients together well, with your hands or a wooden spoon. Pour in the milk, 6 tablespoons at a time, and blend thoroughly after each addition. Then stir in the 2 ounces of melted butter.

Ladle the coconut batter into the prepared tins, filling each of them no more than two thirds full. Bake the bread in the middle of the oven for about 1 hour, until it begins to pull away from the sides of the tins and the top is golden brown and crusty.

Remove the bread from the oven and let it cool in the tins for about 5 minutes, then turn the loaves out onto wire cake racks. Serve the coconut bread either warm or cool.

NOTE: *Seven ounces of desiccated coconut may be substituted. Steep it in the milk for half an hour before draining well and using as described in the method. If the prepared coconut is pre-sweetened (most brands are), reduce the amount of sugar from 14 ounces to 10½ ounces. If you want to reduce the size of the commercially packed flakes to make the bread less crunchy, grind the coconut in the jar of an electric blender by blending it at high speed for a few seconds. It may be necessary to add a little extra milk if the batter is too thick.*

To make 3 small loaves

½ oz. butter, softened, plus
  2 oz. butter, melted
7½ teaspoons plus 1¼ lb. plain flour
14 oz. castor sugar
2½ teaspoons baking powder
½ teaspoon ground cinnamon
¼ teaspoon ground cloves
¾ teaspoon salt
1 large fresh coconut, opened,
  peeled and finely grated (*see
  "Notes on Caribbean Cooking"*)
¾ pint milk

Banana Bread (Jamaica)

Preheat the oven to Mark 4: 350° F. Spread ½ ounce of softened butter evenly over the bottom and sides of a 9-by 5-by 3-inch bread tin, using a pastry brush, and set it aside.

Reserve ¾ oz. of the most perfectly shaped pecan or walnut halves for the garnish. Chop the rest of the nuts coarsely and toss them with the raisins and 1 tablespoon of the flour. Sift the rest of the flour with the baking powder, nutmeg and salt.

Peel the bananas, chop them coarsely, and put them into a small bowl. Mash the bananas to a smooth purée with the back of a table fork. Stir in the vanilla and set aside.

Cream the rest of the butter and the sugar together in a deep bowl, beating and mashing them with a wooden spoon against the sides of the bowl until the mixture is light and fluffy.

Add the egg, and when it is well blended beat in the flour and the bananas alternately, adding about one third of each mixture at a time, and continue to beat until the batter is smooth. Stir in the chopped nuts and raisins, thoroughly but gently.

Ladle the batter into the bread tin and arrange the reserved halved nuts attractively on the top. Bake the bread in the middle of the oven for about 50 to 60 minutes, until a cake tester or a toothpick inserted into the centre of the loaf comes out clean. Remove the bread from the oven and let it cool in the tin for 5 minutes, then turn it out on a wire cake rack.

Serve the banana bread either warm or cool.

To make one 9-by 5-by 2-inch loaf

4½ oz. butter, softened
2¼ oz. unsalted shelled pecans or
  walnut halves
1½ oz. seedless raisins
8 oz. plain flour
2½ teaspoons baking powder
¼ teaspoon ground nutmeg,
  preferably freshly grated
½ teaspoon salt
2 large ripe bananas (about 1 lb.)
½ teaspoon vanilla essence
3½ oz. castor sugar
1 egg

Fiery hibiscus blooms frame three cold fruit sweets (*from left*): mango mousse, coconut sorbet and lime soufflé.

Lime Soufflé (Barbados)

Fold a 24-inch-long piece of greaseproof paper lengthways in half and again lengthways into quarters. Spread the vegetable oil evenly on one side of the folded strip using a pastry brush. Then wrap the paper strip, oiled side in, around the outside of a 1½-pint soufflé dish to make a collar extending about 2 inches above the top edge of the dish. Tie the paper in place with string. Coat the inside of the dish lightly with the rest of the oil and set the dish aside. Pour the lime juice into a heatproof bowl, sprinkle in the gelatine and let it soften for 2 to 3 minutes. Then set the bowl in a shallow pan of simmering water and stir over a low heat until the gelatine dissolves. Remove the pan from the heat, but leave the bowl in the water to keep the gelatine warm. Heat the evaporated milk over a moderate heat in a medium-sized enamel, stainless-steel or glass saucepan until bubbles form around the edge of the pan. Remove from the heat.

Beat the egg yolks with a wire whisk or a rotary egg beater until well blended. Slowly add the sugar and continue beating until the yolks are thick enough to fall in a ribbon when the whisk is lifted from the bowl.

Slowly pour the hot milk in a thin stream into the yolks, beating constantly, then pour the mixture back into the saucepan. Stir over a low heat until it thickens into a custard heavy enough to coat the spoon. Do not let the custard come to the boil or it may curdle. Remove the pan from the heat and stir in the dissolved gelatine and 2½ tablespoons of the lime rind. Transfer the custard to a deep bowl, and set it aside to cool to room temperature.

Beat the egg whites in a separate bowl with a whisk or a rotary egg beater until they form firm peaks on the whisk when it is lifted out of the bowl. Stir about one quarter of the whites into the custard, then pour it over the rest of the egg whites and gently fold them together. Pour the soufflé into the prepared dish and refrigerate for at least 3 hours, until firm. Meanwhile preheat the oven to Mark 3: 325° F. Spread the coconut in a baking tin and toast it in the oven for about 15 to 20 minutes, stirring occasionally until light brown. Remove the coconut from the oven and set it aside to cool.

Just before serving, gently remove the greaseproof collar from the dish and garnish the soufflé with the coconut and the rest of the lime rind.

To serve 6

2½ teaspoons vegetable oil
⅜ pint strained fresh lime juice
¼ oz. unflavoured gelatine
⅜ pint evaporated milk
6 egg yolks
8¾ oz. castor sugar
3 tablespoons finely grated lime rind
4 egg whites
2¼ oz. coarsely grated fresh coconut
(see "Notes on Caribbean Cooking")

Mango Mousse (Barbados)

Peel the mangoes with a small, sharp knife, and cut the flesh away from the large, flat stone inside each fruit. Cut the flesh of 2 of the mangoes into ¼-inch dice and set aside. Chop the 3 remaining mangoes finely and purée them through a food mill set over a bowl. Then stir in the lime juice.

Beat the egg whites with the salt until they are frothy, in a large bowl, using a whisk or a rotary egg beater. Sprinkle in the sugar and continue beating until the egg whites are stiff enough to stand in unwavering peaks when the whisk is lifted from the bowl. Whip the cream in a chilled bowl, with the same whisk, until it is stiff enough to form peaks.

Fold the egg whites into the cream with a rubber spatula. Stir about ½ pint of the mixture into the mango purée, then pour the purée over the rest of the cream and fold them together thoroughly but gently. Carefully fold in the diced mango. Spoon the mousse into individual custard glasses or a large serving bowl. Refrigerate it for 3 hours before serving.

To serve 8

5 medium-sized (about 1 lb. each) ripe mangoes (see "A Note about Mangoes and Pawpaws")
4 tablespoons strained fresh lime juice
2 egg whites
A pinch of salt
2¼ oz. castor sugar
6 tablespoons double cream

Note: If fresh mangoes are difficult to obtain or expensive, canned mangoes or mango purée, usually sweetened or in syrup but occasionally unsweetened can be found in most oriental shops.

that the fish be absolutely fresh and the other that they be cooked very briefly. Madame Elizé placed a few fish in each person's bowl and then tasted the broth still in the pot. Her brow furrowed, and she added salt and some generous squeezes of lime to the liquid. Then she stirred it and spooned the broth over our fish and gave each of us a piece of lime and half a fiery pepper, not to eat but to season the sauce with. The fish was permeated with the aromatic scent of cloves and allspice; sometimes a hint of hot pepper, sometimes the fragrant lime would dominate a bite. I felt I could eat blaff for ever and never be bored with its simplicity, a taste of the sea gracefully modified by the fruits of the tropical soil. With the blaff we drank coconut water from the big green nuts the children had gathered, a cooling sweetness that complemented the spicy fish.

Blaff, still my favourite Caribbean fish recipe, is a speciality of the French islands, but each island has its own method of cooking fish. On Puerto Rico and in the Dominican Republic the most popular way of preparing it is *en escabeche*, a traditional Spanish technique encountered throughout Latin America. An *escabeche* is made by pouring a tangy marinade of olive oil and vinegar, onions, bay or allspice leaves and spices over fillets of grilled or fried fish; the result is eaten either hot or cold. Virtually the same dish is also popular on Jamaica, where it is called escovitch (*Recipe Index*). I have heard that many Jamaicans are not aware of its Spanish origins; they say, jokingly, that escovitch must have been invented by and called after a gourmet Polish sea captain. I like to stop and buy escovitch when I am driving in the countryside where tourist restaurants are virtually non-existent. At roadside stalls in the Jamaican hills the dish is made to order and wrapped up ready to take away; to my mind it is better snack food than the hot dog sold in the United States because it is crisp and spicy and all protein.

I asked a cook at one of the stalls how he made his escovitch and, although I have since read many recipes for it, none was more descriptive than the one he recited. "You make sure the fish is dry by patting it with a towel," he said. "Then you make cuts in it and put in black pepper and salt. Use coconut oil in the pan. But it must be hot; it's got to go *shussh* when you throw in the fish. You got to stand back then, it's going *shussh*! Then you turn it and when it's done, you cut an onion and some pepper, green or red pepper this time, but hot, and fry it in the left-over oil. Then add some vinegar to this. Then put it on top of the fish and cover the dish and let it all sweat inside together. And then you have something wonderful! Then you have escovitch."

In Aruba and Curaçao the most distinctive seafood dish is a chowder called *sopito*. Its special flavour is so hard to achieve consistently that one of the big hotels in Curaçao employs a local chef to make nothing but *sopito*. On Mondays, his day off, there is no chowder, for though the hotel has many chefs the others are not from Curaçao and have never mastered the intricacies of *sopito*.

Sopito differs from other fish chowders in being made with coconut milk. Salt pork or beef, onions, tomatoes, garlic, peppers, fresh cream and a variety of spices are also included. Any of dozens of kinds of fish found in the local waters can be used—as they can in blaff or escovitch. The people of Curaçao buy their fish at the floating market, a fleet of schooners that sails across from near-by Venezuela to supply the island not only with fish but also with the foodstuffs its own arid soil cannot

Continued on page 136

An Abundance of Fishes for Cooking and Looking

From a commercial point of view, the waters of the Caribbean are sadly underdeveloped. They are full of fish, but the primitive methods used in most areas fail to harvest enough to satisfy local demands. Even the spiny lobster, held by some to be superior in flavour to its cold-water cousin, is caught in limited quantities. From a sportsman's point of view, however, the supply of fish is ample. Snorkelling with a spear gun on the coral reefs, trolling in the deep blue of the sea, fly-casting in the shallows of a mangrove inlet—such techniques can yield delicious samples of Caribbean seafood. For those interested more in scenery than in sport, there are other possibilities. At St. Croix in the Virgin Islands an underwater "park" rich in tropical marine life has been set aside for people to watch the fish.

On the beach at Hawksbill Inn in Antigua, an employee dangles two spiny lobsters (*above*) destined for the pot. On the right another member of the Hawksbill staff displays two kinds of edible sea-urchins, or sea eggs. The dolphin (*below*), which changes colour spectacularly when caught, is a fine-tasting game fish.

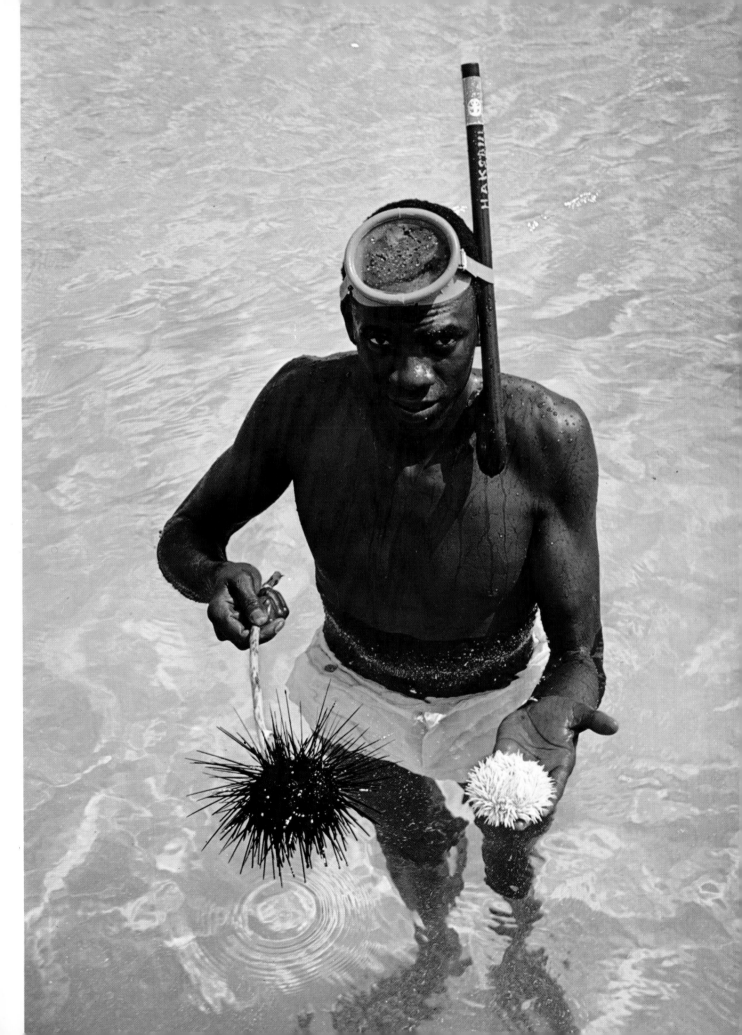

grow. The merchants shout the price of their wares from aboard ship while the buyers on the dock-side jump up and down to get a good look at the grouper, snapper, snook and shark piled on the decks, choosing the ingredients for their *sopito* in a balletic commotion.

At my friend Dolly Delvalle's house in Curaçao, *sopito* is never served as a soup—as it is in hotels and restaurants that skimp on the fish—but as a main dish. Creamy and white, it seems as laden with fish as the schooners of the floating market, and the coconut milk gives it a special smoothness. With it my friend serves Curaçaoan bread, *pan serra*, a compact loaf perfect for scooping up the fishy scraps in the bowl when all the broth has been drunk. I could smell the sea from Dolly's house and that increased the pleasure of my introduction to *sopito*, but I have eaten it since in my New York apartment and found it just as good.

Of the myriad kinds of edible fish in the Caribbean, snapper is the one most often served on restaurant and hotel tables. In the Dominican Republic I ate it topped with a thick layer of capers, olives, garlic and onions; in Jamaica it was served with a stuffing of locally grown cashew nuts. In Trinidad, in fact, a snapper recipe was invented for me and named after me. The people of Trinidad are famous for greeting visitors arriving at the airport with calypsos composed on the spot which have ingenious rhymes based on the tourist's appearance—how tired or excited he looks, his clothing, what he is carrying, the colour of his hair. The chefs of the islands can be just as attentive to the newcomer, and as imaginative as the calypso singers are. Invited to a special dinner given by the National Culinary Arts Association, I was told by my hosts that they regretted it had rained throughout my visit, that I must certainly return—I did, of course—and that meanwhile they intended to provide me with some vicarious sunshine in the main course of the dinner, Red Snapper Sunshine Wolfe. It was a seven-pound snapper stuffed with pigeon peas and salt pork, bathed in lime and orange juice, and rubbed on the outside not only with herbs and spices but with mustard and ketchup as well, to give it a gay sunshiny colour.

Snapper is just as popular on the French islands and, not surprisingly in those outposts of superb eating, the fish is accorded the utmost respect. One evening in Guadeloupe my husband and I were treated to an unforgettable dinner at which every course came from the sea. Our host was a Parisian who had married into a leading local family and had thrown himself into the life and spirit of the islands and become an accomplished Creole-style cook. Because of the constant failures of the telephone service in the Caribbean we had been unable to warn him of our impending arrival; nevertheless, on the day we met he insisted that we come to dinner, though it was already late afternoon. He said he was disappointed that he had not known beforehand because he would have liked to make his speciality, a snapper cooked in the style of the Carib Indians—pit-baked, with thyme and hot peppers placed between the skin and the flesh and a layer of mud packed outside. There was no time for this, he apologized, but he would do what he could.

No apology was needed. Crisply fried little *soleil*, or sun-fish, were followed by fish fritters and then by red snapper *court bouillon*, tingling with spices (*Recipe Index*). Among the Creoles of Martinique and Guadeloupe, *court bouillon* is the name of a dish, not the herb and vegetable-flavoured liquid in which fish or meat is poached in French cooking. The dish is begun by marinating the fish in lime juice and rubbing it with hot peppers. Later it is browned in oil, flavoured with spring onions and then steamed with small tomatoes, onions and more hot peppers. Just before the fish is served it is given a final fillip of flavour by the addition of slices of raw garlic and lime. The spiciness of this dish enlivened our conversation and, indeed, the whole evening. At midnight we all swam off our host's moonlit beach while he gaily pointed out that Creole *court bouillon* was never really good unless the guests felt like taking off their shirts after eating it.

The sea, of course, yields other bounty besides fish. The Caribbean lobster is a superb creature. Its chief difference from the lobster of northern waters is that it has no pincer-like claws. It is also called *langouste*, *langosta* or spiny lobster, and it compensates for its lack of claw meat by the quality of the meat in its tail, acclaimed by its champions as the most delicate meat to be found on any crustacean.

Very few of the lobsters caught in the islands are eaten by fishermen and their families because their catch is sold to meet the demand of establishments catering for tourists. These demands, in fact, often go unsatisfied, even in Jamaica, where half the island's 3,000 fishermen are involved; thus the traveller eager for a taste of the famous spiny lobster is sometimes frustrated. This is true in all the islands except Cuba, which has built up the largest lobster fishery in the whole of the Caribbean and Latin America; lacking a horde of tourists to eat them up, Cubans export lobsters in large quantities.

Cuba has also exported a dish—known variously as *langosta enchilada*, *langosta criolla* or lobster Creole—which is my own favourite elaborate lobster dish, the only way that is good enough to compete with the natural elegance of grilled lobster with butter sauce. In lobster Creole (*Recipe Index*) the lobster tail is fried in hot oil until the shell barely reddens. It is then removed, and into the frying-pan go white wine, tomatoes, onions, sweet green pepper and just enough hot pepper to tangle with the taste of the lobster but not overpower it; finally the lobster is cooked for a few minutes longer in this sauce. The result couldn't be more unlike grilled lobster, but it is just as good because the disguise is not too complicated—beneath it one is always aware of the real thing, the sweet mild chewiness of the lobster meat.

Prawns too are eaten up as fast as they can be caught in the islands. Unfortunately, prawns breed in limited quantities in Caribbean waters; in most places catching prawns is a local, small-scale operation, and tourism has so increased the demand that there never seem to be enough to go around. Indeed, in those islands with the most tourists, such as Jamaica and Puerto Rico, the visitor is likely to find himself eating frozen prawns imported from the United States.

This does not mean that prawns are not highly regarded by the islanders and brilliantly treated in their kitchens. Prawns have been considered a delicacy since the earliest days of the history of the Caribbean. Perhaps the oldest prawn recipe of the islands is for a Jamaican soup that has been handed down in the Pringle family's centuries-old cookery book. The concoction, based on the flesh of the prawn, is strengthened by the addition of the pounded heads, tails and shells and is then given body with a "penny ha'penny worth of salt pork or beef". There is also a host of memorable modern prawn dishes, among them prawns stuffed with anchovy paste, prawn curry and prawn Creole (*Recipe Index*). The latter, which like most Creole dishes is always made

Flying fish are not only exotic but also extremely good to eat. Their wings are actually extended pectoral fins that sustain the fish in a long glide after it leaps from the water when fleeing danger. Common to most tropical waters, flying fish are especially plentiful off Barbados, where this one was caught. The island has even built a cannery and a freezing plant, with the aim of exporting its most elusive delicacy.

with tomato, has become a standing prawn dish in other parts of the world as well.

Perhaps the most famous marine delicacy of the Caribbean is green turtle, the most delicious sea turtle in the World. Its history is an unfortunate one, intimately linked to that of the region. The green turtle used to nest all over the islands in great numbers. When mature, it is as big as a young cow, but it is easy to catch and if turned on its back cannot move; furthermore, it stays alive for months with practically no food. The advantages for transatlantic voyagers were obvious, and so naval and merchant ships of both the British and Spanish fleets carried live green turtles on their journeys home. They proved to be an ideal source of food, providing fresh meat that served both to prevent scurvy and to maintain morale.

So gratifying were the soups and steaks made from the ships' turtle stores that captains began stocking enough not only to feed their crews but to sell, at the high prices imports always commanded, to rich and royal Europeans. Turtle became a dish of ceremonial stature. In England an Alderman's banquet, a traditional feast held by officials of the old City of London guilds, was thought to be inadequate if it did not begin with turtle soup. Eventually the green turtle itself came to be called the London alderman's turtle.

Popular though it may have been, the turtle meat that reached England was not, as a rule, exactly fresh. A traveller to the islands in the middle of the 17th century, promised that she would get so much turtle she would soon be surfeited with it, did not particularly relish the prospect since the turtle meat she had tasted in London, at great expense, had always been old and tough. But it was another story when she got to Antigua. "I have now seen Turtle almost every day," she wrote, "and though I never could eat it at home, am vastly fond of it here . . . where it is indeed a very different thing. You get nothing but old ones there, the chickens being unable to stand the voyage; even these are starved or at best fed on coarse and improper food. Here they are young, tender, fresh from the water, where they feed as delicately and are as great Epicures, as those who feed on them. They laugh at us for the racket we make to have it divided into different dishes. They never make but two, the soup and the shell . . . The shell indeed is a noble dish, as it contains all the fine parts of the Turtle baked within its own body . . . Could an Alderman of true taste conceive the difference between it here and in the City, he would make the Voyage on purpose, and I fancy he would make a voyage into the other world before he left the table."

Inevitably the turtle suffered as a result of its popularity. Though well protected within its shell from most natural predators, it is an easy prey for man. Strong swimmers can catch turtles with little trouble by driving them into large nets. Furthermore, the turtle's eggs, considered as much a delicacy as its meat, are particularly vulnerable—the female lays them in a shallow nest in the sand a few yards from the water's edge, then crawls back to the sea leaving the eggs unguarded. Egg hunters can in effect eliminate a whole generation of turtles on one collecting foray.

As early as 1620 the danger to the species was recognized, and laws were passed in the islands against those "lewd and improvident persons" who would "snatch and catch up indifferentlye all kinds of Tortoyses both yonge and old, little and greate, and soe kill, carrye awaye and devour them to the much decay of the breed . . ." But the laws had only limited effect. Through the following centuries the turtles continued to be caught in such numbers, and their nesting grounds raided so ruthlessly, that the Caribbean green turtle has long been threatened with extinction.

Today there are only two places in the Caribbean where the turtle nests in any number. One is the Bay of Tortuguero on the north-eastern coast of Costa Rica in the western Caribbean; the other is the remote Aves Island near Montserrat in the eastern Caribbean. It is fitting that Aves still provides a home for the vanishing turtle, since it is itself apparently sinking slowly under the sea. Also appropriately, it was at Aves that my favourite raconteur of the old days in the Caribbean, Père Labat, once landed in the company of pirates who rapidly acquired a full load of green turtles. The good priest, although he was keeping bad company at the time, was grateful to God for sending him to so generous albeit barren an island, and he repaid its hospitality by planting orange and lime trees on it.

Today on Aves and at Tortuguero the nesting turtles are effectively protected from modern pirates and over-ambitious fishermen by an international effort—called Operation Green Turtle—aimed at keeping the species from disappearing altogether. And green turtle, while still caught at the right season in Caribbean waters, is now hard to find on hotel and restaurant menus.

I was determined to have some turtle on my last trip to the islands, but the quest was disappointing. In Barbados I had a fine green turtle soup, laced with sherry and tasting rich and salty, but at a famous seafood restaurant in Ponce, Puerto Rico, the turtle steak I had made me decide that the ability to cook turtle correctly is vanishing together with the turtle itself. Although the creature on my plate had the fine, meaty flavour of turtle, it was so swathed in breadcrumbs, onions and garlic that it was smothered. The chief offender was garlic, that Johnny-come-lately to the islands, whose flavour is too potent for the subtle turtle meat.

The Caribbean offers still other fruits of the sea to be sampled. The dolphin, a fish with firm, white swordfish-like flesh, is not related to the endearing mammal known either as dolphin or porpoise, except in one characteristic—like the porpoise it is an inquisitive creature, and when the captains of fishing vessels go looking for it in the Caribbean they go out of their way to troll past any log, box or sunken wreckage where the fish might be exploring. Another local speciality is bone-fish, a skinny, belligerent species that provides spectacular game fishing in the islands' coral shallows. The islanders have an ingenious way of stretching a bone-fish before cooking it in order to remove the many tiny bones from its otherwise excellent flesh.

King-fish, grouper and Spanish mackerel are also succulent Caribbean fish, and so are other denizens of the islands' waters that are harder to identify because the names by which they are locally known are so odd. Jamaicans, in particular, are good at inventing names, and you will not fail to be delighted by their skill even though you may find it difficult to understand just what you are buying at the market. Among my favourite fish names are the go-far, a turbot so called because "it could share to a lot of people"; the John Mariggle, a long tapered fish so called because it is tricky and it "jump and try to shake out hook"; the God-a-me, a small fish that hides in the mud of rivers and is named for its scared-looking expression when caught; and the sea Anancy, a spider crab called after the greatest folk hero in the islands, Anancy, a shrewd half spider, half man whose legendary exploits were told and retold by the African slaves and who is still remembered in all the islands today.

Not only the names of Caribbean fish but their shapes as well can be remarkable and sometimes even bizarre. There is the coffer-fish, which is square-shaped like a chest of buried treasure, the moon-fish, which is round and silvery, and the fish the people on Martinique call *bon-Dié manié moin*—"good God handled me"—which bears unearthly fingerprints along its sides. And among the strangest-looking of all are two creatures that provide some of the finest food from the sea to be had in the Caribbean.

One of these is the conch, called lambi in most islands. Americans know the conch less for its flesh than for its pretty rose-tinted shell, which has become almost a cliché as a symbol of the islands. When the conch itself comes out of its iridescent house it is a veritable monster of the sea, an enormous snail with big horns and a bright golden eye in the tip of each horn. It can be up to a foot long, and its muscular white flesh is almost as compact as cartilage. Before it can be cooked it must be patiently marinated and then furiously pounded with a wooden beater. "He beat him like a lambi" is a phrase that has often been heard in island court-rooms from witnesses testifying in cases of assault and battery. But when the lambi has been marinated and tenderized it can be superb. I have eaten it raw in salads and stewed in chowders on many islands, and often marvelled at how soft and chewy it can become— though I confess that when improperly prepared it can have the consistency of a rubber truncheon. I like it best the way it is done in Guadeloupe, cooked in a brown sauce flavoured with nutmeg, cinnamon, thyme, peppers and lots of sweet lime juice.

Another fearsome-looking but fine-tasting delicacy is the sea egg, a kind of sea-urchin and a cousin of the sinister black urchin whose sharp poisonous spines are a hazard to bathers all over the West Indies. The sea egg is white and lacks the dangerous spines of the black urchin, but I still do not find it a congenial creature. After a day of nervously looking out for sea-urchins and eggs under my feet while swimming from a beach at Barbados I felt quite justified in eating them—when they were first offered to me by a local youth who was catching them barehanded. Deftly splitting them open with a thin stone, he dispensed them with slices of fresh lime, which emphasised their sea-salty taste.

They were intriguing in this natural state, but even better when they were served to me in a private house in Barbados, cooked in the way the islanders prefer—sautéed in butter and well blended with onions. My husband and I had been invited to try them by some friends, and I thought our hostess, a 20 year old newlywed, had overestimated our appetites when she brought to the table a two foot long platter heaped with fluffy yellow sea eggs. "She's a good cook," her husband confided when he saw me staring at the platter, "but she doesn't know how much to make. She never makes enough." I looked at him incredulously, but it turned out he was right. The texture of the sea eggs was so light and airy, almost as insubstantial as candy floss, and their flavour so compelling that I realized it would be almost impossible ever to serve enough of them. We washed them down with mauby, a local drink made from the bark of a tropical tree. Mauby's bitter-sweet taste was just the right accompaniment to the salty, oniony urchins. In no time the four of us had emptied the fat pitcher of mauby and devoured the pile of sea eggs.

Curiously, it is often difficult to obtain fish in the islands. Although there is a great need for protein in the Caribbean diet, relatively little fish is eaten. Sociologists and ethnologists have puzzled over this and one has even reached the stark conclusion that "Caribbean people do not like fish". The truth of the matter is that the resources of the ocean have only just begun to be properly utilized. Fish spoils rapidly in the tropical heat; ice and refrigeration on fishing boats and in markets are even today not commonly available. In the small islands housewives have to go to the town docks or wait on the shore for the little boats to pull in, hoping to be able to buy fish. Often they are turned away because the poverty of the fishermen prevents them from owning any but the simplest and most inefficient equipment; as a result their catch is too small even for their own needs. The most common fishing-boat in the islands is still a narrow craft shaped like a dug-out canoe, varying in length from 10 to 35 feet. Hooks and lines, harpoons, nets made of wire and twine, wooden traps, spears and even bows and arrows are still in common use.

Furthermore, even though the islands are washed by the waters of the Atlantic and Caribbean, many of them, such as Puerto Rico, have virtually no seafaring tradition. The slaves who were taken there came mostly from the African jungle, and for generations afterwards were allowed to do nothing but work in the cane fields. They never acquired the skills of the sea, and many islanders today regard the waters around them as a hostile element.

Many others, however, are as much at home afloat as ashore. In Aruba there are blue-eyed, bronze-skinned fishermen who are said to be descendants of the island's original Indian population and the early European settlers; they handle their cleavers as deftly as Chinese chefs and can slice firm shark meat to precise inch thick fillets on clumsy chopping blocks set up along the beach. Their profession is hereditary and they are extremely proud of their skills. So are the last of the Caribs in Dominica, who still practise their ancient art of building *gommiers*, dug-outs made from huge tree trunks, in which, using only oars and sails, they go out fishing every day.

Perhaps the most famous mariners in the Caribbean are the inhabitants of the tiny Cayman Islands. The inhabitants, superb seamen who have handed down their seafaring skills from generation to generation, were especially gifted at turtle fishing, and they sailed in search of their quarry to every strand, however remote, in the western Caribbean. With the gradual disappearance of turtle fishing, they have gone on to other seafaring work; today they serve aboard the tankers and merchantmen of most of the great maritime nations of the world.

I do not believe that the islanders don't like fish. I wish the sociologists and ethnologists who say they don't could eat in some of the houses I have eaten in and enjoy some of the memorable Caribbean ways of preparing fish, or witness the intense enthusiasm among the village crowds when the fishing boats pull in. But it is true that the supply in many islands is inadequate and that only when the methods of catching and storing fish are improved will Caribbean recipes for cooking fish truly come into their own.

Kershy Yena coe Cabaron (Curaçao)
BAKED EDAM CHEESE WITH PRAWN STUFFING

To serve 6 to 8

Peel the cheese and cut a 1-inch-thick slice off the top. Scoop out the centre of the cheese with a spoon, leaving a boat-like shell about ½ inch thick. Hollow the slice from the top in the same way to make a lid for the shell. Place the lid and shell in a large pan or bowl, pour in enough cold water to cover them by at least 1 inch, and let them soak for 1 hour.

Meanwhile, grate enough of the scooped-out cheese to make ¾ pint and set it aside. Shell the prawns. De-vein them by making a shallow incision down their backs with a small, sharp knife and lifting out their intestinal veins with the point of the knife. If the prawns are small, leave them whole; if they are large, cut them into ½-inch-long pieces.

Remove the cheese shell and lid from the water and invert them on kitchen paper to drain.

Preheat the oven to Mark 4: 350° F. Spread the ½ ounce of softened butter evenly over the bottom and sides of a round baking dish at least 5 inches deep and just large enough to hold the cheese compactly, using a pastry brush. (If the dish is too shallow or too large, the cheese will collapse and spread when it is baked.)

Melt the remaining ounce of butter in the vegetable oil in a heavy, medium-sized frying-pan over a moderate heat. Drop in the onions and cook for about 5 minutes, stirring frequently, until they are soft and transparent but not brown. Watch carefully for any sign of burning and adjust the heat accordingly. Add the tomato, red pepper, salt and a few grindings of black pepper and cook briskly, still stirring, until most of the liquid in the pan has evaporated and the mixture is thick enough to hold its shape almost solidly in the spoon.

Transfer the entire contents of the pan to a deep bowl with a rubber spatula. Add the grated cheese, prawns, breadcrumbs, olives, gherkin, and raisins, and toss together thoroughly but gently. Taste for seasoning, then stir in the beaten egg. Spoon the prawn mixture into the cheese shell, place the shell in the prepared dish, and top it with the cheese lid.

Bake uncovered on the middle shelf of the oven for about 30 minutes, until the top is bubbly and delicately browned. Serve the *keshy yena* at once, straight from the baking dish.

A 4-pound Edam cheese
12 oz. raw prawns
½ oz. butter, softened, plus
   1 oz. butter
2½ teaspoons vegetable oil
¼ oz. finely chopped onions
1 medium-sized firm ripe tomato,
   peeled, seeded and finely chopped
   (*see sopa de gandules*, *Recipe Index*),
   or substitute a 5-oz. can chopped
   drained tomatoes
¼ teaspoon ground hot red pepper
½ teaspoon salt
Freshly ground black pepper
3 tablespoons soft fresh crumbs
   made from white bread,
   trimmed of crusts and prepared
   in a blender or finely shredded
   with a fork
6 small pimiento-stuffed olives,
   drained and finely chopped
2½ teaspoons finely chopped sweet
   gherkin
1½ tablespoons seedless raisins
1 egg, well beaten

Fish Stock

To make about 2 pints

Put the fish trimmings, onion, parsley, bay leaf and salt into a medium-sized glass, enamel or stainless-steel saucepan. Pour in the water and bring to the boil over a high heat. Reduce the heat to low, partly cover the pan, and simmer for 30 minutes.

Strain the stock through a fine sieve set over a deep bowl, pressing down hard on the fish trimmings with the back of a spoon to extract their juices before discarding them. Cover tightly and refrigerate until ready to use. Fish stock may be frozen and stored in the freezer for months; it may be kept in the refrigerator for about a week if brought to the boil every second day.

2 lb. fish trimmings: bones,
   heads and tails from any white-
   fleshed fish
1 medium-sized onion, peeled and
   thickly sliced
4 parsley sprigs
1 bay leaf
1 teaspoon salt
2½ pints water

Curaçao's *keshy yena*, a baked Edam, is shown on the left with prawn filling.

To serve 2

2 uncooked 1½- to 2-lb. lobsters,
    split in half lengthways
2½ tablespoons vegetable oil
    mixed with 1 teaspoon liquid
    annatto
⅜ pint dry white wine
¾ pint *sofrito* (*Recipe Index*)
1 scant teaspoon finely chopped
    fresh hot chillies (*caution:
    "How to Handle Chillies"*)
1 teaspoon salt

Langosta Criolla (*Cuba*)
BRAISED LOBSTER IN CHILLI SAUCE

Remove and discard the gelatinous sac in the head of each lobster and
the long intestinal vein attached to it. Then scoop out and set aside the
greenish brown liver and the black caviar-like eggs (or coral) if any.
Chop off the tail section of each lobster directly at the point where it
joins the body. Twist off the claws and gash the flat underside of each
large claw with a large, heavy knife. Cut off and discard the small claws
and the antennae.

Heat the oil over a high heat in a large, heavy frying-pan until a light
haze forms above it. Add the lobster bodies, tails and large claws and,
turning them constantly, fry them for 3 to 4 minutes, until the shells
begin to turn pink. Transfer the lobsters to a large plate or bowl.

Pour off all but a thin layer of oil from the pan, add the wine, and
bring to the boil over a high heat. Stir in the *sofrito*, chillies and salt,
and return the lobsters and any liquid accumulation around them to the
pan. Turn the pieces over in the sauce to coat them evenly, reduce the
heat to moderate, and cover the pan tightly. Cook for 8 to 10 minutes,
basting the lobsters from time to time with a large spoon.

Just before serving, rub the reserved liver and coral through a fine
sieve with the back of a spoon directly into the sauce. Simmer the sauce
for a minute or so longer, stirring gently, then taste for seasoning. To
serve, arrange the lobster pieces attractively in a large, deep, heated dish
and spoon the sauce over them.

To make about ¾ pint

2 oz. salt pork, finely diced
1 teaspoon vegetable oil, mixed with
    3 drops liquid annatto
6 oz. finely chopped onions
2½ teaspoons finely chopped garlic
2 medium-sized green peppers, the
    seeds and white pith removed,
    and coarsely chopped
4 oz. lean boneless ham, cut
    into ½-inch dice
2 large tomatoes, peeled, seeded and
    coarsely chopped (*see sopa de
    gandules, Recipe Index*), or sub-
    stitute three 8-oz. cans chopped
    drained tomatoes
1¼ teaspoons finely chopped fresh
    coriander (*see Glossary*)
½ teaspoon crumbled dried oregano
1 teaspoon salt
Freshly ground black pepper

Sofrito
SPICED TOMATO COOKING SAUCE

*"Sofrito" is a basic cooking sauce that is widely used in Spain and was brought to
the Caribbean centuries ago by the Spanish settlers. Although some foods require
a special and freshly made "sofrito," many dishes can be based on the all-purpose
mixture below, which can be made ahead in large quantity and either stored in the
refrigerator for a week or two or frozen.*

Fry the salt pork over a moderate heat in a large, heavy frying-pan,
turning the dice over frequently with a spoon until they are crisp and
brown and have rendered all their fat. Remove and discard the dice
with a perforated spoon, and add the annatto-flavoured oil to the fat
remaining in the pan.

Drop in the onions, garlic and peppers and cook for 5 to 10 minutes,
stirring frequently, until the vegetables are soft but not brown. Watch
carefully for any sign of burning and adjust the heat accordingly.

Add the diced ham and stir until all the pieces glisten with oil. Then
stir in the chopped tomatoes, coriander, oregano, salt and a few grindings of black pepper. Reduce the heat to low, cover tightly, and simmer
for 30 minutes, stirring the mixture from time to time to prevent the
vegetables from sticking to the bottom of the pan.

Ladle the *sofrito* into a large, clean jar or bowl, cover tightly, and refrigerate until ready to use. It can be kept for one to two weeks. For
longer storage, ladle the *sofrito* immediately into hot sterilized preserving jars, filling them to within ⅛ inch of the top. Each jar should be
sealed quickly and tightly with a sterilized ring and lid.

In the Caribbean, lobster Creole is made from local *langoustes*, or spiny lobsters, but the big-clawed northern lobster can be substituted successfully as shown here. In the Spanish-speaking islands this savoury blend of seafood, wine, tomatoes, onions and peppers is called *langosta criolla*—a lilting name that can be translated as lobsters in chilli or hot-pepper sauce.

Three members of the onion family—shallots, spring onions and garlic—team up to give pungency to Martinique's *court bouillon à la créole*, a classic dish that superbly blends the fruits of the sea and the land. It may be made either with small fish cut in half (*left*) or with big fish cut into steaks (*right*). In either case, annatto-flavoured oil colours the sauce, and the limes and hot peppers are used as decorations.

To serve 2

1½ pints water
6 tablespoons plus 1 teaspoon
    strained fresh lime juice
2½ teaspoons salt
2 one-lb. firm white-flesh fish,
    each scaled, cleaned and cut
    crosswise into halves, or four 8-oz.
    fish steaks, each cut about 1 inch
    thick
2 oz. finely chopped onions
2½ teaspoons finely chopped garlic
1 scant teaspoon finely chopped
    fresh hot chillies (*caution: see
    "How to Handle Chillies"*)
2 bay rum berries or leaves (*see
    Glossary*)
4 parsley sprigs
½ teaspoon dried thyme

Blaff (*Martinique*)
POACHED MARINATED FISH IN LIME AND HERB BROTH

Put ¾ pint of the water, 6 tablespoons of the lime juice and 1 teaspoon of salt into a large, shallow glass or ceramic baking dish, and stir until the salt dissolves completely.

Wash the fish under cold running water and place them in the juice mixture. The liquid should cover the fish completely; add more water if necessary. Let the fish marinate at room temperature for about 1 hour, then drain off and discard the marinade.

Pour the remaining ¾ pint of water into a heavy, medium-sized frying-pan and add the onions, garlic, chillies, bay rum berries or leaves, parsley and thyme. Bring to the boil over a high heat, reduce the heat to low, cover tightly and simmer for 5 minutes.

Add the fish to the pan and bring to the boil again. Reduce the heat to the lowest possible point, cover, and simmer for about 8 to 10 minutes, until the fish feels firm when pressed lightly with a finger, or the steaks flake easily when prodded with a fork.

Transfer the fish to a deep, heated dish with a perforated spoon. Add the remaining teaspoon of lime juice to the cooking liquid, and taste for seasoning. Pour the broth over the fish and serve at once.

NOTE: Any fish with firm white flesh may be used for either the blaff or the *court bouillon à la créole*. In the islands, these dishes are made with red snapper as well as with more exotic local species.

146

Court Bouillon à la Créole (Martinique)

BRAISED MARINATED FISH WITH TOMATO, SHALLOT AND GARLIC SAUCE

Put ¾ pint of the water, 6 tablespoons of the lime juice and 2½ teaspoons of salt into a large, shallow glass or china baking dish and stir until the salt dissolves. Wash the fish pieces under cold running water and place them in the lime juice mixture. The liquid should cover the fish completely; add more water if necessary. Let the fish marinate for about 1 hour, then pour off the marinade.

Heat the annatto-flavoured oil over a moderate heat in a large, heavy frying-pan until a light haze forms above it. Drop in the shallots, spring onions, 2½ teaspoons of the garlic and the chillies and cook for about 5 minutes, stirring frequently, until they are soft but not brown. Watch carefully for any sign of burning and adjust the heat accordingly. Add the tomatoes, the bouquet, the dried thyme and a few grindings of black pepper and simmer for about 6 to 8 minutes, stirring frequently.

Stir in the remaining 6 tablespoons of water, add the fish pieces and baste them with the sauce. Bring to the boil over a high heat, reduce the heat to low, cover tightly and simmer for about 8 to 10 minutes, until the fish feels firm when pressed lightly with a finger, or flakes easily when prodded with a fork. Do not overcook.

Transfer the fish to a heated dish with a perforated spoon. Add the olive oil, the remaining 2½ teaspoons of lime juice and 1½ teaspoons of garlic to the tomato mixture. Bring the sauce to the boil over a moderate heat, stirring constantly. Taste for seasoning and pour the sauce over the fish. Serve at once.

To serve 4

1 pint water
6 tablespoons plus 2½ teaspoons strained fresh lime juice
2½ teaspoons salt
Two 1- to 1½-lb. firm white-flesh fish, scaled, cleaned and cut crosswise into halves, or four 8-oz. fish steaks, each cut about 1 inch thick
3 tablespoons vegetable oil mixed with 1 teaspoon liquid annatto
4½ oz. peeled finely chopped shallots
1¾ oz. finely chopped spring onions
4 teaspoons finely chopped garlic
1 scant teaspoon finely chopped fresh hot chillies (*caution: see "How to Handle Chillies"*)
3 medium-sized firm ripe tomatoes, peeled, seeded and finely chopped (*see sopa de gandules, Recipe Index*)
A bouquet of 4 parsley sprigs and 1 bay leaf tied together with string
⅛ teaspoon dried thyme
Freshly ground black pepper
1½ tablespoons olive oil

1 large onion, peeled and cut
    crosswise into thin slices
1 medium-sized garlic clove, peeled
    and crushed with the flat side of
    a heavy knife
2 oz. finely chopped carrots
2 oz. finely chopped celery
    including the leaves
1½ tablespoons finely chopped fresh
    parsley
1 medium-sized bay leaf, crumbled
¼ teaspoon crumbled dried thyme
¼ teaspoon crumbled dried oregano
2½ teaspoons salt
5 whole black peppercorns, wrapped
    in a tea towel and crushed
    with a rolling pin
6 tablespoons strained fresh lime
    juice

FISH
A 5- to 6-lb. red snapper or
    striped bass, cleaned and scaled
    but with head and tail left on, or
    substitute any other whole firm
    white-fleshed fish

AVOCADO SAUCE
2 large ripe avocados
2½ tablespoons strained fresh lime
    juice
2½ teaspoons finely grated onion
1 teaspoon salt
Freshly ground black pepper
2½ tablespoons vegetable oil

Pescado con Salsa de Anguacate (*Cuba*)
COLD POACHED FISH WITH AVOCADO SAUCE

Put the sliced onion, garlic, carrots, celery, parsley, bay leaf, thyme, oregano, 2½ teaspoons salt and peppercorns into a fish poacher or a large, deep roasting tin with a cover. Pour in the lime juice and 5 pints of water, and bring to the boil over a high heat. Lower the heat, partly cover the pan, and simmer for 20 minutes. Then let the liquid cool to lukewarm.

Wash the fish inside and out under cold running water. Wrap the fish, without drying it, in a long double-thick piece of cheesecloth, leaving at least 6 inches of cloth at each end.

Twist the ends of the cloth, tie them with string, then place the fish on the rack of the poacher or roasting tin and lower the rack into the poaching liquid. (If you are using a roasting tin, tie the strings at the ends of the cheesecloth to the handles of the pan.) The liquid should cover the fish by at least 1 inch; add water if necessary.

Bring almost but not quite to the boil over a high heat, cover tightly, and reduce the heat to the lowest point. Simmer for about 30 to 40 minutes, until the thickest part of the fish feels firm when pressed with a finger.

Lift the fish from the pan, using the ends of the cheesecloth as handles, and lay it on a large board or dish. Open the cheesecloth and skin the fish with a small, sharp knife by making a cut in the skin at the base of the tail and gently pulling off the skin in strips from tail to gill. Holding both ends of the cheesecloth, carefully lift the fish and turn it over onto a serving dish. Remove the skin on the upturned side.

Let the fish cool to room temperature, cover it with foil or a sheet of plastic, and refrigerate it for at least 4 hours, until it is thoroughly chilled.

Meanwhile, prepare the sauce. Cut the avocados in half. Loosen the seeds with the tip of a small knife, and lift them out. Remove any brown fibres clinging to the flesh. Strip off the skin with your fingers, starting at the narrow or stalk end. (The dark-skinned variety does not peel easily; if necessary use a knife to pull the skin away.)

Chop the avocados coarsely, then purée them through a food mill set over a bowl, or press them through a fine sieve with the back of a spoon. Add the lime juice, the grated onion and salt and a few grindings of black pepper, and mix well. Then beat in the olive oil, a teaspoonful or so at a time. Taste the sauce for seasoning.

The finished sauce should have the consistency of mayonnaise. To prevent it from darkening as it stands, cover the sauce with a sheet of plastic or foil and refrigerate until ready to use.

Just before serving, spread ⅜ pint of the avocado sauce evenly and thickly over the skinned body of the fish. Garnish the dish, as elaborately as you like, with tomatoes, parsley sprigs, olives or sliced lime, and serve the rest of the sauce in a bowl or sauceboat.

Cut the fish into serving pieces as follows: Cut the top layer into individual portions with a sharp knife, without cutting through the spine. Leave the head and tail intact.

Lift out the portions with a fish slice and a fork, and place them on serving plates. Then gently lift out the backbone in one piece, discard it and divide the bottom layer of the fish into individual portions as before. Spoon a little of the reserved sauce over each portion.

Cuba's elegant *pescado con salsa de aguacate* is a cold poached fish, adorned with avocado sauce, tomatoes and cucumbers.

Camarones Rellenos *(Dominican Republic)*
DEEP-FRIED PRAWNS WITH ANCHOVY STUFFING

To prepare the batter, pour the flour into a deep bowl, make a well in the centre and add the egg yolk, beer and salt. Stir the ingredients together and gradually pour in the melted butter. Continue to stir until the batter is smooth. Do not overmix. Let the batter rest for at least 30 minutes. Then beat the egg white until stiff and fold it into the batter.

Cream the butter with a wooden spoon in a mixing bowl, mashing and beating it against the sides of the bowl until light and fluffy. Beat in the anchovy paste, onion, lime juice and a few grindings of pepper. When the mixture is smooth, stir in the breadcrumbs, a few tablespoons at a time. Refrigerate the stuffing for at least 20 minutes, until fairly firm.

Shell the prawns. Make an incision about $\frac{1}{4}$ inch deep down their backs with a small, sharp knife and lift out the intestinal vein with the point of the knife. Be careful not to cut too deeply or the prawn may split in half.

Fill a deep-frying pan or large saucepan with vegetable oil to a depth of 3 inches and heat the oil to a temperature of 350° F.

With your fingers, force about 1 teaspoon of the anchovy stuffing into the cavity of each prawn and press the openings together to enclose it. Dip the prawns in the remaining 4 ounces of flour and lightly shake off the excess. Place the prawns, two at a time, in a perforated spoon and immerse them in the batter. Immediately drop the prawns into the hot oil and deep-fry them for 6 to 7 minutes, turning them over occasionally until golden on all sides. Transfer them to kitchen paper to drain as they brown. Serve at once.

To serve 4

BATTER
4 oz. plain flour
1 egg yolk
$\frac{3}{8}$ pint flat beer
1 teaspoon salt
1 oz. butter, melted
1 egg white

STUFFING
2 oz. butter, softened
3 tablespoons anchovy paste
1½ tablespoons finely grated onion
1½ tablespoons strained fresh lime juice
Freshly ground black pepper
1 oz. fresh soft crumbs, made from white bread, prepared in a blender or finely shredded with a fork

PRAWNS
2 lb. large raw prawns (12 to 15 per lb.)
4 oz. plain flour
Vegetable oil for deep frying

149

VII

Tourism: Mother of Culinary Invention

Fancy-dress desserts, as well as picture-book sunsets, are part of the glamour of Caribbean hotels. At the Miramar in Barbados the desserts range from a chocolate mousse called Pitch Lake pudding (*top left*) to an island-inspired cake (*bottom right*) called corn pone (*Recipe Index*). With them are a fruit trifle (*top right*), a coconut pie (*centre*) and a tray of candied coconut.

There are two Caribbeans—the mythical one and the real one. The mythical Caribbean is a string of island paradises always fertile and free of rain and peopled by happy islanders trilling calypso songs day and night. In the myth the sea is so filled with fish and the fruit trees are so laden that a hungry man has to do little more than stretch out his arm to satisfy his every need.

The makers of this myth are travel agents, travel writers and hotel and airline representatives, and most people are all too willing to believe their story. I have some friends who, though ordinarily quite realistic, fell total victims to it. In a travel article about picturesque Dominica they read that although there were no restaurants in the rugged interior, it was possible to walk across the island and fill oneself by eating fruit off the trees. My friends forthwith decided to holiday in Dominica and to walk across it, eating fruit.

Naturally they came right up against the real Caribbean. There was very little fruit to be picked off the trees. Tropical fruits, like northern fruits, are seasonal; they are not ripe all the year round. Moreover, tropical society, like northern society, is capitalistic. Most fruit trees grow on land that is owned by someone, therefore out-of-bounds to would-be fruit pickers. My friends discovered this in time, and on their walks they sensibly took ham sandwiches with them. However, although it was February and the height of the tourist season, the rain fell steadily for four days and they were forced to turn back several times. They returned to New York soggy, disappointed and untanned, having set out for the mythical Caribbean and having spent their holiday in the real one—which *is* beautiful, to be sure, but no help-yourself paradise.

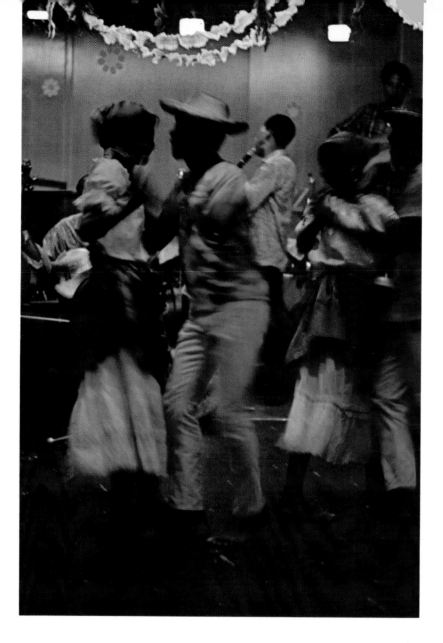

Nearly 80,000 cruise-ship passengers visit Martinique in a year, and many of them are entertained by these lively dancers, who are members of the Groupe Folklorique Martiniquais. Dressed in cheerful island costumes, they perform both at the tourist hotels and aboard vessels moored at Fort-de-France, diverting tourists with traditional dances.

The real Caribbean, on the contrary, is a region of distressing poverty. In many of the islands the economy has been languishing for a hundred years. Agriculture is not only poorly organized and handicapped by old-fashioned farming and marketing techniques but it is constantly threatened by hurricanes, plant diseases and serious soil deficiencies. There is not much fish to be had in the markets because the fishing industry is underdeveloped. Very little cattle is raised on the islands and, where it is, the meat obtained is often sold before being properly hung and is invariably badly butchered. As for calypso songs, they began as songs of protest against the conditions of Caribbean life. Many islanders emigrate, when they can, to more prosperous parts of the world. And of course it does rain, even in the holiday season.

I do not want to be a myth maker about the food of the Caribbean. The cooking at most hotels and restaurants still has a long way to go before it can match the menus in other celebrated tourist centres of the world. But the process is under way, encouraged by the interaction of two groups who make odd collaborators, the tourists and the islands' political nationalists.

Getting a meal of local food in the Caribbean has been a problem for the traveller for a long time. When Anthony Trollope visited Jamaica in 1859 he complained that his hosts sneered at the local fruits and recipes he had longed to try, and fed him on canned meats and canned potatoes. He had steak and onions for breakfast, a veritable ocean of oxtail soup at mid-day, and imported cheeses to end the meal. It was because of sheer snobbery, he concluded, that nothing was considered of value by the colonials in the islands unless it came from Europe.

When the modern age of tourism began almost a century later, hoteliers took up the same attitude. They did not serve indigenous food partly because it was difficult to obtain in reliable quantity and of consistent quality, but mostly because they felt that the local cooking simply was not interesting enough to serve in their dining-rooms. Furthermore they believed that the sort of tourist who came to the Caribbean, obsessed with sun and sand and indifferent to experiment, would not want to try the local cooking anyway.

There was, in fact, some truth in this. Large-scale tourism in the Caribbean is a fairly new phenomenon. The first commercial flight from the United States was made in 1928, in a three-engined Fokker aeroplane that carried seven passengers from Key West to Havana. Before that, and for a long while afterwards as well, Americans visiting the islands went as Columbus had, by ship. They were likely to be older people with money and plenty of leisure, and they also were likely to regard the region as a kind of tropical rest home. When they wanted adventure they went to Europe; when they wanted to rest and recuperate they went to the Caribbean.

Jet air strips have been built on dozens of islands and direct flights from the United States now penetrate to the furthest corners of the Caribbean and a network of air routes reaches even to tiny outposts like Anguilla and Little Cayman. From England British Airways and other major airline carriers operate direct services to the Bahamas, to Kingston and Montego Bay in Jamaica, to Barbados, Antigua, St. Lucia and to San Juan in Puerto Rico. Tourism increased greatly in the 1960s and 1970s and in the early 1980s is around 7.0 million a year. The main tourist invasion is from the United States and Canada, with the numbers from Europe and Great Britain rising more slowly in recent years as the tying of the Caribbean currencies to the U.S. dollar has had the effect of making the area more expensive to non-North American visitors.

Compared to the pre-war tourists, most of the new travellers are younger, less wealthy and more adventurous. They want sun and sand, of course, but they want something else as well. They are bent on experiencing a way of life different from the one they know at home. Since one of the most pleasant ways to learn about a new culture is quite literally to taste it, the tourists themselves have begun asking hotel owners why their restaurants serve imported pears instead of pawpaw, fillet of sole instead of local snapper, baked potatoes instead of breadfruit.

And at the same time as the tourist is seeking to experience Caribbean culture, the culture itself is changing. In the 1950s the Caribbean urge for independence grew to epidemic proportions; more and more, the islanders took control over their islands and their destinies. Newly conscious of their heritage, however un-European it might be, they were determined to emphasize it. The results are apparent everywhere in the Caribbean today, both in the newly independent islands and in

Continued on page 156

153

How a Local Pumpkin Made Good as Cinderella's Coach

Unlike Cinderella's pumpkin, which was round and orange, the Jamaican variety looks like a large green marrow with a long neck. Despite its differences, Lucille Tyson turned it into a fairy-tale coach that won a prize in the Jamaican Culinary Arts Competition. Her first step was to prepare the pumpkin by scrubbing it clean and cutting it in half lengthways. She chose the handsomer half for the coach, scraped out the seeds and the stringy fibres to create a hollow shell, and notched the edge in a saw-tooth pattern to make a decorative rim round it. Here, she rubs the cut surfaces with a piece of lime to prevent discoloration.

To fill the shell, Miss Tyson invented a rice, prawn and coconut-milk mixture; here she is squeezing the milk from the freshly grated coconut. Next she boiled some prawns to use as the coachman and horses, and she marinated others for a garnish.

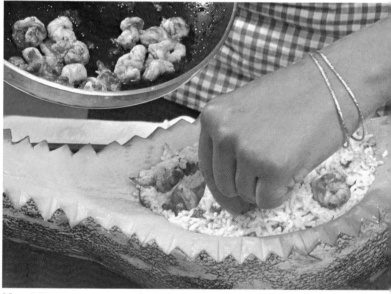

To precook the body of the coach, Miss Tyson has set the pumpkin in a large pan, immersed it in water to its neck, and is simmering it for 30 minutes. The trick is to make the pumpkin tender but keep the shell firm enough to hold the filling without collapsing. After cooking, the pumpkin was turned upside down to drain.

Now Miss Tyson works on the filling. She has already sautéed the marinated prawns in one pan until they turned pink. In another pan, she cooked a little of the raw pumpkin in the coconut milk, and seasoned the mixture with tomatoes, spring onions and rum before adding rice. When the rice was almost tender, she stirred in fresh prawns and some lime juice and simmered them all until cooked. Here, having spooned the filling into the hollow of the pumpkin, she arranges the sautéed prawns over it. The next step is to bake the stuffed pumpkin until it becomes tinged with gold.

154

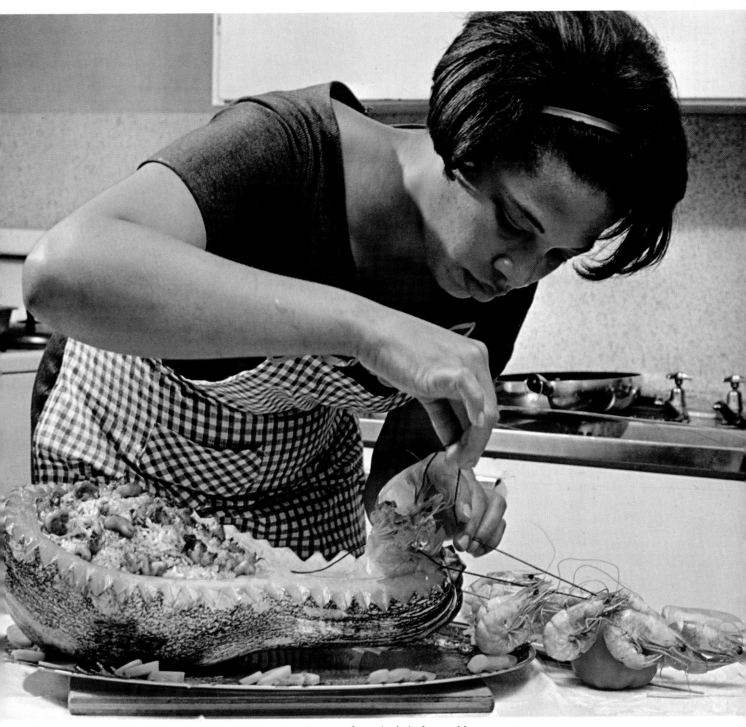

Finally, Miss Tyson adds the finishing touches that transform the baked pumpkin into a proper coach. Here she places a boiled prawn at the front of the pumpkin neck to sit as Cinderella's coachman, in front of a lettuce leaf that represents the back of his seat. The remaining boiled prawns serve as horses; they are held in place with lengths of coconut fibre as reins, and the pair in front is propped up on a tomato. Later Miss Tyson pinned four large slices of tomato to the sides of the pumpkin with toothpicks to simulate wheels and complete the illusion of Cinderella's coach. The complete recipe is in the Recipe Booklet.

those that retain their ties with Europe. Trinidad shows the tourist its way of life by arranging for visitors to stay with local families in Port of Spain during the carnival. The French islands promote handicrafts to acquaint the traveller with local skills. In Martinique, for example, a local arts centre subsidized by the island government sells visitors an impressive variety of wood carvings, paintings and pottery. Some of it is first rate, such as the cane weaving and appliquéd wall hangings, or the cribs made of hollowed-out coconut husks that house dozens of tiny hand-painted figures of the Holy Family and their attendants. Martinique's awakening to its own talents also is seen in the existence of an exuberant group of young dancers, the Folklorique, who perform sprightly, graceful and comic dances based on island folklore.

And everywhere, food is beginning to be seen as a great maker of friends, a way of bridging the gap between the mainlanders and the islanders. The most outstanding efforts to achieve local gastronomic excellence are being made by jamaica, the largest of the English speaking independent islands. This is all the more creditable because many Jamaicans are, for a number of reasons, in two minds about the tourist industry. A remark attributed to the Bishop of Jamaica probably best reflects their attitude; he is reported to have said that if the tourist industry thrived in Jamaica he hoped that the tourists would be changed by the island rather than the island by the tourists. The islanders, who tend to be conservative in their behaviour, are worried by the tourists' informal dress and manners, but there is something more fundamental involved. The big hotels and cottage developments have tended to isolate themselves from the rest of island society, and have their staffs, their architecture and their menus from Europe or America. The island's political leaders recognize the economic advantages of the hotel business but in their newly asserted pride of race they have attempted to make it function profitably for Jamaicans and not just for foreign hotel owners. Their goal is to develop hotels and hotel restaurants as an outlet for Jamaican talent and as a way of bringing the tourists and the Jamaicans closer together.

To this end the Jamaican government sponsors an annual Culinary Arts Competition, an event patronized by women of all ages and social classes. The purpose of the competition, "the preparation of Jamaican food and drinks in new recipes", is so important to Jamaicans that provision was made for the competition in the five-year master plan adopted when Jamaica became independent in 1962. Thus the aura that surrounds the annual competition is one of proud nationalism. The women who take part feel that apart from winning prizes for themselves they are doing a service for their country. Not only are they reviving long-forgotten culinary traditions but, as Hugh Nash, a director of the competition, put it, they are creating "more palatable and delicious indigenous dishes to replace imports, dishes which in due course will become household words to Jamaicans and welcome fare for visitors to our island".

I was very impressed with the spirit of the contestants when I attended the July finals of a Culinary Arts Competition. It was held in the big Sheraton Hotel in Kingston, now the Wyndham Hotel, where some 100 women presented more than 230 dishes. And these were only the finalists in a competition that had begun the previous winter and had drawn on the cooking skills of thousands of women.

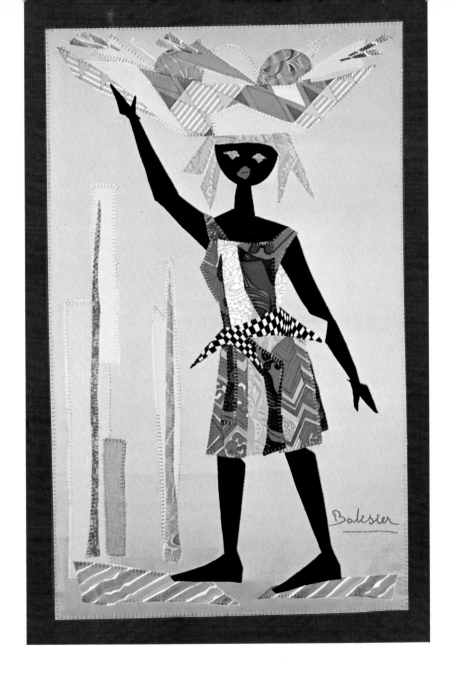

Bright and bold, appliquéd tapestries with local motifs like this one have become a collector's item for visitors to Martinique. An old art in the island, tapestry making has been given a fresh impetus by government support. Many of the hangings are sold in a State-owned crafts shop in Fort-de-France; the profits are invested in a number of schemes to encourage native arts.

The judging-day excitement started at dawn when cars, some of which had been travelling all night from towns on the other side of the island, began pulling up in front of the low, sprawling hotel. They deposited cartons of cakes and confections, huge tureens of soup and platters of parboiled seafood; husbands emerged sleepy-eyed from the cars to help their nervous wives to carry their creations, along with bags stuffed with fruits and props and leafy decorations.

From 9 until 11 the Sheraton's kitchens, thrown open to the contestants for last-minute preparations, were a scene of sweltering anguish. Round each of the seven huge stoves, some for baking and some for grilling and roasting, clustered dozens of women. Like a toreador, each contestant had her band of hangers-on and helpers—the woman who invented a dish did the final arrangement of it, but her crew sautéed the onions, cut the peppers, stirred the butter and flour. Competition at the burners and sinks was frantic and there were some tearful moments. One little nine-year-old, helping to strain a pepper-pot soup, was crying

Continued on page 160

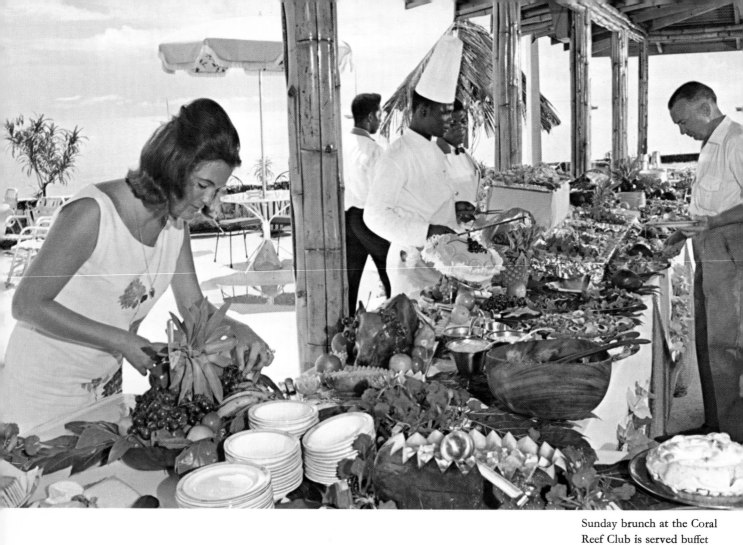

Sunday brunch at the Coral Reef Club is served buffet style on a terrace overlooking the Caribbean. Amid all the fruits and flowers and salads are a roast sucking pig and a whole red snapper.

Along Barbados' "Platinum Coast," Decorative Food Is Everyday Fare

At such luxurious establishments as the Coral Reef Club (*above*) and the Miramar Hotel (*opposite*), pampered travellers can dine in the grand style. Both resorts are in St. James on the western coast of Barbados—locally referred to as the Platinum Coast because of the elegance of the hotels and the wealth of their patrons. In surroundings like these the menus are made up mainly of Continental dishes: jellied consommé, *coq au vin*, grilled steak, lobster salad and the like, with an English-inspired trifle or a French-style cold fruit soufflé for dessert. While local fruits and fish have always graced such tables, it has only been in recent years that the restaurants of the most luxurious Caribbean hotels have begun to feature favourite native dishes like the simple *asopao* and *picadillo* illustrated with recipes at the end of this chapter. The result is that at long last any tourist in whatever income bracket can eat his way through the islands without feeling that he never left home.

158

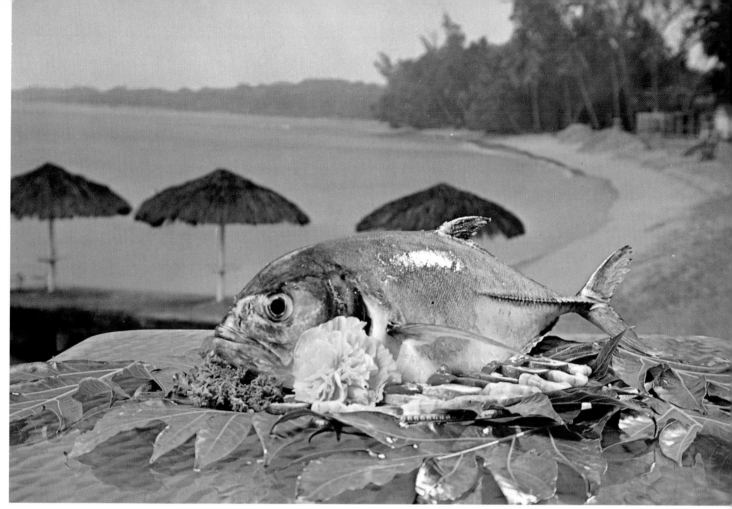

This jack-fish has been poached, chilled and painted with clear aspic, but its chief virtue is that it is only a few hours out of the sea.

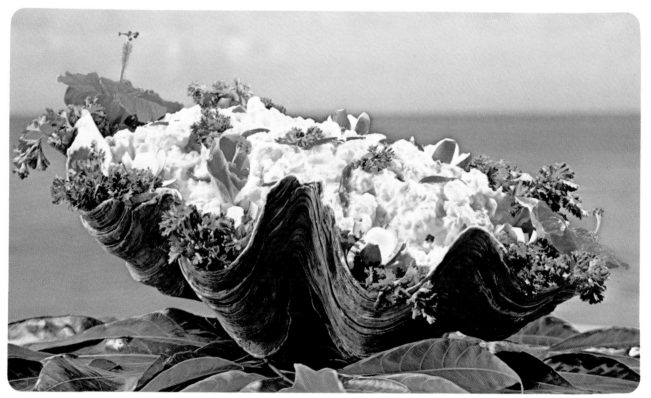

A lobster salad at the Miramar is presented in a giant clam shell and embellished with radish roses and hibiscus blossoms.

so much with excitement that her mother kept begging her to stop her tears lest they make the soup too salty.

Promptly at 11, all the dishes were laid on long tables in the ballroom of the Sheraton, ready for the critical palates of the judges. There were steaming soups, like crayfish and okra gumbo, and prawn and pumpkin chowder; there were curries of goat and poultry and jack-fruit, unusual dishes of baked fish cooked in coconut sauce or combined with bananas or citrus fruits, pineapples stuffed with local delicacies like prawns or avocado. There were ancient recipes like tum-tum—boiled bread-fruit beaten into an elastic dough—an African dish still eaten in the native village of a very old contestant but unknown to most of the city women; and there were wonders never seen before like a cake, fully four feet by five, on which an intense lady from the distant parish of Westmoreland had created out of batter and coloured icing, an entire Jamaican village, complete with cabins, out-buildings, animals, bushes and grass, bananas and even a garden of yams twisting their delicate vines of icing along an icing trellis.

While the tasting and judging were taking place I talked to many of the contestants and learned that most of them had never studied cookery. They had become interested in the contest when government representatives visited their towns and villages and encouraged their creative instincts. They all spoke with great feeling about their creations. One young woman, Lucille Tyson, who is a secretary with an insurance company in Kingston, told me that since the inception of the contest she had longed to compete but that until the year before she had had no idea that she considered good enough. Then, one day, she was inspired while reading the story of Cinderella to her two young nephews. They could not see how a pumpkin could turn into a coach. Lucille, an indulgent aunt, decided to demonstrate how it could indeed resemble one: she opened a Jamaican pumpkin—we would call it a large green marrow—and hitched a matched team of prawns to the front of it. The children were delighted, and Lucille realized she had an idea worthy of the culinary competition.

She perfected it and presented it as Cinderella's coach—a baked pumpkin with wheels of tomato slices, drawn by prawns with coconut strips for reins, and filled with sautéed prawns and rice cooked with coconut milk, tomatoes and spring onions (*pages 154-155*). The judges' appreciation was as great as that of Lucille's nephews, and perhaps more substantial, for they awarded the creation a silver medal.

Lucille was so encouraged by her award that she immersed herself in cooking and devoted all her spare time in the following year to reading cookery books and perfecting her skills. At the competition I attended, her second, she won prizes for every dish she entered. They included a mammoth stuffed and curried lobster, a graceful swan, two and a half feet high, made of a new Jamaican crop, Irish potatoes, and a spectacular drink named fire on ice, a fruit punch containing otaheite apple, garden cherry and orange juice mixed with sugar, strong green tea, rum and bitters. The drink was poured over ice cubes made of coconut water and then flamed with 32-proof rum just before it was presented.

When the winners of the competition were announced there were a few tears, but the scene was mostly one of hugs, kisses and joyful satisfaction. The recipes not only of the winners but of all the entrants in the finals were to be printed and circulated by the government; representatives of many of the island's hotels had seen or tasted the food, and presumably these dishes were on their way to becoming "household words to Jamaicans and welcome fare for visitors . . ."

The movement to explore and exploit local culinary resources is growing throughout the Caribbean. Trinidad holds a competition like the one in Jamaica, although on a more modest scale, called the Better Villages Competition. On Puerto Rico a food contest, open to hotel chefs rather than amateurs, changed its emphasis in 1968 from international to Caribbean cooking; the new rules specified that either local products *or* local themes must be stressed. Since most hotel chefs are artists at heart, the contest turned up not only edible food but such creations as a lard sculpture of an Arawak woman meditating, and a detailed map of Puerto Rico executed in rice and beans.

Food and politics seem to go together in all the islands. Fidel Castro makes a point of encouraging Cuban consumption of local foods by setting the example of eating them with gusto himself. An amusing tale about sharing dinner with Castro is told by Lee Lockwood, a photojournalist who spent seven days with the revolutionary leader in 1964. They were encamped in the hills, and on the table were roast pig, ham sandwiches, squash-like malanga and foo-foo. Lockwood was baulked at trying the foo-foo, which is made of mashed plantains and which, according to him, looked like "sticky balls, the size of matzoh balls"; he

Now well into its second century, La Mallorquina is the oldest restaurant in San Juan; within its cool white walls generations of Puerto Rico's gentry have come to eat and talk. It is a particular favourite of politicians; legend says that Luis Muñoz Rivera, the great Puerto Rican leader of the late 19th and early 20th centuries once had so heated a political argument in the restaurant that he swung his cane and cracked one of the ornate vases that stand on the pedestals in the corners of the room.

avoided them, and concentrated on the meat. But Castro ignored the meat and piled his plate high with malanga and foo-foo. After a while he took second helpings of these and, noticing that his visitor hadn't even tried them, ladled some foo-foo on to Lockwood's plate. Lockwood found the foo-foo "extremely bland, and its texture like that of raw dough". Apparently Castro was disappointed, for he told his guest, "You must eat foo-foo. It is a great delicacy. Very healthy too, very full of vitamins. We practically lived on it in the sierra. For us, it was our steak. Now that I live in Havana I miss foo-foo very much."

Castro, of course, likes steaks too, as did his predecessor, Fulgencio Batista, although Batista seems to have had no penchant for Cuban dishes. I had a long chat with his former chef, Ramón Torres, who after leaving Cuba had started a tiny Cuban restaurant called Bambu in New York; although Ramoncito spoke glowingly of the pheasant and caviar and squab that always graced his employer's table, he was hard put to think of any Cuban dish admired by the dictator. "Oh yes, rice and black beans," he remembered at last, "we sometimes served that."

Most islanders, however nationalistic, will admit that the tourists cannot be expected to like all the local foods, that salt-fish fritters will never drive out *sole meunière* nor okra replace green beans. But advocates of the Caribbean cuisine want not just to revive traditional dishes but to use local products in interesting new combinations; not, for instance, to popularize foo-foo but to find new and more attractive ways of serving plantains.

The hotels are joining in the effort to add. Some of the small hotels are particularly hard hit by the high costs of importing frozen foods, and, out of convenience and economic necessity, have developed menus based on local ingredients such as fish and poultry. For others, like the Young Island Hotel in a tiny island just off St. Vincent, the policy of fostering local cooking and using freshly grown native ingredients is a matter of philosophy and deliberate choice. At the Young Island Hotel the menu emphasizes freshly caught lobster and local fish prepared in a dozen interesting ways, including tree-tree cakes, a delectable fritter made of tiny, salty, fresh fish that taste something like caviar. Within a short time of its opening in 1965, the hotel had achieved a reputation for serving some of the finest food in the Caribbean.

According to local legend, Young Island was a gift to an English planter in St. Vincent from a Carib chieftain in the 1700s. The Carib had longingly admired the white stallion that Young was riding, and Young, anxious to maintain good relations with the rebellious Indians, said, "If you like it, it is yours". Some time later he happened to remark to the Carib chief how pretty he found the little island, just 200 yards off St. Vincent. The chieftain, according to the legend, said, "If you like it, it is yours". Eventually it passed from Young to the St. Vincent government, and recently it was leased to John Houser, a former executive of Hilton Hotels International and always a spokesman for the new, more adventurous American tourist. Turning the entire island into an elegantly designed hotel property, Houser continued the complementary exchange begun two centuries ago between outsider and islander by using the local St. Vincent chefs to develop his menu.

St. Vincent achieved independence in 1969, and to celebrate the occasion the kitchen at Young Island Hotel, manned by 40 local cooks, turned out a feast for 300 distinguished islanders and visitors. Every

Opposite: Cool and uncluttered, this tiled and whitewashed kitchen, now an exhibit in the Museum of the Puerto Rican Family in Old San Juan, shows the kind of kitchens used in 19th-century Puerto Rico. The stove, equipped with a hood to trap smoke and cooking smells, was fuelled with charcoal pushed through the square holes in front.

dish, from sucking pig and an array of almost 50 vegetable creations, to the local rum drinks with floating hibiscus flowers, was prepared from island-grown ingredients.

Larger hotels in the Caribbean usually serve a good deal of meat, but most of them now carefully highlight their menus with local products. The Montego Beach Hotel renamed Jack Tar in Jamaica, for example, serves a great deal of American beef prepared according to French recipes for its main courses, but offers a good selection of native fruits for breakfast and serves many traditional soups like pepper-pot, pumpkin and red pea. The hotel's local chefs have developed excellent chewy coconut breads, fragrant banana rolls and island-inspired hors d'oeuvre ranging from fried, salted coconut chunks to spicy pastry-wrapped meat patties and a baked delicacy of bacon-wrapped banana titbits.

Frequently hotel owners develop their own recipes. The owner of the Spice Island Inn in Grenada was the inventor, so far as I have been able to track it down, of a cold bread-fruit soup (*Recipe Index*) that is now served in many island hotels. The owner of the Sign Great House in Jamaica has contributed a dish called chicken patois that combines layers of sliced chicken with grapefruit, oranges, pineapple, prunes, mango chutney and green peppers. This colourful concoction somewhat resembles a traditional Jamaican dish that Sign Great House also serves: "pork downtown" (sometimes called "pork in the country", depending upon where you are), which features layers of roast pork with bananas, pawpaws and prunes.

Indeed, it is becoming difficult to single out those hotels that rely on local dishes to make their menus interesting, because the movement to do so is growing by leaps and bounds. Each year sees a greater increase in the hotels' ratio of local to imported chefs, foods and recipes. It is still somewhat difficult, however, to find restaurants which serve local specialities, places away from the hotels that the tourist can visit for an interesting, well-prepared meal. The Caribbean—except for a few islands—does not have a restaurant tradition. There is one old restaurant, perhaps the oldest in the Caribbean, for which I, together with many others, have a special affection: the La Mallorquina in San Juan. In a city increasingly dedicated to what is new and up-to-the-minute, La Mallorquina remains drowsily unselfconscious, cherishing its giant ceiling fans in defiance of air conditioning and proudly displaying its ornate vases, mirrors and carved wooden tables, once the possessions of a Spanish marquis who lived in Puerto Rico in the early 1800s.

Opened in 1848 by a Spaniard from Majorca, the restaurant is responsible for popularizing a number of Majorcan recipes in Puerto Rico, among them chewy *pan de majorca*, known in Majorca as *enseimadas*, an irresistible sweet breakfast roll baked with lard and dusted with powdery sugar. At the turn of the century, when life on Puerto Rico was more leisurely, members of prominent San Juan families used to take a late morning breakfast of local coffee and *pan de majorca* at La Mallorquina. The restaurant no longer serves breakfast, but *pan de majorca* has become a San Juan tradition and several bakeries in the narrow streets of the old city bake the rolls daily.

As the island loosened its ties with Spain, La Mallorquina too became more Puerto Rican than Spanish. Today it still serves *gazpacho* and garlic soup and *paella*, but it emphasizes a wide selection of *asopaos*. *Asopao*, related to *paella* but with a character all its own, is truly Puerto Rican, in-

164

vented on the island itself. *Asopao* means soupy, but I do not know whether to define it as a stew-like soup or a soup-like stew. It is made with chicken, prawn, lobster, squid or land crab, simmered with annatto-flavoured rice and combined with tomatoes, onions and other seasonings. It is an earthy dish but holds its own with the more sophisticated fare on La Mallorquina's menu.

In recent years other restaurants that purport to be Spanish have opened in the narrow streets of Old San Juan with less legitimate credentials than those of La Mallorquina. Their Puerto Rican or American owners seem to assume that visitors to the island really planned a trip to Spain but could not afford the fare. To make up for this misfortune the new restaurants serve Spanish garlic soup, *gazpacho* and *paella*, and tend to ignore true Puerto Rican dishes.

One charming exception is La Fonda del Callejon, a dark-beamed, white-washed restaurant so determined to be Puerto Rican that it serves only traditional island dishes: salt-fish fritters (*bacalaitos*), spicy blood sausages (*morcillas*), crescent-shaped meat patties in a crisp dough made of green plantain and taro flour (*pastelillos*), fried plantains (*tostones de plátano*), and many others. The restaurant is in Old San Juan in a restored colonial building that also houses the Museum of the Puerto Rican Family, furnished with antiques gathered from the old estate houses on the island.

La Fonda del Callejon is assisted by a government subsidy, an arrangement also enjoyed by Devon House, a restaurant in Kingston sponsored by the Jamaican government. This impressive place too is part of a museum displaying the treasures of colonial days, a reconstructed great house complete with antiques, formal gardens and fountains. At Devon House you can eat traditional soups like conch or turtle, or the delightfully named coo-coo roo, a chicken chowder also called cock soup, or the thin spicy fish broth known as fish tea. The main courses at Devon House are usually skewered beef or American filet mignon. But at the end of the meal you will be served one of Jamaica's finest culinary delights, a cup of Blue Mountain coffee. This rich coffee is a much prized local product that grows in the Blue Mountains of Jamaica at an altitude of over 3,000 feet. The mountainous area, with its cooler temperature and moderate rainfall, is superbly suited for coffee growing. Produced only in small quantities. Blue Mountain coffee is a connoisseur's treat and for a long time was hard to find in Jamaica itself because it was so much in demand abroad. Devon House always has it, served not only as part of a meal but also as a dessert, and some visitors come just for the coffee; it may be flavoured with orange rind or cinnamon stick, allspice or ginger, or gilded with whipped cream, frozen coconut cream, dark rum, or burnt sugar flamed with rum.

But the best place of all to find good local restaurants in the Caribbean is on the islands owned by France. The French concern with fine food and their predilection for dining out have, happily, long since left their mark, on Martinique and Guadeloupe. In the 1880s the American writer Lafcadio Hearn spent two years in the French West Indies and was fascinated by the food. He ate *manicou* and callaloo and *poule-épi-diri*, a chicken and rice dish similar to New Orleans jambalaya. Hearn wrote that Martinicans thought *poule-épi-diri* to be such a delicacy that "an over-exacting person, or one difficult to satisfy, is reproved with the

Blue Mountain coffee, grown high in the hills of Surrey County in the eastern part of Jamaica, is considered one of the world's finest varieties. Jamaicans are proud of it but find it something of a luxury since so much of the crop is exported to Japan—which pays the highest prices—England and Italy. Only small amounts reach the United States. Two stages in processing are shown above: in the bag are coffee "cherries" with their skins on; the others are "parchment" or cherries whose skins have been removed.

Overleaf: Given the shade they need by the broad leaves of banana trees, coffee trees grow abundantly on the Wallingford estate in the Blue Mountains of Jamaica. Coffee trees bear fruit for more than 20 years.

165

simple question, '*Ça ou lè 'ncò—poule-épi-diri?*' ['What more do you want —chicken and rice?']" Hearn's encounter with Martinican food so stimulated him that later in life he, like the French writer Alexandre Dumas, became that rare creature, a novelist turned cookery book writer. His *Creole Cooking* was published in New Orleans in 1885.

Today Martinique is a particularly good hunting ground for restaurants that feature specialities like blaff and *court bouillon* and that have always done so, tourists or no tourists. Several of the villages in the island—Saint-Pierre in the north and Sainte-Anne in the south, for instance—boast small restaurants where the food is simple but splendid and where tourists are welcome but still in the minority. Martinique can also boast an array of first-class restaurants that serve fine French food as well as local fare. Establishments have their ups and downs, of course, but the last time I was in Fort-de-France, Le Foyal and La Louisiane were particularly impressive.

Nevertheless, my favourite restaurant of all is in Guadeloupe: Le Pergola, famous throughout the Caribbean for the imagination and perfectionism of its owner, Mario Petreluzzi. His menu includes sea eggs, hearts of the local cabbage palm, conch, various local fishes, pretty desserts like banana and coconut pancakes, and several outstandingly good dishes using the native land crab. Although I have eaten land crab in a wide variety of ways since my first encounter with it back in 1958 in Puerto Rico, nowhere was it so delicious and so tasty as in Le Pergola's *omelette de crabe du terre*. The omelette is made with great skill, the whites and yolks being beaten separately to form a puffy pillow that is then stuffed with the downy crab meat, enhanced with chives and parsley.

Despite his Italian name M. Petreluzzi's Guadeloupian ancestry dates back 300 years on his mother's side, and he cares passionately about the island and its food. He grows angry at the mere mention of one of the new luxury hotels that serve only European food. "It is a tradition in France, an unwritten law," he argues, "that a regional restaurant must serve the regional specialities. Show me any restaurant in Michelin which will be praised if it does not serve the traditional foods and dishes of the region."

Each year more and more hoteliers and restaurateurs agree with M. Petreluzzi. True, those who want to serve local foods still find many stumbling blocks in their way. It will be a long time before restaurants and hotels can rely on a steady supply of local fruits and vegetables, meat or even fish and other seafood of consistently high quality, because the island economies need much more developing. But at least the snobbery that Trollope encountered more than a century ago is on the wane. Nowadays everyone connected with the islands—governments, hotels, restaurants, even airlines—seems bent upon perfecting the island cooking. This is no myth, it is reality, and the tourist can take credit for much of what is happening. It was he who brought about the change by insisting on being allowed to experience the culture of the islands as well as their climate.

Opposite: In a bay on the west coast of Antigua, a party of tourists aboard skipper Hugh Bailey's sturdy charter yacht *Sagittarius* sip a glass of white wine before tucking into a feast of freshly caught lobster. *Sagittarius*, out of English Harbour, Antigua, is a familiar sight in the islands, where sailing—and catching their own dinner—are great major attractions for the visitor.

Asopao (*Puerto Rico*)
CHICKEN AND RICE STEW

To serve 6

1 teaspoon coarsely chopped garlic
½ teaspoon crumbled dried oregano
1 teaspoon salt
A 2½- to 3-lb. chicken, cut into
   6 to 8 serving pieces
1½ oz. lard
2 oz. finely chopped onions
3 oz. finely chopped green peppers
2 oz. lean boneless ham, cut
   into ¼-inch dice
4 medium-sized firm ripe tomatoes,
   peeled, seeded and finely chopped
   (*see sopa de gandules, Recipe Index*), or
   substitute three 8-oz. cans chopped
   drained tomatoes
13 oz. uncooked long-grain white
   rice
2½ pints chicken stock
Freshly ground black pepper
1 ten-oz. packet frozen peas,
   thoroughly defrosted
1¼ oz. freshly grated Parmesan
   cheese
1½ oz. small pimiento-stuffed green
   olives
2½ teaspoons capers, rinsed
1 whole canned pimiento, drained
   and cut lengthways into ½-inch
   strips

Mash the garlic, oregano and salt to a smooth paste with a pestle and mortar or in a small bowl with the back of a spoon. Pat the pieces of chicken completely dry with kitchen paper and rub them with the paste.

Heat the lard over a high heat in a large, heavy casserole until a drop of water flicked into it splutters instantly. Brown 3 or 4 pieces of chicken at a time, starting them skin side down. Turn the chicken carefully and adjust the heat so that the pieces brown quickly and evenly without burning. Transfer the pieces to a plate as they brown.

Add the onions and green pepper to the fat remaining in the casserole and cook for about 5 minutes, stirring frequently, until the vegetables are soft but not brown. Stir in the ham, then add the tomatoes and cook briskly until most of the liquid in the pan evaporates and the mixture is thick enough to hold its shape lightly in a spoon. Return the chicken to the casserole and turn the pieces over and over to coat the chicken well with the tomato mixture. Reduce the heat to low, cover tightly, and simmer for about 30 minutes, until the chicken is tender. Transfer the bird to a plate and remove the meat from the bones and cut it into 2-inch squares, when cool enough to handle.

Meanwhile stir the rice, stock or stock and water, and a few grindings of pepper into the tomato mixture remaining in the casserole and bring to the boil over a high heat. Reduce the heat to low, cover tightly, and simmer for about 20 minutes, until the grains are completely tender. The mixture will be soupy—which is what *asopao* means—when the rice is cooked.

Stir in the peas, the grated cheese, the olives and capers. Mix well, then add the chicken and arrange the pimiento strips on top. Cover and simmer for 2 to 3 minutes longer to heat the peas and chicken through. Taste for seasoning and serve at once, straight from the casserole.

Corn Pone (*Barbados*)
CORNMEAL CAKE WITH RAISINS AND CHERRIES

To make 1 eight-inch round cake

1 tablespoon plus ½ lb. butter,
   softened
9 oz. yellow cornmeal
8 oz. plain flour
8 oz. sugar
¼ teaspoon vanilla essence
¼ teaspoon ground nutmeg,
   preferably freshly grated
A pinch of salt
6 eggs, lightly beaten
⅜ pint milk
1½ tablespoons light rum
5¼ oz. seedless raisins
1¼ oz. glacé cherries, coarsely
   chopped

Preheat the oven to Mark 4: 350° F. Spread ½ ounce of softened butter over the bottom and sides of an 8-inch springform cake tin, using a pastry brush.

Sift the cornmeal and flour together. Cream the remaining ½ pound of butter, the sugar and 1½ tablespoons of the cornmeal mixture together, in a deep bowl, by beating and mashing them against the sides of the bowl with a wooden spoon until they are light and fluffy. Add the vanilla, nutmeg and salt and slowly pour in the eggs in a thin stream, beating constantly. Beat in about 4 ounces of the cornmeal mixture, then 3 tablespoons of the milk, and continue adding alternately until all the cornmeal and milk have been mixed in.

Stir in the rum, raisins and cherries, and pour the batter into the prepared tin. Bake in the middle of the oven for about 1½ hours, until the top of the cake is golden and a cake tester or toothpick inserted in the centre comes out clean. Let the cake cool for 4 to 5 minutes before removing the sides of the springform. Then slide it off the bottom of the tin on to a cake rack to cool completely, with the aid of a large metal palette knife.

Asopao, a chicken and rice stew, now gives an authentic local flavour to the menus of many Puerto Rican hotels.

Concombres en Salade

CUCUMBER SALAD

Peel the cucumbers and cut them in half lengthways, using a swivel-bladed vegetable parer or a small, sharp knife. Seed them by scraping the tip of a small spoon down their centres. Then cut the cucumbers crosswise into ¼-inch-thick slices.

Put the cucumber slices into a bowl, add the salt, and turn the slices over and over with a spoon to coat them evenly. Let the cucumbers stand at room temperature for about 30 minutes, then drain off all the liquid accumulated around them and pat them dry with kitchen paper.

Drop the cucumber slices into a serving bowl, add the chillies, lime juice and garlic, and toss until all the ingredients are thoroughly blended. Cover the bowl tightly with foil or a sheet of plastic and marinate the salad at room temperature for at least 1 hour. Just before serving, remove and discard the garlic and sprinkle the top of the salad with a few grindings of pepper.

To serve 4

2 medium-sized firm fresh cucumbers
1¼ teaspoons salt
1½ teaspoons finely chopped fresh hot chillies (*caution: see "How to Handle Chillies"*)
1½ teaspoons strained fresh lime juice
1 large garlic clove, peeled and crushed with the flat side of a large, heavy knife
Freshly ground black pepper

171

To serve 8 to 10

STUFFING

A 1-lb. loaf of white bread, sliced

3 oz. pitted green olives, finely
chopped

¾ oz. finely chopped fresh chives

1 teaspoon crumbled dried thyme

½ teaspoon salt

¼ teaspoon freshly ground black
pepper

1½ oz. butter

4 oz. finely chopped onions

2½ teaspoons finely chopped garlic

3 tablespoons milk

SUCKING PIG

A 10- to 12-lb. oven-ready
sucking pig

1½ tablespoons coarse salt, or
substitute 2½ teaspoons table salt

Freshly ground black pepper

3 tablespoons vegetable oil

1 fresh lime

To serve 4 as a main course or 6 as
a first course

MAYONNAISE

2 egg yolks

½ teaspoon white wine vinegar

⅛ teaspoon crumbled dried thyme

1 teaspoon salt

¼ teaspoon white pepper

⅜ pint vegetable oil

3 tablespoons soured cream

1 tablespoon strained fresh lime juice

LOBSTER

2 lb. freshly cooked, frozen or
canned lobster meat, drained,
picked over to remove all bits of
shell and cartilage, and cut into ½-
inch cubes

3 hard-boiled eggs, peeled and
coarsely chopped

2 oz. finely diced celery

¾ oz. finely diced spring onions,
including 1 inch of the green tops

Roast Sucking Pig with Bread and Olive Stuffing *(Barbados)*

Preheat the oven to Mark 2: 300° F. First prepare the stuffing in the following way: Trim the crusts from the bread with a sharp knife. Arrange the slices side by side on one or two large baking sheets and toast in the middle of the oven for 5 minutes on each side. Remove the toast from the oven and raise the heat to Mark 4: 350° F. Tear the slices of toast into ½ inch pieces and drop them into a deep bowl. Add the olives, chives, thyme, salt and pepper, and toss thoroughly together.

Melt the butter over a moderate heat in a heavy, medium-sized frying-pan. When the foam begins to subside, add the onions and garlic and cook for about 5 minutes, stirring frequently, until they are soft and transparent but not brown. Watch carefully for any sign of burning and adjust the heat accordingly. Add the entire contents of the pan to the toast mixture, stir in the 3 tablespoons of milk and toss together until all the ingredients for the stuffing are well blended. Taste for seasoning.

Wash the pig quickly under cold running water and pat it dry inside and out with kitchen paper. Sprinkle the abdominal cavity and skin with salt and liberal grindings of pepper, then fill it loosely with the stuffing mixture. Close the opening by lacing it with skewers and kitchen string or by sewing it up with thick white thread.

Crumple a sheet of aluminium foil into a ball the size of the lime and insert it in the pig's mouth to keep it open as it roasts. Cover the ears with small squares of foil to prevent them from burning. Brush the pig all over with vegetable oil and place it on a rack set in a large shallow roasting tin. If the head extends beyond the edge of the tin, double a strip of foil under it to catch any drippings.

Roast the pig undisturbed in the middle of the oven for 1½ hours, then remove the foil from the ears, and continue roasting for 15 to 20 minutes longer. To test for doneness, pierce the thigh with the point of a small, sharp knife. The juice should spurt out a clear yellow; if it is slightly pink, roast the pig for another 5 to 10 minutes.

Transfer the roast pig to a large heated dish and replace the ball of foil in its mouth with the whole fresh lime. Let the pig rest at room temperature for about 10 minutes for easier carving.

Lobster Salad *(Barbados)*

First prepare the mayonnaise in the following way: Warm a large mixing bowl in hot water, dry it thoroughly but quickly, and drop in the egg yolks. Beat the yolks vigorously for about 2 minutes with a whisk or a rotary egg beater, until they thicken and cling to the whisk. Stir in the vinegar, thyme, salt and white pepper. Beat in 5 tablespoons of the oil, ½ teaspoon at a time; make sure each addition is absorbed before adding more. By the time 6 tablespoons of oil has been beaten in, the sauce should be the consistency of very thick cream. Pour in the rest of the oil in a slow, thin stream, beating constantly. Stir in the soured cream and lime juice, and taste for seasoning.

Just before serving, put the lobster, eggs, celery and spring onions into a large chilled bowl and toss them together thoroughly but lightly. Then add the mayonnaise and turn the lobster mixture over and over in it with a spoon to coat the pieces evenly.

Christophene au Gratin (Martinique)

BAKED CHRISTOPHENES WITH ONION AND CHEESE FILLING

To serve 4

Wash the *christophenes* or courgettes under cold running water, drain, and cut them lengthways into halves. Drop them into enough lightly salted boiling water to cover them completely and cook briskly for about 30 minutes, until they are tender and show only slight resistance when pierced with the point of a small, sharp knife.

Drain them and, when they are cool enough to handle, remove and discard the seeds and hollow out each half with a small spoon to make boat-like shells about ¼ inch thick. Set the shells aside on kitchen paper to drain completely and chop the scooped-out pulp coarsely.

Preheat the oven to Mark 4: 350° F. Melt the 2 ounces of butter over a moderate heat in a large, heavy frying-pan. When the foam begins to subside, drop in the onions and cook for about 5 minutes, stirring frequently, until they are soft and transparent but not brown. Watch carefully for any sign of burning and adjust the heat accordingly. Add the chopped vegetables, ¾ ounce of the cheese, the salt and a few grindings of pepper. Cook briskly, still stirring, until most of the liquid in the pan has evaporated and the mixture is thick enough to hold its shape lightly in the spoon.

Fill the 4 courgette shells with the onion mixture, patting it in firmly. Arrange them side by side in a shallow baking dish large enough to hold them comfortably and dot the tops with the ½ ounce of butter pieces. Sprinkle with the rest of the cheese and bake in the middle of the oven for about 20 minutes, until the tops are a delicate golden brown. Serve at once, straight from the baking dish.

2 large *christophenes* (*see Glossary*), each about 12 oz., or substitute two 12 oz. courgettes
2 oz. butter, plus ½ oz. butter cut into ¼-inch pieces
6 oz. finely chopped onions
1 oz. freshly grated Parmesan cheese
1 teaspoon salt
Freshly ground black pepper

Pitch Lake Pudding (Barbados)

MOCHA MOUSSE WITH ORANGE LIQUEUR

To serve 8

Melt the butter over a moderate heat in the top of a double boiler. Set the pan over barely simmering (not boiling) water and stir the coffee into the butter. Sift in the cocoa, about 1 ounce at a time, beating constantly with a wire whisk or large spoon, and beat until the mixture becomes a smooth paste. Reduce the heat to the lowest possible point and keep the cocoa paste warm.

Beat the egg yolks with an electric or a rotary egg beater in a deep bowl, for about a minute. Beat in the sugar, 2 ounces at a time, and continue beating until the yolks become pale yellow and thick enough to fall back in a ribbon when the whisk is lifted from the bowl. Beat in the cocoa paste, about 6 tablespoons at a time, then the liqueur. Set aside.

Beat the egg whites and salt together in a separate large bowl, with a wire whisk or a rotary egg beater, until the whites are stiff enough to stand in firm, unwavering peaks when the whisk is lifted from the bowl. Stir about one quarter of the whites into the cocoa and egg yolk mixture, then pour it over the remaining egg whites. Fold them together, thoroughly but gently using an over and under cutting motion rather than a stirring motion.

Ladle the Pitch Lake pudding into a 1½-pint soufflé dish, a large serving bowl, or eight individual pudding dishes and refrigerate for at least 3 hours, until thoroughly chilled. Just before serving, spread the whipped cream lightly over the pudding, or, if you prefer, spoon the whipped cream into a bowl and present it separately.

6 oz. butter, cut into small pieces
2½ tablespoons instant coffee, preferably instant *espresso*, dissolved in 9 tablespoons boiling water
12 oz. unsweetened cocoa
6 egg yolks
14 oz. superfine sugar
4 tablespoons Curaçao, Grand Marnier or other orange-flavoured liqueur
6 egg whites
A pinch of salt
⅜ pint chilled double cream, stiffly whipped

Picadillo *(Cuba)*

SPICED CHOPPED BEEF WITH OLIVES AND RAISINS

To serve 4

Place the beef in a large, heavy saucepan, add 1 teaspoon of the salt and a few grindings of pepper, and pour in enough water to cover the meat by at least 2 inches. Bring to the boil over a high heat, meanwhile skimming off the foam and scum as they rise to the surface. Reduce the heat to low, partly cover the pan and simmer for about 1½ hours until the beef is tender and shows no resistance when pierced with the point of a small, sharp knife. Drain the beef and chop it coarsely, when cool enough to handle.

Heat the oil over a moderate heat in a large, heavy frying-pan until a light haze forms above it. Drop in the onions, garlic, pepper and chillies and cook for about 5 minutes, stirring frequently, until the vegetables are soft but not brown. Watch carefully for any sign of burning and adjust the heat accordingly. Add the tomatoes, cloves, the remaining 1½ teaspoons of salt and a liberal grinding of black pepper. Cook briskly, still stirring, until most of the liquid in the pan has evaporated and the mixture is thick enough to hold its shape almost solidly on the spoon.

Add the olives, raisins and vinegar and stir for a minute or two. Then add the chopped beef and stir until the meat is heated through. Taste the *picadillo* for seasoning and serve, attractively piled up on a heated dish or individual plates.

In Cuba each serving is traditionally topped with deep-fried eggs (*huevos estilo cubano, Recipe Index*). *Picadillo* may also be accompanied by such dishes as fried plantains, *riz et pois, quingombós cocidos (Recipe Index)*, boiled rice or *concombres en salade (Recipe Index)*.

2 lb. lean boneless beef, preferably chuck, trimmed of excess fat and cut into 2-inch cubes

2½ teaspoons salt

Freshly ground black pepper

3 tablespoons vegetable oil mixed with teaspoon liquid annatto

4 oz. finely chopped onions

1½ teaspoons finely chopped garlic

4 medium-sized green peppers, the seeds and white pith removed and finely chopped

2½ teaspoons finely chopped fresh hot chillies (*caution: see "How to Handle Chillies"*)

6 medium-sized firm ripe tomatoes, peeled, seeded and finely chopped (*see sopa de gandules, Recipe Index*), or substitute two 1-lb. cans chopped drained tomatoes

¼ teaspoon ground cloves

2 oz. small pimiento-stuffed green olives

1¼ oz. seedless raisins

1½ tablespoons white distilled vinegar

Chilled Breadfruit Soup *(Grenada)*

To serve 6

Melt the butter over a moderate heat in a large, heavy saucepan. Add the onions and garlic and cook for about 5 minutes, stirring frequently, until they are soft and transparent but not brown. Watch carefully for any sign of burning and adjust the heat accordingly.

Stir in the chopped breadfruit and the chicken stock, and bring to the boil over a high heat. Reduce the heat to low, cover tightly, and simmer for about 20 minutes, until the breadfruit is tender enough to be easily mashed against the sides of the pan.

Pour half the mixture into the jar of an electric blender, add 6 tablespoons of the cream, and blend at high speed until the mixture is reduced to a smooth purée. Scrape the purée into a bowl or tureen with a rubber spatula. Then purée the rest of the breadfruit mixture with the rest of the cream. (If you do not have a blender, force the breadfruit mixture through a fine sieve set over a deep bowl, pressing down hard on the vegetables with the back of a spoon. Or purée the mixture through a food mill set over a bowl. Stir the cream into the purée.)

Season the soup with salt and pepper, and refrigerate for at least 3 hours, until thoroughly chilled. Taste for seasoning, and serve the soup from a chilled tureen or in individual soup plates. Sprinkle the soup with the chopped chives before serving.

2 oz. butter

4 oz. finely chopped onions

1 scant teaspoon finely chopped garlic

6 oz. peeled, cored and coarsely chopped fresh breadfruit (*see Glossary*), or 4 slices canned breadfruit, thoroughly drained and coarsely chopped

1½ pints chicken stock

⅜ pint single cream

1 teaspoon salt

¼ teaspoon freshly ground black pepper

2½ teaspoons finely chopped fresh chives

Picadillo, almost a national dish in Cuba, is a glorified version of beef hash, lavishly seasoned with a tomato and pepper sauce, and garnished with olives and raisins. With it are a cool cucumber salad and beer.

VIII

Rum, the Elixir of the Islands

The tourist who steps out of his plane at a steamy Caribbean airport still dressed in his northern winter clothes invariably feels hot and sticky. Fortunately two reliable cures await him. The first is a swim, which for maximum effect should be taken within one hour of arrival. The second is a cooling, energy-restoring rum drink.

There is something magical about rum. It combats heat in the tropics and cold in northern regions. Planter's punches and hot toddies are completely different except that they are both based on rum, but that similarity is enough to make them both great restoratives. In the islands, the original home of rum, the spirit comes in endless surprising varieties. The Scotch, gin or bourbon drinker, accustomed to the subtle, and sometimes imaginary, differences among the various brands of his favourite spirit, is amazed to discover not only that there are hundreds of different kinds of rum—most of them never encountered at home—but that by and large they taste noticeably different from one another. The casual drinker quickly becomes fond of the many mixed drinks made with the rums of the different islands, while the connoisseur is delighted to find rums that are so mellow and smooth that, like cognac, they can be sipped neat. Both types of imbiber, impelled perhaps by the high cost of whisky and gin, quickly learn in the land of rum to drink and enjoy the local speciality.

Not only does every major island have its own rums and varieties of rum, but every island has its own favourite rum drinks; and so, in fact, does every house, every hotel and every hotel barman. Planter's punch, a drink that people innocent of Caribbean ways often assume to be the name of a specific drink, can be anything that makes use of both rum

Arch-symbol of Caribbean hospitality, the planter's punch has almost as many versions as there are barmen. But some kind of rum and fruit juice are basic to the punch, and it is often festooned with fresh fruit. This version, which has dark rum floating on top and a pineapple spike as a garnish, is accompanied by a basket of crisp plantain crisps (*Recipe Index*).

177

and fruit juice. Nowadays the rum can be light or dark, but the traditional rum for planter's punch is dark. And any kind of fruit juice can be used, from the exotic guava and mango to the more commonplace pineapple and orange.

At one time, however, the name did stand for a specific drink, and, if you are fortunate, you may still encounter the ancestral planter's punch. The recipe for this classic punch is expressed in a venerable jingle that goes, "One of sour, two of sweet, three of strong and four of weak," or one part of fresh lime juice, two parts of sweetening, either sugar or sugar syrup, three parts of rum and four parts of water or ice. Sometimes the classic recipe calls for a fifth ingredient, powdered nutmeg, to be sprinkled sparingly on top of the drink. In Barbados there is an excellent museum with exhibits relating to early life in the islands, and one of them displays some 18th-century punch-making equipment: elegant crystal bowls and silver pocket-sized nutmeg graters. According to the museum, which, despite its palm-studded gardens, is as authoritative and musty in its way as its London counterparts, the word punch comes from a Hindustani word, *panch*, which means five. And five were the ingredients necessary in a punch: lime juice, sweetening, spirits, water and spice. What I gathered from the exhibition is that the wide-ranging British learned the word for punch in India and the method of making the spirit for it in the islands, and that thus planter's punch evolved, a felicitous example of imperial eclecticism.

A cousin of planter's punch is the classic Martinican drink called *petit punch*, a name which usually comes out sounding something like "tee-paunsh". It can be made with either light or dark matured rum but it is diluted by only two things, a few drops of fresh lime juice and *sirop*, a heavy cane sugar concentrate that smells of the cane fields. The charm of the "little punch" is enhanced by the traditional, almost ceremonial way in which it is served. A tray is passed round bearing two bottles of rum, light and dark, a small bottle of *sirop*, a dish of very small wedges of lime, small glasses and a bucket of ice. Each drinker makes his own, varying the proportions as he likes, but generally pouring about two parts of rum to one of *sirop* with a few drops of lime juice. Visitors usually have ice to cut the sweetness of the drink, but most Martinicans prefer it sweet, as if to emphasize their pride in their bountiful sugar. Not too long ago one paid only for the *sirop* when drinking rum punch in a bar. The rum itself was left indifferently on the counter and, like the water, was free. The *petit punch* goes down very smoothly, and seems almost immediately to enhance the spirits of the guests.

Very like *petit punch* in basic ingredients but quite different in its concept is the Daiquiri, the most popular rum drink in the United States. The Daiquiri uses lime juice, sugar and rum, each in a greater amount than the last, but then it is shaken and strained through cracked ice.

The man who invented the Daiquiri was an American mining engineer, a man of some considerable refinement and social prestige, a friend of the American artist Frederic Remington. His name was Jennings Cox and in the 1890s he was supervisor of several copper mines in the eastern part of Cuba near the little town of Daiquiri. His granddaughter Carmen, whom I met in the islands, told me how her grandfather invented the drink one day in 1896 when important and unexpected visitors from the States arrived in Daiquiri. Cox, a gin drinker, was out of his favourite potion. He sometimes drank the local

Cuban rum but he feared that it would not be to the taste of the Americans. To disguise the rum a little, he picked limes from a tree in his garden, added their juice and some sugar to his rum; then he chilled and tentatively served the result. It was an immediate success. For many years Cox derived much gratification from his fame as the inventor of the Daiquiri and, although few people today know his story, his granddaughter zealously guards his memory. His monument is a big, old-fashioned scrap-book in which she has kept the yellowed photographs, letters and cuttings that tell the tale and recount the praise of the great and the famous for Cox's "invention".

One cutting contains a Rear Admiral's account of his first encounter with it. Admiral Lucius Johnson and his men had landed on the beach at Daiquiri in June 1898 during one of the major campaigns in the short-lived Spanish-American War—the blockade of Cuba that forced Spain to relinquish the island. "That beach at Daiquiri seemed hot, desperately hot to us," the Admiral recalled. But he and his officers soon got over their discomfort when a "tall well-tanned man whose urbane and genial manner is still a pleasant memory" invited them all for a drink "that he had put together to make the locally produced rum more agreeable to the foreign taste". When the war ended, the men took gallons of the rum home with them, introduced the Daiquiri to the Army and Navy Club in Washington and thus launched its successful career in America.

When Carmen showed me her grandfather's scrap-book we reflected sadly on how fleeting the fame of celebrities often turns out to be, and were touched and amused by the gentle effort of Cox's wife Isabel to immortalize his name. In 1909 she proudly presented him with a prettily decorated hand-lettered valentine with a poem of her own composition:

> *There was a gay man from a Mine*
> *Liked Life, Laughter and Wine*
> *A memory retentive*
> *His nature inventive*
> *Gave the world the "Daiquiri" fine.*

If *petit punch* and the Daiquiri are the first cousins of planter's punch in its original form, the drink that is usually known as planter's punch today seems almost to be no relation at all. You cannot be sure what you will get when you order a planter's punch nowadays. Some recipes call for both light and dark rum. Some even call for three rums, light, medium and dark. Island-made liqueurs or Angostura bitters from Trinidad may be added. Grenadine, spices, coconut cream, fruit juice and raw fruit often make the punch seem more like a salad than a drink. Since rum mixes well with many other flavours and since in every man there is apparently something of the inventiveness of a Jennings Cox, new rum drinks are devised by the hundred each year. The Mai Tai, invented at the bar of a Trader Vic's Restaurant, calls for a rum specially blended by the Trader Vic company from a selection of Caribbean rums to produce the right texture and bouquet for the cocktail. In the Jamaica Arms restaurant in New York, where superb rums from all the islands can be sampled neat—some of them matured like brandies for up to 20 years—the mixed drinks include yellow bird, in which rum and fruit juice are combined with Italy's golden syrupy Galliano liqueur, and Lady Nugent's tulip, a presumably lady-like drink which can produce unlady-like after effects through its heady mixture of rum and brandy.

In the islands themselves there are innumerable rum drinks with colourful names like white witch and brown skin gal, ginnal general, beach lamour and moonshot.

But most true rum drinkers consider it superfluous to mix rum with other spirits, for rum is not only a delicious drink in itself, but is also notoriously potent. This was made known as early as 1651 by Richard Ligon, a pioneer traveller to Barbados, who wrote, "The chiefe fudling they make in the Island is Rumbullion, alias Kill-Devill, and this is made of suggar canes distilled, a hot, hellish and terrible liquor."

And kill-devil, alias rumbullion, alias rum, has had a hot, hellish and terrible history. Although one of Alexander the Great's generals noted during the Greek conqueror's campaign in India in 325 B.C. that there was in that country a drink made of fermented sugar-cane, historians believe that the drink in question was most likely a kind of beer, and that the first distilled sugar-cane spirit was produced in Barbados in about 1630. Its quality was questionable to say the least. So high was the alcoholic content of this formidable beverage that Ligon tells the story of a slave who lost his life carrying it from the still to the drinking room. "In the night, not knowing the force of the liquor he carried [he] brought the candle somewhat nearer than he ought, that he might better see how to put it into the Funnel which conveyed it into the Butt. But the Spirit being stirr'd by that motion, flew out, and got hold of the flame of the Candle, and so set all on fire, and burnt the poor Negre to death, who was an excellent servant."

Others lost their lives through drinking the fiery and usually immature spirit, and still others in the raucous after-effects of rum drinking. Indeed, although a few scholars suggest that the name rum came from an abbreviation of the Latin word for sugar, *saccharum*, most believe that the word is a shortening of the 17th-century English words rumbullion and rumbustion, which meant tumult, rumpus. There is no question that both the spirits and its effects were held in very low esteem by many thoughtful people of the time. As an English archbishop, Thomas Tenison, put it, it was "destructive to Nature, wasting the Vitals and an enemy of Propagation".

Rum's fierce reputation was not improved by the company it kept. The famous skull and cross-bones flag was sometimes supplemented on pirate ships by an even more fearful pennant, which showed a skeleton holding in one hand a dagger and in the other a glass known as a "rummer". In fact, pirates seem to have preferred brandy when they could get it, by hook or by crook, but the pirates and rum association is a strong one. Robert Louis Stevenson strengthened it when, inspired by the name of an island in the West Indies called Dead Man's Chest, he wrote in *Treasure Island* the lines that have frightened four generations of children: "Fifteen men on the Dead Man's Chest, yo-ho-ho, and a bottle of rum! Drink and the devil had done for the rest—yo-ho-ho, and a bottle of rum."

Rum was even more shamefully associated with the slave trade. New England merchants imported West Indian molasses and manufactured their own rum from it, then shipped the rum to the west coast of Africa. There it was used as currency to purchase human cargo, then sold to the West Indian planters in exchange for more molasses. This 17th and 18th-century practice has gone down in history as the famous—or infamous —"triangular" trade.

Continued on page 184

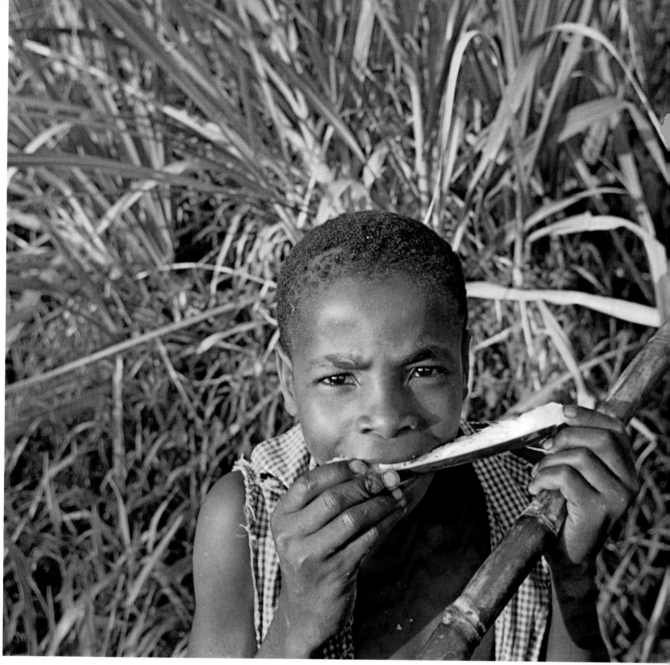

Where Rum Begins—in a Forest of Cane

For 30 gallons of rum, you need about a ton of sugar. For this amount of sugar, about 10 tons of sugar-cane. And for 10 tons of sugar cane, about an acre of prime plantation land. That, in brief, is the equation that helps to explain the green forests of spiky cane that cover so much of the West Indies. Some of the cane goes to make small boys happy; and much of it, of course, goes into sugar. But millions of acres of cane go into the ocean of rum produced each year in the Caribbean—the dry Cuban and Puerto Rican varieties; the darker Barbadian and Martinican potions; the heavy Jamaicans and Demeraras. All rum, whether distilled from cane juice or molasses, comes from sugar-cane. And connoisseurs everywhere acclaim it as the noblest contribution of the cane.

Standing in a sugar-cane field not far from where Napoleon's Empress Josephine was born, a young Martinican enjoys his version of an afternoon candy bar by sucking the sweetness from a juicy cane stalk, a pleasure shared by children and adults all over the Caribbean.

Overleaf: On a hillside overlooking the sea in Barbados, workmen stack cane on a lorry bound for a sugar mill for processing.

181

Many New England fortunes were built on the triangular trade, and the merchants were brazen about it. One notorious slave trader, Simeon Potter of Bristol, advised his agents on the Gold Coast of Africa to "Make yr chief Trade with the Blacks and Little or none with the white people" because slaves purchased from independent black chiefs could be bought for less than those purchased from organized companies of white traders. Potter had other instructions for his lieutenants too: "Worter yr Rum as much as possible and sell as much by the short measur as you can."

The rum made in the Caribbean islands was at first given only to slaves and servants, partly as a way of making them more content with their fate; their masters preferred imported brandy and Madeira. But eventually even the planters, as well as Englishmen and Americans in increasing numbers, began to enjoy the drink. Some people were scandalized by its popularity. The American Quaker John Woolman vainly urged the boycotting of rum not only because he thought it so bad for people but also because it was produced "by the labour of those who are under such lamentable oppression". But most people liked the drink so much that they found plenty of excuses for drinking it. The 18th-century English poet William Cowper light-heartedly expressed the general attitude of his day in these lines:

> I own I am shocked at the purchase of slaves;
> And fear those who buy them and sell them are knaves;
> What I hear of their hardships, their tortures and groans
> Is almost enough to draw pity from stones.
> I pity them greatly, but I must be mum,
> For how could we do without sugar and rum?

One reason for the popularity of rum in Cowper's time was that the drink had gradually become associated with British valour at sea. In the previous century sailors of the Royal Navy had been allowed beer, which often went sour after a few weeks on board. Then it was discovered that rum not only kept well in casks, but that its flavour and body actually improved with age. In 1655 the Navy began to issue rum to its men. Thirty years later Samuel Pepys, as Secretary to the Navy, expressed his scepticism as to whether "Rumm" was as suitable to the "Health and Satisfaction of our Seamen" as brandy, and requested that an inquiry be held into the effects of the rum issue. Despite his concern, rum continued to be issued in ever more generous amounts, until the official Navy rum ration, dispensed in equal tots twice a day—the first was taken in the morning on an empty stomach—was equivalent to six double whiskys.

Then, in 1731, the tide turned. Admiral Edward Vernon, Commander-in-Chief of His Majesty's Naval Forces in the West Indies, decided that while rum might produce courage and contentment in some sailors, it also caused illness and severe disciplinary problems. Vernon, a thoughtful and brave man—George Washington was so impressed by the Admiral that he called his house after him—defied the fury of his men in the interest of their health and ordered that their rum ration be diluted in the proportion of one part of rum to three of water. The sailors had already nicknamed the admiral Old Grog, from his habit of coming aboard his ships wearing a distinctive cloak made of a coarse material called grogram. When he watered down their rum ration they dubbed the new drink grog. For many years the word was widely used to mean not only rum and water but any alcoholic drink. We rarely use it any more, but we still use the adjective groggy to describe the effects of drinking.

In America grog became a patriot's drink. Washington was elected to the Virginia House of Burgesses in 1758 not so much by political campaigning as by distributing 70 gallons of rum among the voters. Paul Revere might never have roused the Massachusetts sharpshooters on the night of his famous ride had not it been for rum. Events, it seems, did not happen as Longfellow described them in his famous poem. Revere started his ride silently, simply in order to warn a few patriotic friends that the British might be up to something. But he was chased by two enemy horsemen. He eluded their pursuit but, upset by his near-capture, stopped in at the home of Isaac Hall, a friend and local rum manufacturer. Hall poured Revere several draughts of heavy Medford rum; Revere tossed them down and what happened after that is history.

Eventually rum became elevated to a gentleman's, even a prince's, drink. Its rise to this eminence culminated in 1892 when the physician to the Court of Spain prescribed Cuban rum for a 6-year-old royal prince suffering from a severe attack of influenza complicated by high fever and insomnia. Immediately the fever began to abate and the boy fell asleep. He soon regained his health—and subsequently became King Alphonso XIII—and the Bacardi family, manufacturer of the health-restoring rum, was granted permission to use the Spanish coat of arms on its label.

The rum we drink today differs considerably from the spirit that spurred on Paul Revere. What Isaac Hall produced in his Massachusetts distillery was heavy-bodied, pungent and dark in colour; since the late 19th century, rums on the whole have been of higher proof, lighter in colour and texture, and more varied. They can generally be divided into three categories, light, medium and heavy. Light rum, almost as dry in flavour as vodka, is primarily used in cocktails. The more traditional heavy rum, full-bodied, pungent in bouquet and usually dark in colour, is most often used for punches, where it must compete with other flavours. In the middle is a wide spectrum of versatile light to middle-bodied rums, ranging in colour from golden to ruby to deepest mahogany; they can be used in cocktails or punches, or treated like liqueurs and drunk neat.

The British taste in rum has been traditionally for the dark, heavy, Navy-issue type or the fruitier, more aromatic medium rums associated in this country with Trinidad. But British tastes often follow American preferences and the popularity of light-bodied drinks in the United States is reflected in the steadily increasing demand for white rums in Britain today. All this is a matter of custom, and custom is subject to change. Heavy rum was preferred in America until around the start of World War I; after that there was a shift to lighter-bodied rums. Today interest seems to be growing in the medium rums, perhaps as a result of the sophistication caused by travel. Visitors to the Caribbean have tasted rum in the way the islanders prefer it, not in cocktails but in drinks in which the *taste* of rum predominates. A mild but well-flavoured rum is essential for this kind of appreciation.

However much it may vary, rum owes its distinctive taste to its origin in sugar-cane. Most distilled spirits are made from grain, some from

Old San Juan's La Fonda del Callejon is renowned not only for its Puerto Rican food but also for its rum drinks; the speciality of the house is the *coqui*, photographed here in the inner courtyard of the restaurant. Unlike the fruity rum drinks made with lime, pineapple or banana, *coqui* is a smooth, creamy tipple concocted from two kinds of rum and enriched with fresh coconut cream (*Recipe Index*). The ingredients grouped round the glass include, from the right: rum, evaporated milk, coconut, vanilla, nutmeg, egg yolk and Triple Sec, an orange-flavoured liqueur.

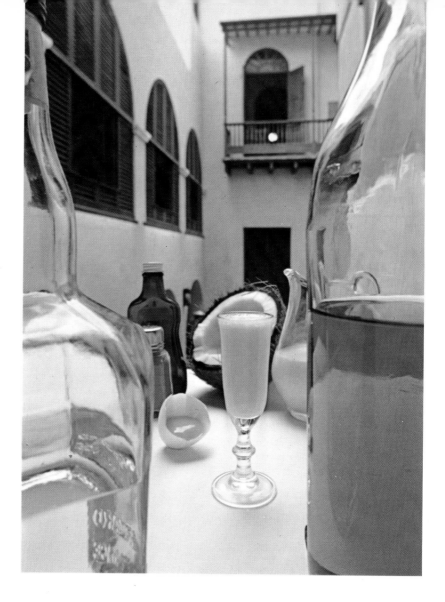

grapes or other fruit; only rum comes from sugar-cane. It is sometimes distilled directly from fresh cane juice, but more often it is a by-product of sugar production. In making sugar, the stalks of the sugar-cane are crushed until they exude a sweet juice. The juice is boiled and the sugar in it crystallizes, leaving various impurities that remain as a thick, sticky, dark brown semi-liquid—molasses. It is at this point that most rum making starts. Molasses left lying in the tropical sun will ferment readily and actively, and it is believed that rum production began in the early 1600s when a Barbadian sugar planter got the idea of carrying the process another step and distilling his naturally fermented molasses.

Today the fermentation process is started either by the addition of dunder, a residue left from a previous distillation, or by the addition of yeast. Rum makers are reticent about their techniques, particularly when it comes to the yeasts that they use. It has been said of a leading Puerto Rican rum company that it breeds its yeast in secret, like Derby runners, staking everything on the yeast's individuality. A prominent Haitian rum manufacturer grows mystical when talking about his yeast, attributing the excellence of his rum to the fact that the yeast and sugar-cane he uses both grow in the same part of the island; this, he asserts, produces a natural harmony that is reflected in the taste of his rum.

Once the molasses is fermented the distillation process begins. Either a pot still or a continuous still may be used. Pot stills distil at a lower proof and remove fewer of the congenerics that impart taste and aroma to spirits, and thus the rum that results—the traditional rum—tends to be heavier in flavour and bouquet. But however distilled, the rum that emerges can hardly be called rum. Like all spirits at this stage, it is colourless and its flavour is undeveloped. It is the maturing process that gives most rum its distinctive character. For a light rum the spirit is placed in ordinary oak casks or simply in covered tanks; for a heavier rum, charred oak casks are used. Caramel is added to give the desired colour and the rum is left to age. Some rums are bottled without being matured; some are barrel-aged only for a few months, others for as long as 25 years; sometimes batches of different ages are blended.

Rum distilled in a continuous still is drawn off at a very high proof—that is, with high alcoholic content—and is eventually reduced by the addition of distilled water. Most rums are between 70 and 100 proof—between 35 and 50 per cent alcohol—but several distillers also produce an over-proof rum, bottled at 132 proof, or more. This would be extremely dangerous to drink, but used in desserts or flambéed dishes it is excellent. A curious story told about this rum is that the original demand for it came not from people in the Caribbean but from whalers and trappers in Canada's icy Hudson Bay where, when winter sets in, ordinary rums will freeze and break their containers. Supposedly out of sympathy for their frustration the tropical islanders began to manufacture over-proof rum, whose alcoholic concentration makes it as easy to pour as anti-freeze even at the North Pole.

Light rum has long been associated with Puerto Rico and Cuba, where it was first developed in the late 19th century, and dark, heavy rum of the kind that, until 1970, was regularly dispensed as the British Navy's rum ration. Today most islands produce light, heavy and intermediate rums. Among white rums, Bacardi reaches the British market not from Puerto Rico but from Mexico and the Bahamas, Daiquiri—the white rum, not the bottled cocktail—from Guyana; Jamaica exports a 101 proof white rum and there have been white rums from Cuba on the market as well.

The British, who are quite considerable rum drinkers, do not, in fact, import many of the rums that are popular on the United States market with the distinguished exceptions of dark Myers rum, golden Appleton Estates and full-bodied Lemon Hart, all from Jamaica, and the drier Mountgay from Barbados. Most British rums come from Jamaica, Barbados, Trinidad and Guyana. These last are usually referred to as Demerara rums and include such household names as Lamb's Navy Rum. Anejo, a long-matured liqueur rum, is exported by the Bacardi company and rums from the French islands are represented only by Negrita which reaches Britain via Bardinct of Bordeaux. The famous Barbancourt of Haiti, long the favourite of American connoisseurs, is unobtainable. This is a medium-bodied, pleasantly flavoured variety of rum that reflects the French skill in brandy making in that it, like brandy, is double-distilled. It is interesting that, while the product of the second distillation is the favourite with connoisseurs, the first distillation is sometimes bottled and sold domestically as the most powerful means of propitiating the local voodoo gods. Unaged and called *clairin* because it is colourless, it is the libation poured upon the ground in voodoo ceremonies.

My own favourite rums come from Martinique, where a few distilleries make their rum not from molasses but directly from cane juice. St. James—the only brand easily available in the United States—Bally and Clément are all excellent examples of sugar-cane rum made on Martinique. The companies that produce these rums operate on a smaller scale than do most of the distilleries using molasses. Since they do not make sugar and therefore have no molasses set aside, they manufacture their rum only during the actual sugar-cane cutting season. But the rum they produce is superb; its admirers poetically claim that it has more of the sun and the fragrant earth in its bouquet than any other.

Having enjoyed both Bally and Clément rums, I eagerly accepted the offer of a Martinican friend who knew both proprietors to take me to see their distilleries. At both the cane was being brought in on battered lorries or even wearier looking mules. The yards outside the distilleries were littered with scraps of cane, and for miles around the air was laden with the ripe, sickly-sweet smell of the sugar-cane being crushed. The machinery in the distilleries seemed to me like a nostalgic exhibit of old locomotives—hissing pistons, huge iron fly-wheels, clacking valves. The buildings themselves were wooden, with creaky steps and roofs that revealed occasional patches of the hot blue tropical sky.

My Martinican friend was embarrassed by the old machinery and said apologetically, "You as an American will probably view this as a sort of handicraft." But I explained that I found something wonderful in its simplicity, and in the way in which the relationship of the raw sugar to the finished rum was almost tangible. There is a bit of the craftsman in me as there must be, I think, in anyone who likes cooking. The great resurgence of interest in cooking today seems to me an almost deliberate courting of the old ways, a defiance of the technology that gives us frozen tacos, packaged chicken pies and canned vichyssoise. I tried to make this clear to my friend but he, as a man keenly interested in the economic development of his island, was more concerned with a future that would put modern machines at the service of his island's traditional art.

Some time later I visited the Bacardi distillery in Puerto Rico and was impressed but oddly disappointed by the huge, 55,000-gallon molasses fermentation vats two storeys high that froth like some giant child's bubble bath, and by the white-coated technicians and the computers they used to control the distilling process. But at the end of the tour I recovered my appreciation for the art of rum making when I was introduced to a shy quiet man in sloppy work clothes, a member of the Bacardi family, who was seeing to the blending of rums of various ages and proofs that produces the various Bacardi products. Like a wine-taster in a vineyard cellar, he was using what is in the end the only standard of excellence, his own taste and judgement. I talked to him for a time and later wrote to my Martinican friend that perhaps the making of all good rum, like all good food, is a handicraft.

Handicraft or not, the production of rum is certainly an industry at which the islanders excel. Although Britain imports rum from only seven places in the Caribbean—Puerto Rico, the Virgin Islands, Jamaica, Trinidad, Barbados, Haiti and Martinique—a great many other islands manufacture their own rums.

A number of them also manufacture excellent liqueurs from tropical plants other than sugar-cane. The orange liqueur of Curaçao made from the bitter oranges that grow there is perhaps the most famous, although Jamaica's sweet rum-based Tia Maria, flavoured with Blue Mountain coffee, is fast becoming a rival. Jamaica also makes Pimento Dram, a liqueur based on the oil of the allspice berry, which is known as pimento on that island. Chococo from St. Croix is a coconut liqueur delicately flavoured with chocolate. Puerto Rico uses its plentiful pineapples and bananas to make delicious liqueurs. These are used in Haiti too, as well as mangoes and pawpaws, and—even here there is a fragrant liqueur made from hibiscus flowers.

But rum is of course the triumphant alcoholic offering of the islands. Wherever your plane lands, one of the first questions you will be asked is, "Have you tasted our rum?" And whether because you are hot or excited by travel, or just responding to the questioner's enthusiasm, as soon as you do sample the local rum you discover that it tastes better than any rum ever tasted at home. It is the perfect drink for the climate, heady and compelling. Your plane has physically taken you to the tropics but your mind still lingers in the north. The first rum on arrival completes your voyage by transporting you psychically. Cold and cares are forgotten. The second rum is hypnotic. Its golden colour reflects the sunshine all around you, and its bouquet is redolent of graceful cane fields. Rum in hand, you find yourself at rest, ready to rejoice in the mere contemplation of the island-strewn Caribbean.

Honeymooners sipping tall rum drinks (*above*) share a view and a hammock at the Caneel Bay Plantation in St. John in the United States Virgin Islands.

Overleaf: The montage of labels represents just a sample of the hundreds of rums produced in the Caribbean. Included are labels for Tia Maria (*top centre*), a Jamaican coffee-flavoured liqueur made with rum, and Angostura bitters (*top right*), a Trinidad flavouring added to many rum cocktails. In the foreground is a row of rum-based drinks (*from left*): a pitcher of rum punch, a Bacardi cocktail, dark rum on the rocks with lime juice, and beside it, a frozen daiquiri made with light rum, a pony of Tia Maria, a tall rum Collins and, on the top right, a banana daiquiri, a peach daiquiri and a Blue Mountain cocktail (*recipes on following pages*).

To serve 2

1 fl. oz. strained fresh lime juice
2½ teaspoons castor sugar
3 fl. oz. light or dark rum
4 fl. oz. water
3 or 4 ice cubes
2 thin orange slices

To make 2 cocktails

3 fl. oz. medium-dark rum
1½ fl. oz. vodka
1½ fl. oz. Tia Maria or other coffee
    liqueur
2 fl. oz. strained fresh orange juice
1 fl. oz. strained fresh lime juice
3 or 4 ice cubes

To serve 2

7 fl. oz. dark rum
2 fl. oz. strained fresh lime juice
3 tablespoons castor sugar
A dash of Angostura bitters
⅜ pint crushed or finely cracked ice
Freshly grated nutmeg

GARNISH (OPTIONAL)
2 maraschino cherries and 2 fresh
    pineapple or banana strips, or 2
    thin lime or orange slices

To make 2 cocktails

6 fl. oz. light rum
1 fl. oz. strained fresh lime juice
1½ teaspoons castor sugar
3 or 4 ice cubes

To make 2 cocktails

4 fl. oz. light rum
1 fl. oz. strained fresh lime juice
1½ teaspoons castor sugar
¾ pint finely cracked ice.

Rum Punch

Put the lime juice, sugar, rum, water and 3 or 4 ice cubes into a mixing glass, and place a bar shaker on top of the glass. Grasping the glass and shaker firmly together with both hands, shake them vigorously 9 or 10 times. Remove the shaker and place a strainer over the mixing glass. Pour the punch into 2 tall, chilled glasses filled with ice cubes, garnish with orange slices, and serve at once.

Blue Mountain Cocktail

Put the rum, vodka, coffee liqueur, orange juice, lime juice and ice into a mixing glass, and place a bar shaker on top of the glass. Grasping the glass and shaker firmly together with both hands, shake them vigorously 9 or 10 times. Remove the shaker and pour the cocktail unstrained into 2 chilled 8-fluid ounce tumblers. Serve at once.

Planter's Punch

Put 6 fluid ounces of the rum, the lime juice, the icing sugar, bitters and cracked ice into a mixing glass, and place a bar shaker on top of the glass. Grasping the glass and the shaker firmly together with both hands, shake them vigorously 9 or 10 times.

Remove the shaker and pour the contents of the glass, unstrained, into 2 tall, chilled, half pint glasses.

Place a teaspoon upside down in each glass in turn and very slowly pour ½ fluid ounce or more of the rum over the back of the spoon, letting it trickle off on to the surface of the drink so that the rum floats on top. Grate a little nutmeg over the drink and serve at once.

Planter's punch is often served garnished with some kind of fresh fruit. If you like, add a maraschino cherry and a pineapple or banana strip to each drink, or slit the lime or orange slices from peel to centre and stand them on the rim of each glass.

Daiquiri

Put the rum, lime juice, sugar and ice cubes into a mixing glass, and place a bar shaker on top of the glass. Grasping the glass and shaker firmly together with both hands, shake them vigorously 9 or 10 times. Remove the shaker, and place a strainer over the mixing glass. Pour the Daiquiri into 2 chilled 4-fluid ounce cocktail glasses, and serve at once.

Frozen Daiquiri

Put the rum, lime juice, sugar and cracked ice into the jar of an electric blender, and blend at medium speed for about 20 seconds. Pour the contents of the jar, unstrained, into 2 chilled 6-fluid ounce champagne glasses and serve with short drinking straws.

Pineapple Daiquiri

Put the pineapple juice, rum, lime juice and Cointreau into the jar of an electric blender, and blend at high speed for about 20 seconds. Taste and stir or blend in a little castor sugar, if you find it necessary. Pour the Daiquiri into 2 chilled 8 to 10-fluid ounce tumblers filled with ice cubes, and serve at once.

To serve 2

⅜ pint canned pineapple juice
4 fl. oz. light rum
½ fl. oz. strained fresh lime juice
1 teaspoon Cointreau
Castor sugar

Banana Daiquiri

Put the banana, rum, banana liqueur, lime juice and ice into the jar of an electric blender, and blend at high speed for 20 to 30 seconds, until the banana is completely puréed and the mixture smooth and frothy. Taste and add castor sugar if necessary. Pour the Daiquiri into 2 chilled 8-fluid ounce tumblers and serve at once.

To make 2 cocktails

½ medium-sized ripe banana, peeled
    and coarsely chopped
4 fl. oz. light rum
½ fl. oz. banana liqueur
½ fl. oz. strained fresh lime juice
6 tablespoons crushed or finely
    cracked ice
Castor sugar

Peach Daiquiri

Put the peach, rum, Cointreau, lime juice, sugar and ice into the jar of an electric blender, and blend at high speed for about 20 seconds, until the peach is completely puréed and the mixture smooth and frothy. Pour the Daiquiri into 2 chilled 6-fluid ounce champagne glasses, and serve at once.

To serve 2

½ medium-sized firm ripe peach,
    peeled, seeded and cut into chunks
1½ fl. oz. light rum
½ fl. oz. Cointreau
1 fl. oz. strained fresh lime juice
1 teaspoon castor sugar
⅜ pint crushed or finely cracked ice

Cold Rum Soufflé (Jamaica)

Sprinkle the gelatine over the cold water and set it aside to soften. Meanwhile beat the egg yolks and 2 ounces of the sugar together in a mixing bowl with a whisk or a rotary egg beater, until the yolks are pale yellow and thick.

Pour the evaporated milk and the cornflour mixture into a fairly large enamel, stainless-steel or glass saucepan. Stir over a low heat until the milk thickens enough to coat the spoon heavily. Remove the pan from the heat and add the egg yolks and the softened gelatine, beating constantly. Return the pan to a low heat and continue to stir until the mixture is smooth and thick enough to coat the spoon heavily. Do not let the custard come anywhere near boiling point or it will curdle; if it seems to be getting too hot, lift the pan off the stove to cool it. It must, however, be sufficiently hot to thicken.

Strain the custard through a fine sieve into a large mixing bowl. Then warm the rum in a small pan over a low heat. Set light to the rum, off the heat, with a match and shake the pan gently to and fro until the flames die out. Stir the rum and vanilla into the custard.

Wash and dry the whisk or beater; then beat the egg whites, in a separate bowl, until they are frothy. Add the remaining 2 ounces of sugar and the salt, and continue beating until the whites are stiff enough to stand in firm, unwavering peaks on the whisk when it is lifted from the bowl.

Set the bowl of custard into a pan or another larger bowl filled with crushed ice or ice cubes and cold water. Stir the custard for about 4 to 5 minutes, until it is quite cold and beginning to thicken. Scoop the egg whites over the custard and fold them in thoroughly but gently with a rubber spatula.

Ladle the soufflé into a 1½-pint soufflé dish and refrigerate for at least 3 hours, until firm and set.

To serve 6

¼ oz. powdered gelatine
3 tablespoons cold water
4 egg yolks
4 oz. sugar
⅜ pint evaporated milk
2½ teaspoons cornflour blended
    with 5 teaspoons cold water
3 tablespoons dark rum
¼ teaspoon vanilla essence
4 egg whites
A pinch of salt

To make 2 cocktails

4 fl. oz. light rum
2 fl. oz. strained fresh lime juice
1½ teaspoons grenadine
1 teaspoon castor sugar
3 or 4 ice cubes

To serve 2

5 fl. oz. canned pineapple juice
4 fl. oz. light rum
2 fl. oz. bottled coconut syrup
2 fl. oz. strained fresh lime juice
3 or 4 ice cubes

To serve 2

8 fl. oz. medium-dark rum
2 eggs, lightly beaten
1½ teaspoons castor sugar
2 dashes Angostura bitters
⅜ pint crushed or finely cracked ice
Freshly grated nutmeg

To serve 1

3 fl. oz. medium-dark rum
1 fl. oz. strained fresh lime or lemon
  juice
1 teaspoon castor sugar
2 or 3 ice cubes
6 fl. oz. cold soda water
1 thin orange slice (optional)
1 maraschino cherry (optional)

To make about 1½ pints

1 oz. fresh ginger root, in one
  piece (about 1½ inches long and
  1 inch in diameter), peeled and
  crushed with the flat side of a
  cleaver or large, heavy knife
The rind of 1 medium-sized lime
4 tablespoons strained fresh lime
  juice
4 oz. sugar
1½ pints boiling water
1 teaspoon dried yeast
3 tablespoons lukewarm water (110°
  to 115°F.)

Bacardi

Put the rum, lime juice, grenadine, sugar and ice cubes into a mixing glass, and place a bar shaker on top of the glass. Grasping the glass and shaker firmly together with both hands, shake them vigorously 9 or 10 times. Remove the shaker and place a strainer over the mixing glass. Pour the Bacardi into 2 chilled 4-fluid ounce cocktail glasses, and serve at once.

Piña Colada

Put the pineapple juice, rum, coconut syrup, lime juice and 3 or 4 ice cubes into a mixing glass, and place a bar shaker on top of the glass. Grasping the glass and shaker firmly together with both hands, shake them vigorously 9 or 10 times. Remove the shaker and place a strainer over the mixing glass. Pour the *piña colada* into 2 chilled, tall, 8-fluid ounce glasses filled with ice cubes, and serve at once.

Rum Flip

Put the rum, beaten eggs, sugar, bitters and ice into a mixing glass, and place a bar shaker on top of the glass. Grasping the glass and shaker firmly together with both hands, shake them vigorously 9 or 10 times. Remove the shaker and pour the rum flip, unstrained, into 2 chilled, tall, half-pint glasses. Grate a little nutmeg on top and serve at once.

Rum Collins

Place the rum, lime or lemon juice and sugar in a 14-fluid ounce Tom Collins glass and stir with a bar spoon to dissolve the sugar. Add the ice cubes, fill the glass with cold soda water and stir briefly. Garnish the drink, if you like, with an orange slice and or a cherry.

Ginger Beer (Trinidad)

Starting a week in advance, put the ginger, lime rind, lime juice and sugar into a large earthenware bowl, and pour the boiling water over them. Stir until the sugar dissolves completely, then let the mixture cool to room temperature.

Sprinkle the yeast over the lukewarm water in a small bowl or cup. Let it stand for 2 to 3 minutes, then stir to dissolve the yeast completely. Set the bowl in a warm, draught-free place for about 5 minutes, until the mixture begins to bubble and almost doubles in volume. (If no bubbles develop, discard the mixture and repeat the process with yeast from a fresh packet.) Add the yeast to the ginger mixture and stir thoroughly.

Cover the bowl tightly with foil or a sheet of plastic, place it in a warm, draught-free place, and let the mixture ferment for a week. Stir the ginger beer every other day. After a week the mixture will be mildly carbonated.

Strain the ginger beer through a fine sieve and, using a funnel, pour the liquid into a 1½ pint glass or stone bottle and cork it tightly. Let the beer ferment at room temperature for 3 or 4 days longer, then refrigerate until it is thoroughly chilled.

Serve the ginger beer in chilled tumblers, with or without ice cubes.

Cruzan Dawn

Put the ice cubes, rum and vermouth into a 6-fluid ounce tumbler and stir briefly with a bar spoon. Serve at once.

To make 1 cocktail

2 or 3 ice cubes
2 fl. oz. Cruzan Clipper rum, or substitute any other medium-dark rum
1 fl. oz. sweet vermouth

Coqui

RUM AND COCONUT CREAM DRINK

Put the coconut cream, evaporated milk, egg yolks and vanilla into the jar of an electric blender, and blend at high speed for about 30 seconds, until the mixture is smooth. Add the dark rum, the medium-dark rum and the Cointreau, and blend for a few seconds longer. Refrigerate the *coqui* for about 4 hours, until it is thoroughly chilled.

To serve, pour the *coqui* into chilled punch glasses and sprinkle the top lightly with nutmeg.

To make about 1½ pints

½ pint coconut cream made from 5 oz. coarsely chopped fresh coconut and ½ pint single cream (*see "Notes on Caribbean Cooking"*)
9 tablespoons evaporated milk
2 egg yolks
½ teaspoon vanilla essence
⅜ pint dark rum
⅜ pint medium-dark rum
1½ tablespoons Cointreau or other orange-flavoured liqueur
Freshly grated nutmeg

Floating Island (*Jamaica*)

Put the egg yolks and sugar into a heavy, medium-sized saucepan and beat with a whisk for 2 to 3 minutes, until they begin to thicken. Slowly pour in the cream, whisking constantly. Place the pan over a low heat and simmer for about 10 to 12 minutes, stirring constantly and deeply with a wooden spoon, until the custard is thick enough to coat the back of the spoon. Do not allow the mixture to come anywhere near boiling point or it may curdle. Let the custard cool to room temperature, then pour it into a serving dish about 8 or 9 inches in diameter, and refrigerate for at least 3 hours, until it is completely chilled.

Just before serving, melt the guava jelly in a small shallow pan over a low heat. Remove the pan from the stove. Beat the egg whites with a wire whisk or a rotary egg beater until they are stiff enough to stand in unwavering peaks when the whisk is lifted from the bowl. Pour the melted jelly slowly over the whites in a thin stream, beating constantly, and continue to beat until the jelly and the whites are well blended.

To make the "floating islands" after which the sweet is named, scoop up about 3 tablespoons of the beaten egg whites in a ladle or serving spoon and drop it gently on the surface of the custard, spacing the islands about an inch or so apart.

Beat the double cream in a chilled bowl, with the same beater, until it begins to thicken. Add the icing sugar and the rum, and continue beating until the cream is stiff but not buttery. Place a heaped teaspoon of the whipped cream on each of the islands and serve at once.

To serve 4

4 egg yolks
3 tablespoons sugar
¾ pint single cream
4 tablespoons guava jelly
2 egg whites
6 tablespoons double cream
1½ tablespoons icing sugar
3 tablespoons dark rum

Caribbean Cocktail

Put the pineapple juice, rum, lime juice, bitters and ice into a mixing jar, and place a bar shaker on top of the glass. Grasping the glass and shaker firmly together with both hands, shake them vigorously 9 or 10 times. Taste and add castor sugar, if desired.

Remove the shaker and pour the cocktail, unstrained, into 2 chilled 8-fluid ounce tumblers. Add enough soda water to fill each glass to the brim. Grate a little nutmeg on top and serve at once.

To serve 2

6 tablespoons canned pineapple juice
2 fl. oz. medium-dark rum
2½ teaspoons strained fresh lime juice
About ¼ teaspoon Angostura bitters
⅜ pint crushed or finely cracked ice
Castor sugar
Soda water
Freshly grated nutmeg

An Island Eating Guide

Here is a traveller's guide to eating in the Caribbean islands. It is not a comprehensive list of all available dishes but represents some of the local specialities, offered by specific islands, that have been enjoyed by those who worked on this book. The fresh fruits, fish and shellfish are superb throughout the islands. The same vegetables (under many different names) grow and are prepared in various ways on most of the islands. Be sure to sample them and then ask for some of the dishes listed here. (Many of them are described in detail in the Glossary or the text; *see General Index*.)

Antigua, Montserrat, Nevis

Boija (coconut-cornmeal bread)
Funchi (cornmeal pudding)
Fish soup
Pepper-pot soup
Stuffed crab back
Pumpkin soup
Salt fish with avocado or aubergine

Aruba and Curaçao

Keshy yena (stuffed Edam cheese)
Sopito (chowder)
Calas (bean fritters)
Tripe soup
Stobá (lamb or goat stew)
Boterkoek (butter biscuits)
Funchi
Pastechi (meat-stuffed turnover)
Cachapas (cornmeal pancakes)
Ayacas (leaf-wrapped meat rolls)

Barbados

Flying fish
Sea eggs (sea-urchins)
Conch fritters
Jug-jug (cornmeal Christmas pudding)
Conkies (cornmeal and meat pies)
Pudding and souse (black pudding brawn)
Pepper-pot stew
Turtle steak
Sea moss jelly

Cuba

Moros y Cristianos (beans and rice)
Black bean soup
Green plantain soup
Ajiaco (spicy meat stew)
Langosta enchilada (lobster in spicy sauce)
Picadillo (spicy minced meat)
Ropa vieja (shredded beef)

Dominica

Tannia soup (taro soup)
Mountain chicken (frogs' legs)

Dominican Republic

Carne mechada (stuffed beef roast)
Locrios (rice and meat stew)
Sopón (soupy rice casserole)
Pastelitos (meat-filled turnovers)
Mofongo (plantain balls)
Sancocho (meat stew)

Grenada and the Grenadines

Callaloo (soup with greens)
Flying fish
Carrot soup
Jacks and bluggoe soup (fish and banana soup)
West Indian plum pudding
Sour-sop fool
Bread-fruit soup
Lambi souse (marinated conch)
Guava and nutmeg jellies
Turtle soup

Guadeloupe and Martinique

Sea eggs
Soupe de poisson (fish soup)
Land crab omelette
Acrats de morue (codfish fritters)
Blaff (fish in broth)
Court bouillon (fish in Creole sauce)
Colombo (curry)
Callaloo with crab
Hearts of palm vinaigrette
Crab stew
Pâté en pot (thick meat soup)
Boudin (black pudding)

Haiti

Riz au djon djon (rice and black mushrooms)
Tassau de dinde (dried turkey)
Griots de porc (fried pork)
Sauce Ti-Malice (tart sauce)
Codfish salad
Acrats de morue (codfish fritters)
Stuffed crab
Flambéed lobster
Crab stew

Jamaica

Pepper-pot soup
Curried goat
Salmagundi (herring salad)
Salt fish and akee
Baked black crab

Stamp and go (codfish fritters)
Brown fish stew
Duckunoo (sweet-potato pudding)
Cassava cakes
Jerk pork (barbecued pig)
Matrimony (star apple and orange drink)
Akkra (pea or bean fritters)
Red pea soup
Pumpkin soup
Escovitch (marinated fish)
Mackerel run down (fritters)
Rice and peas

Puerto Rico

Land crab in the shell
Land crab pie with yuca
Baby goat fricassée
Ostiones (mangrove oysters)
Surrullitos (corn and cheese sticks)
Mofongo con chicharrones (plantain with crackling)
Arroz con pollo (chicken and rice)
Asopao (thin rice and meat or seafood stew)
Pasteles (leaf-wrapped meat pies)
Piononos (meat-stuffed plantains)

St. Martin (France and the Netherlands)

Steak Creole
Soupe de poisson

St. Vincent

Stewed shark
Bread-fruit sweets
Callaloo
Arrowroot sponge

Trinidad and Tobago

Rice and peas
Sancocho
Pepper-pot
Pudding and souse
Pelaus (rice with meat or seafood)
Mangrove oysters
Roti (Indian bread with various fillings)
Shark meat on hops bread
Roast pork with rice and red beans

Virgin Islands

Meat patty
Callaloo
Salt fish and rice
Herring gundy (herring salad)
Fish chowder
Tannia soup
Turtle or lobster stew
Conch salad

Glossary

ACHIOTE: *See* ANNATTO.

AKEE (ackee): Oblong or egg-shaped fruit of an evergreen tree widely cultivated in Jamaica. The scarlet pod encloses cream-coloured flesh whose bland texture and taste is often compared to scrambled eggs. It is traditionally served in Jamaica with salt fish. Available canned in some West Indian shops.

AKKRA (accra, acrat): Originally a West African fritter, made throughout the islands. The traditional Jamaican akkra is a fritter made of ground blackeyed peas or soya beans; the same thing is known as *cala* on the Dutch Islands. Akkras are also made of a heavy batter into which a variety of ingredients are mixed, salt cod being the most popular. This mixture is called stamp and go in Jamaica, *acrat de morue* in the French islands and *bacalaitos* in Puerto Rico.

ALLSPICE (pimento): Dark-brown berries of an evergreen tree native to the West Indies. The berries resemble smooth over-sized peppercorns and their aroma and flavour suggest a blend of cloves, cinnamon and nutmeg.

ALLSPICE OIL: Oil extracted from the leaves of the allspice tree and used in making a Jamaican liqueur called Pimento Dram.

ANNATTO (*achiote*): Rusty-red dried seed of a tropical American tree. It is used primarily to colour cooking oil or lard a bright orange yellow, but also lends a delicate flavour. Liquid annatto is available on order from chemists' shops. Keeps indefinitely in a well-sealed bottle. Shake the bottle thoroughly before use. No substitute.

APIO (*arracacha*): Root of a tropical plant popular in the Caribbean, used as a starchy vegetable and as an ingredient in SANCOCHO.

ARROWROOT: Starch obtained from the roots of a plant native to tropical America. Finely ground to the consistency of cornflour, it is used as a flavourless thickening agent in light sauces and glazes.

ASOPAO: The word literally means "soupy" in Spanish and is used to describe a thin stew made with rice and with chicken, meat or seafood; a traditional Puerto Rican dish.

BAKES: Fried baking-powder biscuits, a speciality of Trinidad.

BAY RUM: Evergreen tree related to myrtle and allspice, native to the West Indies. The spirit distilled from its leaves is used in cosmetics. The small dark berries, also called malagueta pepper, are used in a way similar to ALLSPICE.

BEANS: Islanders use the term peas (or *pois*) for both beans and peas of various kinds. For instance, the Haitian *riz et pois* is a dish of rice and red kidney beans. The beans used in the recipes in this book are dried and available in most groceries. *See* GANDULES, HABICHUELAS, FRIJOL NEGRO.

BLAFF: Fresh fish poached in a clear stock seasoned with hot peppers. Traditional in the French islands.

BREAD-FRUIT: Round or oblong fruit with a tough, yellowish-green and bumpy or prickly skin. It may measure up to 8 inches in diameter and weigh as much as 10 pounds. The flesh is cream-coloured and has a flavour and texture that is often compared to wholegrain bread. It is eaten like a starchy vegetable, boiled, roasted or fried. Available in West Indian shops, July to September.

CALABAZA (West Indian pumpkin, green pumpkin): Pumpkins belong to the squash family, and in most parts of the Caribbean the term calabaza, or pumpkin, is used to mean a squash. Sizes, shapes and skin colouring vary, but calabazas usually have firm yellow flesh and a delicate flavour somewhat like that of Hubbard or butternut squash. Available in West Indian shops.

CALLALOO: Caribbean soup made in all the islands from callaloo greens and crab meat. The word may also be used to mean CALLALOO GREENS.

CALLALOO GREENS: The term is used both for the young leaves of the DASHEEN or TARO plant and for the Oriental pot-herbs known as Chinese spinach. Available in some West Indian shops.

CAPSICUM: *See* PEPPERS.

CASHEW: Evergreen tree and shrub native to the West Indies. It bears a tart, reddish, pear-shaped cashew apple, from the bottom of which grows the kidney-shaped nut, edible only when roasted.

CASSAREEP: Juice squeezed from freshly grated cassava root, which is boiled down and used as a thickening agent and a bitter-sweet flavouring in Trinidadian PEPPER-POT.

CASSAVA (manioc, yuca, mandioca): Long, irregularly shaped root at least 2 inches in diameter with a dark-brown rough bark-like skin and hard white starchy flesh. The bitter variety is poisonous until cooked. It is the base for tapioca and manioc meal, but in the Caribbean is chiefly used to make starch. The root used in the recipes in this book is the sweet variety, which is available throughout the year in most West Indian shops. The root will keep safely for 2 to 3 weeks in the refrigerator.

CHAYOTE: *See* CHRISTOPHENE.

CHICHARRONES: Fried pork crackling available in packets in most Latin American shops in the U.S.A. Not yet imported into the U.K.

CHILLIES: *See* PEPPERS.

CHOCHO: *See* CHRISTOPHENE.

CHORIZO (Spanish sausage): Lightly smoked sausage of coarsely chopped pork, seasoned with garlic, sweet red pepper and hot paprika. Available in 4-inch links or canned, packed in lard, at Spanish grocers' shops and in any delicatessens.

CHRISTOPHENE (*chayote*, chocho): Tropical squash, round or pear-shaped, ranging from white to dark green; 3 to 8 inches long. It may be smooth or corrugated and is sometimes covered with soft spines. The firm, crisp flesh is more delicate in flavour than courgettes. Available in some West Indian shops throughout the year.

CILANTRO: *See* CORIANDER.

COCIDO: Spanish word for stew.

CONCH (lambi): A large edible mollusc with a beautiful spiral shell found throughout the islands; its firm flesh is generally tenderized by pounding before being served in salads or chowders. Usually pronounced "conk" in the Caribbean.

CONKIES: Cornmeal mixed with chopped meat, raisins, coconut and spices, wrapped and cooked in envelopes of banana leaves. A traditional Barbadian speciality.

CORIANDER (*cilantro, culantro,* Chinese parsley): Aromatic herb that resembles flat-leaf parsley in appearance, but has a much more pungent flavour. It is sold fresh by the bunch in Greek, Cypriot and Chinese shops. Do not wash the leaves or remove the roots before storing; it will keep for about a week if refrigerated in a plastic bag.

COURT BOUILLON: In the French islands of the Caribbean, the term describes a traditional recipe for poached fish. Not to be confused with the classic court bouillon of French cooking: the liquid in which fish or other food is poached.

CRAPAUD: French for the large frog found on Dominica and Montserrat, where it is also called mountain chicken and considered a delicacy.

CUMIN SEED: Yellowish-brown seed of a plant of the parsley family. Shaped like a miniature corn kernel, it is aromatic and reminiscent of caraway. Often used in curries. Available whole or ground.

CURAÇAO: Liqueur produced in the Dutch islands from the rind of bitter oranges.

DASHEEN: *See* TARO.

DJON DJON: Tiny Haitian mushrooms with small caps. They give off a dark brownish-black liquid and colour when cooked. Dried European mushrooms can be substituted.

ESCABECHE: The word literally means "pickled" and is used to describe a Spanish and Portuguese method of preparing fish, seafood, poultry or game birds. Recipes vary, but typically the food is cooked and then pickled in a vinegar marinade.

ESCOVITCH: The Jamaican version.

FARINE: On the French islands, a shortened form of *farine de manioc*, or cassava meal.

FLOATS: Fried yeast buns, a speciality of Trinidad. Tradition-

ally served with codfish AKKRAS.
FRIJOL NEGRO (black bean, turtle bean): Small, flat charcoal-coloured bean not more than $\frac{1}{2}$ inch long. It is a native of the Americas and related to the common haricot and kidney bean. Available dried in most groceries. *See* BEANS.

FRUTA BOMBA: Cuban name for PAWPAW.

FUNCHI (fungee): Cornmeal pudding, like Italian *polenta*.

GANDULES: Spanish name for PIGEON PEAS. *See* BEANS.

GINGER ROOT: Gnarled brown root with a moist firm yellow flesh. It is about 3 inches long with a more pungent flavour than dried ginger. Available in Indian and Far-Eastern shops throughout the year. The fresh root will keep for 2 to 3 weeks if wrapped in a plastic bag and refrigerated.

GUAVA: Oval or more or less pear-shaped fruit of an evergreen tree native to tropical America. Guavas are usually from 2 to 5 inches in diameter and their skin is thin and a pale yellow. Guavas taste sweet and are eaten raw or stewed. They are also made into jams, jellies and guava paste, a rich preserve, often eaten in the islands with cream cheese. Fresh guavas are sometimes available in Indian shops. Canned guavas, guava paste and guava jelly are available in many good grocers' shops. Very occasionally it is possible to obtain canned seedless guavas.

HABICHUELAS: Spanish name for red kidney beans. *See* BEANS.

JACK-FRUIT (*jaquier, jaca*): Oblong fruit with green, lumpy skin, closely related to the breadfruit but enormous—it sometimes weighs as much as 70 pounds. Though the fruit is malodorous, its soft flaky yellowish pulp is sweet, and can be eaten raw or cooked; it is especially popular in curries. Available occasionally in West Indian shops.

KACHOURI: Deep-fried fritter of Indian origin made with chick-pea meal and chopped spring onions.

KESHY YENA: The term, from the

Spanish, means, literally, "stuffed cheese". A speciality of the Dutch islands, it is made with Edam cheese and various mixtures of meat, poultry, fish or seafood. Traditionally the cheese is hollowed out, stuffed and baked.

LANGOSTA (*langouste*): Spiny lobster, native to Caribbean waters, highly prized for the meat of its tail. It lacks the large claws of the northern lobster.

LECHOSA: Spanish word for PAWPAW.

LOQUAT: Small yellow-orange stoned fruit the size of an apricot with something of the flavour of a peach. Available canned in some grocers' shops and Oriental stores.

MACE: *See* NUTMEG.

MALAGUETA PEPPER: Name given to the small dark berry of the bay rum tree used in such dishes as BLAFF: *See* BAY RUM.

MALANGA: Member of the TARO family.

MAMEY APPLE: Large tropical fruit, related to the mango, with thick brown skin and sweet orange-red pulp, eaten raw or cooked.

MANGO: Fruit of an evergreen tree taken from India to the West Indies about 200 years ago. Mangoes range in size from plum-sized varieties to those weighing 2 or 3 pounds. Usually oval in shape. The skin is smooth and yellow or yellowish green, often with a splotch of scarlet; the stone inside is long and flat. When ripe, the yellow flesh is sweet and juicy. Available in better greengrocers' shops between April and September.

MANIOC: *See* CASSAVA.

NASEBERRY (sapodilla): Tropical fruit about 3 inches in diameter with a brown rough skin and a sweet brownish-purple pulp. Available in better greengrocers' shops in the summer.

NUTMEG: Brown oval seed of the fruit of the nutmeg tree, which flourishes on Grenada. When ripe, the nutmeg is covered with a thin black shell surrounded by a red lacy network, or aril, which is mace. Covering both is a thick fleshy

pericarp that can be used to make jelly or ice-cream. Both nutmeg and mace are fragrant and slightly bitter, but mace has a more pronounced aroma and flavour. Mace is generally available ground; nutmeg is available whole or ground.

OTAHEITE APPLE: *See* POMERAC.

PALM HEARTS: Tender ivory-coloured hearts or shoots of palm obtained from the core at the crown or top of the palm tree. Used as a vegetable or salad ingredient. Available canned in most better grocers' shops.

PASTELES (*ayacas*): Puerto Rican speciality made of a stuffing of meats with raisins, olives, capers, almonds in cornmeal or mashed plantain wrapped in a plantain leaf and steamed. Found in all Spanish-speaking islands.

PASTELITOS (*pastelillos, pastechi, patty*): Small meat-filled turnovers baked in a pastry crust.

PÂTÉ EN POT: Traditional dish of the French islands; a very thick soup made of finely chopped lamb, offal and vegetables.

PAWPAW (papaya, *lechosa, fruta bomba*): Large cylindrical melon-like fruit of a tree native to the West Indies. Pawpaws range from 3 to 20 inches in length and may weigh as much as 10 pounds. The skin is thin and smooth and, when the fruit is ripe, both skin and flesh are orange yellow to deep orange; inside is a mass of small blackish seeds. Pawpaw flesh is rather sweet, with a slight musky taste, and is eaten raw or used in cooking. When green, the fruit is made into chutney. Available both ripe and green in some greengrocers' and West Indian shops.

PELAU (pilaf, pilau): An Indian dish consisting of rice cooked with meat, fowl, fish or seafood.

PEPPER-POT: In Trinidad, a highly seasoned stew made with meat, game or fowl, and thickened and flavoured with CASSAREEP. In Jamaica, a spicy soup made with meat or fowl and vegetables.

PEPPERS: Every podded pepper —sweet, pungent or hot—is a member of the *Capsicum* family and a native of the New World. Hot peppers, or chillies, vary

enormously in shape, colour, size and degree of hotness. Most ripen from green through orange yellow and then to red; colour does not indicate pungency, but fully ripened ones may have a more pronounced flavour. Chillies lose their flavour quickly and must be stored in the refrigerator. They are available from some greengrocers, specialist delicatessens and West Indian shops. (*Caution: see How to Handle Chillies.*)

PICADILLO: Highly seasoned hash-like meat dish made with raw minced beef or cooked beef. The Cuban version, with olives and raisins, is especially famous.

PICKAPEPPA: Brand name of two Jamaican sauces: Pickapeppa sauce, a sweet mango sauce, and Pickapeppa hot pepper sauce, a hot chilli sauce resembling Tabasco.

PIGEON PEAS (*gandules*, goongoo or gunga peas): Round seeds the size of a small garden pea. Young pigeon peas may be eaten green, but the seed is usually used mature and dry, when it is brownish in colour with flecks of grey. Canned green pigeon peas are sometimes available in West Indian shops; the dried variety is generally available. *See* BEANS.

PIMENTO: *See* ALLSPICE.

PIONONOS: Puerto Rico's deep-fried plantain rings filled with spiced minced beef.

PLANTAIN (*plátano*): Fruit of the banana family, similar in shape, but larger and not so sweet; must be cooked before eating. Often available in West Indian shops in all degrees of ripeness from green through yellow to dark brown. Plantains ripen at room temperature, but may be kept at a desired stage for 2 to 3 days if refrigerated.

POLOURI: Small fritter of Indian origin made with split-pea meal.

POMELO: *See* SHADDOCK.

POMERAC (Otaheite apple): pear-shaped red fruit about 3 to 4 inches long with white flesh, eaten raw or cooked and made into jam.

ROSELLE (*rosella*): *See* SORREL.

SAHINA: Deep-fried fritter of Indian origin made from TARO leaves and split-pea meal.

SANCOCHO (*sancoche*): Stew of the

Spanish-speaking islands made with a variety of meats and vegetables.

SAPODILLO: *See* NASEBERRY.

SEA EGG: Island name for a white sea urchin, the ovaries of which are considered a delicacy.

SHADDOCK (pomelo): Thick-skinned citrus fruit, from which the grapefruit was developed, with sharp-tasting, reddish flesh; introduced into the islands in the 17th century.

SHROB (shrub): Liqueur made on the French islands from rum and the rind of bitter oranges.

SOFRITO: The term literally means lightly fried and describes a basic sauce used in Spanish and island cooking. Always made with either onions or garlic and often with both, a *sofrito* usually contains tomatoes, peppers, herbs, spices and ham. Its ingredients are chopped, then cooked in oil.

SOPITO: A creamy fish chowder made with coconut milk; a speciality of the Dutch islands.

SORREL (roselle, *rosella, flor de Jamaica*): Tropical flower grown throughout the islands. Its fleshy sepal (the leaf-like calyx or cup beneath the blossom) has a faintly acid taste and is used in making drinks, jams, jellies and sauces. Sorrel sepals are available dried in West Indian shops.

SOUR-SOP: Large dark-green heart-shaped fruit with spiny skin. Its pithy flesh has black seeds and is slightly acid. Often made into a drink or an ice-cream.

STAMP AND GO: Jamaican fried codfish cakes; made of a heavy batter flavoured with annatto, onions and chillies.

SURULLITOS: Puerto Rican fried cornmeal and cheese sticks.

SWEET POTATO (*boniato*): Tuberous vegetable native to the Americas. Its skin colour ranges from nearly white to brown, pink, magenta and even purple. The flesh may be white, yellow, orange or purple. Yellow- and orange-fleshed varieties are popular in the United States and are available in most grocers' shops; white sweet potatoes may be found in West Indian shops. Often confused with YAM.

TAMARIND: Brown pulp of the seed pod of a tree cultivated throughout the tropics; used for flavouring. The pod is brittle, cinnamon-coloured and shaped somewhat like a pea pod, but is up to 8 inches long. The pulp has a somewhat acid taste.

TANGELO: Hybrid fruit created in the 1890s by crossing a tangerine with grapefruit. It can be round or pear-shaped, with rough or smooth orange-coloured skin. The flesh of some is rather acid tasting; others are sweeter.

TARO (dasheen, tannia, malanga, elephant's ear, *yautía*): Tuberous edible plant root, about the size of a large baking potato with dark-brown bark-like skin. The firm flesh can be white, green, grey or violet and has a some-what nutty taste. The word taro can also refer to the leaves of the plant. These, also known as CALLALOO and elephant's ears, are green, roughly heart-shaped, and may be as much as 3 feet long; their flavour is faintly bitter and reminiscent of spinach. Leaves and roots are available throughout the year in West Indian and Far-Eastern shops.

UGLI: A thick-skinned hybrid citrus fruit that was developed in Jamaica. A cross between grapefruit, orange and tangerine, it is called ugli because of its lumpy appearance.

WEST INDIAN PUMPKIN: *See* CALABAZA.

YAM: Large tropical tuberous vegetable that occasionally may weigh as much as 100 pounds. It has a thick, rather hairy skin. The flesh may be white, yellow or red and is starchy and slightly sweet. Available in West Indian shops. (In the United States the terms yam and Louisiana yam are often erroneously applied to the soft orange-coloured sweet potato; they do not belong to the same botanical family.)

Shopping for Caribbean Ingredients

There are a large number of specialist food shops catering for West Indian customers in various parts of the United Kingdom. The main retail shop for fresh, dried and canned Caribbean foods in London is Food Stores Ltd., 189 Shepherd's Bush Market, London, W.12. Dien's also supply goods by mail order.

Certain ingredients are also to be found in Indian and Far Eastern food shops. Evans, Gray & Hord of 110 Cannon Street, London, E.C.4 are importers of West Indian canned foods and may be able to advise where they are to be found in different parts of the country.

Dien Brothers (Food Importers Ltd.) Coal Wharf Road, W.12 can also supply a list of their outlets.

Recipe Index: English

NOTE: An R preceding a page refers to the Recipe Booklet.

Recipe Index: Caribbean

General Index

Numerals in italics indicate a photograph or drawing of the subject mentioned.

Picture Credits and Acknowledgements

The sources for the illustrations in this book are given below. Credits for the pictures from left to right are separated by commas, from top to bottom by dashes. All photographs are by Richard Meek except: page 4—top right Salvatore Fragliossi for SPORTS ILLUSTRATED —Charles Phillips, Phillip Dowell. 12, 13—Map by Mary Sherman. 14, 15—Michael Rougier. 36—Drawing by John Frederick. 38, 39—Drawings by Robert Geissman. 50 —Manuel Millan. 55—Drawing by Robert Geissman. 86, 87—Derek Bayes courtesy the Trustees of the British Museum. 106—Richard Meek courtesy Hart Preston Collection. 119—Drawings by Robert Geissman. 158 —Michael Rougier. 189—Michael Rougier.

For their help in the production of this book, the editors wish to thank the following: on *Antigua*: William DeCoudres, The Hawksbill; Gwendolyn Tongue, Government Supervisor of Home Economics; on *Barbados*: Clenell Bynoe, Barbados Tourist Board; in *California*: Louise Hartmann, Dole Pineapple Co., San Jose; John Scelsa, Calpac Corp., Santa Ana; on *Curaçao*: Sarita Brandão; Edsel Jesurun, Curaçao Tourist Board; Delia Maduro; Olga and Alfred Morón; Bep Newton; in *Detroit*: Sister Karen Kennelly; on *Dominica*: Phyllis and Robert Allfrey; in the *Dominican Republic*: Armando D'Alessandro; Adria de Manón; on *Grenada*: Lloyd Charles; Raymond Harford, Grenada Nutmeg Assn.; Alan Krassner; Gertrude Protain, Grenada Tourist Board; on *Guadeloupe*: Robert Chéenne, Roger Fortuné, Guadeloupe Tourist Board; Jeanette Reignard; in *Ithaca, New York*: Dr. Robert Smock, Cornell University; on *Jamaica*: Doreen Kirakadie and Desmond Henry, Jamaica Festival Office; Myrtha Swire, Jamaica Tourist Board; in *Litchfield, Conn.*: the White Flower Farm; on *Martinique*: Jacques Alexandre, Association of Sugar Cane Planters and Manufacturers; Robert S. Barrett IV, U.S. Consul; Denise and Max Elizé; in *New York City*: The American Sugar Assn.; Sam Aaron, Sherry Lehmann Inc.; Alexis Bespaloff; Dorothy Bowes; British Overseas Airways; Dennis Brown, The Bronx Botanical Gardens; Bessie Byam; Pearl Cameron, Trinidad and Tobago Tourist Board; Byron Clement, French Government Tourist Office; Norman Cooper, Rums of Puerto Rico; Peter Davis, Jamaica Arms Restaurant; Frank Doherty, Ross Associates; Eastern Airlines; Pierre Edugene; Charles Elliott; Andrew Geller, Raymond Loewy-William Snaith Inc.; Georg Jensen; Mary George; Hammacher Schlemmer; Joseph Hidalgo, U.S. Dept. of Agriculture; Eugene Lamour; Macy's; Vincent Manchusi; Dorothy Newman; Pan American Airways; Mme. de la Pine, French Government Cultural Service; Plummer McCutcheon; Lewis Politi, New York Botanical Gardens; The Pottery Barn; RMH International; Frederick Ruoff, Jamaica Tourist Office; Nicole Scott; Lyonelle Singer; Dr. C. Lavitt Smith, The Museum of Natural History; John Squire, The Rock Corporation; Mirtha Stengel; Lillian Stuckey, Bernard Lewis Agency; Carmen and Luis Valldejuli; Hendriena van Hoboken, Curaçao Tourist Board; Robert C. Warner, Robert F. Warner Inc.; José Wilson; on *Puerto Rico*: Ellen Hawes; Roberto Huyke and Dr. Jesús Vélez-Fortuño, The University of Puerto Rico; on *St. Croix*: Walter Lewisohn, The St. Croix Landmarks Society; on *Trinidad and Tobago*: Sylvia Hunte; Dr. Joan Kazim; Therese Mills; Naomi Osborne, U.N. Information Centre; Derek Walcott; in *Washington, D.C.*: The Distilled Spirits Institute; Norbert D. Roche, U.S. Treasury Department; William Roland, The United Fresh Fruit and Vegetable Assn.; Gordon Webb, U.S. Department of Agriculture.

Sources consulted in the production of this book include: *The Making of the West Indies* by Augier, Hall, Gordon and Reckford; Longmans, London. *Sources of West Indian History* by Augier and Gordon; Longmans, London. *The Story of Sugar* by Aykroyd; Quadrangle Books, Chicago. *History of the British West Indies* by Burns; Allen and Unwin, London. *Jamaica Talk* by Cassidy; Macmillan, New York. *West Indian Cookery* by Clark; Nelson, Edinburgh. *The Memoirs of Père Labat* tr. by Eaden; Constable, London. *The Traveller's Tree* by Fermor; Harper and Row, New York. *The World of Vegetable Cookery* by Hawkes; Simon and Schuster, New York. *Two Years in the French West Indies* by Hearn; Harper and Row, New York. *The Barbados Book* by Lynch; Toplinger, New York. *The West Indian Scene* by Percy; Van Nostrand, New York. *The Caribbean* by Rodman; Hawthorn, New York. *Cooking the Caribbean Way* by Slater; Paul Hamlyn, London. *Caribbean Cook Book* by Springer; Evans, London. *Rum, Romance and Rebellion* by Taussig; Minton Balch, New York. *Caribbean Here and Now* by Ullman and Dinhofer; Macmillan, New York. *The Art of Caribbean Cookery* by Valldejuli; Doubleday, New York. *Journal of a Lady of Quality, 1774-1776* ed. by Walker; Yale University Press, New Haven. *Documents of West Indian History* by Williams; PNM Publishing, Trinidad.